Documents in Crisis

SUNY series in Latin American and Iberian Thought and Culture

---

Jorge J. E. Gracia and Rosemary Geisdorfer Feal, editors

Documents in Crisis

Nonfiction Literatures in Twentieth-Century Mexico

Beth E. Jörgensen

SUNY PRESS

Published by State University of New York Press, Albany

Printed in the United States of America

For information, contact State University of New York Press, Albany, NY
www.sunypress.edu

Production by Eileen Meehan
Marketing by Michael Campochiaro

Library of Congress Cataloging-in-Publication Data

Jorgensen, Beth Ellen.
Documents in crisis : nonfiction literatures in twentieth-century Mexico / Beth E. Jörgensen.
p. cm. — (SUNY series in Latin American and Iberian thought and culture)
Includes bibliographical references and index.
ISBN 978-1-4384-3939-6 (hardcover : alk. paper)
ISBN 978-1-4384-3938-9 (pbk. : alk. paper)
1. Mexican prose literature—20th century—History and criticism. 2. Literature and history. 3. Mexico—History—20th century—Sources. 4. Mexico—History—20th century—Historiography. 5. Autobiography—Mexican authors—History and criticism. 6. History in literature. I. Title. II. Title: Nonfiction literatures in twentieth-century Mexico.

PQ7118.J67 2011
860.9'9720904—dc22 2011005035

Contents

Acknowledgments vii

Introduction 1

1 The Distinction of Nonfiction: Toward a Theoretical Framework 11

2 Writing the Mexican Revolution of 1910 27

3 Living Stories, Telling Lives: Autobiographical Writings of José Vasconcelos and María Luisa Puga 69

4 Life Writing from a Popular Perspective 107

5 Chronicling Crisis: Late Twentieth-Century Manifestations of the Literature of Encounter 137

6 Making History: Subcomandante Marcos in the Mexican Chronicle 161

Conclusions: Thinking Back, Looking Ahead 191

Notes 201

Works Cited 211

Index 221

Acknowledgments

I would like to thank a number of colleagues who share my interest in both nonfiction modes of literature and Mexican literature and culture, and who have encouraged my own research and writing through their scholarly work and their friendship. Ignacio Corona's invitation ten years ago to co-edit the volume *The Contemporary Mexican Chronicle* led to a deeper engagement with the theory and practice of the chronicle, as well as opening up connections to the wonderful group of contributors—chroniclers and scholars—who made our volume possible. Other colleagues near and far have generously included me in projects that allowed me to develop different aspects of my work on Mexican nonfiction literatures. Mary Long, Linda Egan, Ryan Long, Nuala Finnegan, and Jane Lavery are at the top of that list of valued intellectual collaborators.

These acknowledgments would not be complete without thanking two remarkable women: Elena Poniatowska for her writing and for the support and friendship that she has extended to me since I first met her three decades ago, and Rosemary G. Feal for the work that she does at the MLA to benefit our entire profession and the mentoring that she generously provides to so many individuals.

Finally, my family—Paul, Megan, and Ben—always keep me going and make the journey a true adventure.

Introduction

More than twenty-five years ago when I first read Elena Poniatowska's highly acclaimed book *Hasta no verte, Jesús mío*, I read it rather unproblematically as a novel. That is, I read it as a work of fiction, which I took to mean that its narrated world, while it might have a connection—even an easily recognizable one—to what we call reality, did not bear any particular responsibility to that reality. As a novel, its story could not be held up for scrutiny or subjected to a process of verification concerning the accuracy of its information or its claims about the present or the past. The format and the marketing of Poniatowska's book, and the narrator-protagonist's improbable opening salvo—"Esta es la tercera vez que regreso a la tierra . . ." (9) [This is the third time that I have returned to earth]—invited its reading as a work of imaginative literature, autonomous from the "real world" and employing language and literary conventions to inscribe its own internal logic and coherence. My role as a reader was to discern and to enjoy the textual construction of character, dialogue, place, time, and action as a process of making meaning through storytelling. However, I was soon to discover that other readers, better informed than I about how the book had been conceived and written, were examining it as a "true-life" story, a *testimonio* within the tradition of contemporary Latin American writing. While I was preparing to undertake an analysis of *Hasta no verte, Jesús mío* as a work of fiction, others were busy debating to what degree the published text was faithful or responsible to the interviews that Elena Poniatowska had carried out with a living, identifiable woman—"known," albeit mistakenly, by the name of Jesusa Palancares. At stake was an argument over whether to classify the text as a *testimonio* or a novel, or perhaps a *testimonio novelado*.

I have told the story of the multiple critical readings of *Hasta no verte, Jesús mío* in my book *The Writing of Elena Poniatowska: Engaging Dialogues*, and I will not reiterate that work here.[1] Nevertheless, I mention this bit of my own history as a reader, because my engagement with what I have called the "creative confusions" surrounding the writing and the reception of *Hasta no verte, Jesús mío*, and my study of Poniatowska's other, more transparently fact-based works such as *La noche de Tlatelolco* and *Nada, nadie: las voces del temblor* awakened an interest in thinking more deeply and more critically about the categories of fiction and nonfiction, to use the most commonly accepted terms in literary studies. Questions of what might differentiate nonfictional discourse from fiction, and how and why the distinctive textual practice of nonfiction matters to writers and readers alike were my points of departure for an inquiry that I soon found would not lead to ready-made answers. In reviewing the existing criticism, I encountered a general acknowledgment among scholars that in the world of literary history and analysis both in Mexico and in the United States, the fictional narrative genres of the novel and the short story regularly attract far more attention than the traditionally conceived nonfiction forms such as autobiography, biography, and chronicle. The extensive attention given to testimonial literature has been the outstanding exception to this rule in studies of Latin American literature of the past thirty years,[2] an exception that proved that nonfiction writing comprised a field of research with ample room to roam and to explore.

The most acknowledged foundational account of the difference between fiction and nonfiction in the Western literary and philosophical tradition is the passage in Aristotle's *Poetics* in which he distinguishes between poetry and history writing. "It also follows from what has been said that it is not the poet's business to relate actual events, but such things as might or could happen in accordance with probability or necessity. A poet differs from a historian, not because one writes verse and the other prose . . . but because the historian relates what happened, the poet what might happen. This is why poetry is more akin to philosophy and is a better thing than history; poetry deals with general truths, history with specific events" (18). This passage gives the basic criterion upon which our culture's commonsense notion of fiction and nonfiction is still grounded today: the difference between telling general truths or "what might happen," and relating "actual events." Across the centuries, it has proved to be a durable distinction that readers and writers continue to employ in the process of creating, receiving, classifying, and interpreting the verbal and visual texts that surround us.

At the same time, in the twentieth century, certainly, and even much earlier, this convenient and apparently "natural" distinction has been a highly contested issue in Western theories of representation. In the past one hundred years, the boundaries between fiction and nonfiction, the nature of facts, the relationship between linguistic representation and the lived reality it might claim to imitate, and the status of knowledge-producing discourses including the quantitative and the human sciences, have been subjected to an intense process of critical scrutiny. Modern linguistics and the transformations that it has inspired in the study of all aspects of human society and culture, have created a deep skepticism regarding what we know about the world and how we know it. This skepticism toward the reliability of knowledge and the attainability of truth is in constant tension with an equally urgent desire and need for what we can consider to be accurate knowledge about past and present realities outside of our immediate experience. I believe that the tension between our desire to know and our skepticism toward how knowledge is produced and organized in language is particularly acute in our reading of nonfiction texts, and in this book I examine a number of narratives produced across a century of Mexican literature in order to explore the distinction of nonfiction as a practice of writing and reading. The first chapter of the book treats a variety of theoretical approaches to key concepts in the discussion of nonfiction writing, concepts that are useful for formulating questions and strategies for the textual analyses in the chapters to follow. In this introduction, however, I wish to establish the continuing relevance of the fiction/nonfiction binary, however contested it is, for contemporary readers.

The importance of the distinction for U.S. writers, publishers, marketers, cataloguers, and readers (both academic and popular) is easy to demonstrate, because it is visible in the cultural marketplace in a number of ways. Best-seller lists, book advertisements, book stores, and libraries all rely on the categories of fiction and nonfiction to organize their materials for consumption, and the division is taken quite for granted until something occurs to violate its parameters. For example, in the 1960s and 70s the rise of the North American New Journalism and the proliferation of the documentary novel and other hybrid forms of narrative challenged the prevailing ideas about journalism and nonfiction writing in the United States, and both book reviews and scholarly studies questioned what was happening to long-established literary conventions. Indeed, over thirty years ago E. L. Doctorow announced the demise of the categories of fiction and nonfiction as meaningful ways to organize literature when he said that, "There's no more fiction or nonfiction now, there's only narrative."[3] However, as Phyllis Frus McCord points out in her 1986 article on the nonfiction novel, Doctorow's statement was neither prophetic nor performative, and it did not abolish the effective force of the fiction-nonfiction distinction for American writers and readers.

In 2006 the controversy that raged in the print and the electronic media over the "memoir" *A Million Little Pieces*, shows that readers take very seriously a book's claim to nonfiction status, and they don't like to be fooled. In this brouhaha, the public indignation over the author James Frey's inventions and exaggerations of episodes of his "life story," which was sold to publishers as a memoir only after it was rejected as a novel, occupied our notoriously short national attention span for several weeks. The popular talk show host Oprah Winfrey, who had promoted the title in her on-air book club in October 2005, at first spoke out in Frey's defense. She called in to the January 11, 2006 taping of *CNN Larry King Live* to affirm that in spite of numerous factual inaccuracies, "The underlying message of redemption in James Frey's memoir still resonates with me."[4] However, when public opinion turned more strongly against the book and against her endorsement of it, the talk show host recanted her previous support and excoriated Frey during a second appearance by the author on her show later in the same month. More recently, *Three Cups of Tea*, Greg Mortenson's wildly popular account of his experiences traveling in Pakistan and Afganistan and his mission to build schools in rural areas there, was subjected to an exposé done by the television show *60 Minutes* in April 2011. Their investigation into significant distortions and misrepresentations in the book created a particularly strong reaction in light of the author's use of the book in order to raise tens of millions of dollars for the charity that he directs. People felt fooled and betrayed on various levels by the blurring of fact and invention in this putatively "true story."

Although I am not carrying out a comparative study of nonfiction in the United States and Mexico, these examples of popular debates over nonfiction literature and its transformations have relevance for my project. In general terms, U.S. cultural productions are seen to have a strong influence on Mexican writers, and North American popular culture permeates the Mexican market, including in the form of the sale of translations of U.S. best sellers. More specifically, the lessons of the New Journalism have been absorbed and transformed by Mexican writers of chronicles, a prominent form of nonfiction that I examine in Chapters 5 and 6 of this book.

The debate over holding nonfiction literature to a high standard of "truth telling" has played out in regard to several prominent Spanish American texts as well. In the Mexican context, Elena Poniatowska's *La noche de Tlatelolco* was subjected to a public critique by Luis González de Alba, one of the student movement leaders interviewed by the author, who was not satisfied with the accuracy of some of the material used in the book. In an article published in the magazine *Nexos* in October 1997, González de Alba identifies twenty-eight paragraphs of testimony that he asserts are incorrectly attributed. That is, he says that Poniatowska, as editor, attached the names of the wrong individual witnesses to some passages of testimony, and he demanded that a new, revised edition of the canonical text about 1968 be issued. A far more widely known and hotly discussed controversy arose over the accuracy of certain episodes in Rigoberta Menchú's *Me llamo Rigoberta Menchú y así me nació la conciencia* with the publication of anthropologist David Stoll's research in 1999. These controversies have made questions about the reliability of memory and eye-witness testimony and the relative responsibility of nonfiction writers to accuracy as opposed to aesthetics or a more poetic concept of truth, visible for a wide reading public outside of academic circles.

An overall evaluation of the status of nonfiction discourse in Mexico reveals a somewhat different situation than that encountered in the United States, without implying that the distinction has been in any way abolished for Mexican readers. In Mexico, the term nonfiction is less consistently used as a tool to classify works of narrative literature than what is common practice north of the border. Nonfictional discourses appear to be primarily the preserve of historians and other social scientists, while literature is not systematically divided into fiction and nonfiction texts. For example, best-seller lists that I have consulted place all books into one ranking without distinction as to form. A May 1, 2006 list that I located online at the "buscabiografías" Web site, included among its ten titles the novel *El león, la bruja y el armario* by C. S. Lewis, alongside *México, lo que todo ciudadano quisiera (no) saber de su patria* by Denisse Dresser and Jorge Volpi, which is a history text, albeit one that takes a rather unconventional approach; and Erick

Guerrero Rosas's political essay *Perredistas al poder*. This is typical for the several months that I checked the online list in early 2006.[5] The Web site for the Fondo de Cultura Económica (FCE) makes available a monthly "Boletín de Novedades" and a list of "lo más vendido" (best sellers). The "Boletín" features new FCE publications grouped into the following categories: Ciencia y Tecnología, Economía, Historia, Lengua y Literatura, Niños, and Política. The language and literature section presents scholarly work in linguistics and literary criticism and theory, as well as an inclusive mix of fiction and nonfiction literary genres: autobiography, essay, novel, short story, drama, and poetry. A perusal of shelves at the well-known Gandhi bookstore in Mexico City reveals a similar organizational strategy, somewhat complicated by the tendency to group books according to publisher rather than by topic or genre. All of this is simply to make the point that on the surface it can appear that the Mexican book industry is not particularly invested in a distinction that is usually clear-cut and widely employed in the United States.

Moving from the selling of books to the academic study of literature, a review of several standard histories of Mexican literature confirms the impression that nonfiction is not generally regarded as a distinct literary practice requiring a mode of reading attentive to its specific demands. Ermilo Abreu Gómez's anthology *Cuatro siglos de literatura mexicana* published in 1946 divides its selections by genre and by century, such that poetry, theater, novel, short story, and *relato* (account, story, or tale) are treated in chronological order from the colonial period to the 1940s. Surprisingly, the chronicle of the conquest is excluded entirely, but under "relatos" of the nineteenth and twentieth centuries one finds some narrative nonfiction in the forms of biography and memoir. José Luis Martínez's history *Literatura mexicana, siglo XX, 1910–1949* (published in 1949), also organizes its material according to the traditional genres, but he includes a miscellaneous category of "Varios" where he curiously accommodates indigenous literature and writing by women. Finally, the extensive *Mexican Literature: A History* (1994) edited by David William Foster opens the door to significant examples of nonfiction in the chapter on the colonial period, in which a discussion of historical writings, legal documents, and ethnographic compilations predominates. The chapters on Romanticism, realism, Modernismo, and literature of the twentieth century, however, overlook such nonfiction forms as essay, chronicle, and autobiography in favor of a focus on the novel, poetry, and theater.

Nevertheless, Mexican literature since the colonial period contains a wealth of well-known and influential texts produced in dialogue with the traditional fact-based genres of autobiography, biography, chronicle, essay, ethnography, memoir, testimony, and travel writing. These works acknowledge the conventions of nonfiction writing as it is constituted in Western culture both by conforming to established expectations and by challenging and stretching their limits. The letters of Hernán Cortés, Bernal Díaz del Castillo's *Historia verdadera de la conquista de la Nueva España*, Fray Bernardino de Sahagún's collaboratively produced ethnographic writings, and Sor Juana Inés de la Cruz's essays are only a few of the best-known examples of nonfiction writing that are part of the canon of Mexican literature and that demonstrate its diverse forms and uses. Clearly, Mexican writers have always been well aware of contemporary debates over nonfiction literature, and they have creatively contributed to the ongoing innovations and transformations of these genres. In the textual analyses to follow, I will frequently make references to the authors' own prefaces, essays, and interviews in which they reflect on the practice of nonfiction writing for insights that have been overlooked by the literary histories.

In a further effort to create a context for my study, I examined book reviews in search of the assumptions—explicit and implicit—that inform the reading of nonfiction literature in Mexico. In almost thirty years of the monthly journal *Vuelta*, reconceived as *Letras Libres* in 1999, its substantial book review section demonstrates that nonfiction texts occupy a prominent place among those titles chosen for review by the professional reader. History books are particularly favored, but chronicles, biography, and autobiography are also prominently featured. Based on the many reviews that I read (without my making this an exhaustive project in itself), I can offer several observations. First, the terms "no-ficción" or "no-ficticio" never appeared, their absence substituted by phrases such as "historia verdadera," "personajes de carne y hueso," "vivencia personal," "base documental," and "respeto a la verdad" [true story, flesh and blood characters, personal experience, documentary basis, respect for the truth]. Second, when reviewing histories and biographies, regular contributors such as Christopher Domínguez Michael, Adolfo Castañón, and Fabienne Bradu repeatedly attest to the value of in-depth research and knowledge of the documentary archive when writing nonfiction, as well as the imperative to avoid "myth," "legend," and "speculation" in favor of a strictly fact-based account. However, the questions of what constitutes a fact, a document or a historical source, and how reality is rendered by language do not generally arise. One can only suppose that a series of unspoken assumptions are at work that take for granted popularly accepted notions of these key critical terms. Interestingly, reviews of historical novels were sometimes the site of inquiry into the distinctions between history and novel, or reality and fiction, although these inquiries did not delve very far into the matter. Even keeping in mind the length limitations of a typical book review, the overall failure to acknowledge the complexity and ambiguity inherent in terms like fact, document, and true story is striking.

In the study that follows, I undertake an analysis of the practices of nonfiction narrative literature in twentieth-century Mexico within a broad conceptual framework derived from theories produced in Mexico, the United States, and Europe. It is not a survey in the sense of a comprehensive treatment of a large number of texts throughout the given time period, but rather, it examines selected titles, some well-known and firmly ensconced in the canon of Mexican literature, and other less widely regarded and even marginalized by the standard literary histories. The specific modes of writing that I have included under the rubric of nonfiction narrative literature include autobiography, ethno-autobiography, memoir, historical essay, and chronicle, as the following outline of the book's six chapters shows.

Chapter 1 presents contemporary theories of nonfiction literary writing, which are often conceived in relationship to theories of historiography, in order to formulate pertinent questions and to define necessary terms and concepts for the textual analyses. Chapter 2 treats nonfictional representations of the Revolution of 1910, with a particular emphasis on the figure of Pancho Villa. Primary attention is given to *Memorias de Pancho Villa* by Martín Luis Guzmán, *Apuntes sobre la vida militar de Francisco Villa* by Nellie Campobello, and *The Wind That Swept Mexico* by Anita Brenner, supplemented by references to Guzmán's and Campobello's novels, *El águila y la serpiente* and *Cartucho*. Guzmán's wholesale appropriation of Villa's voice through a kind of textual ventriloquism, the tension between the legendary and the historical dimensions of the figure of Villa, and Brenner's incorporation of the visual into the verbal through the reproduction of documentary photographs are unique features of these texts that appeal to and challenge the reader's expectations.

Chapter 3 studies the elite production of autobiographical writing by considering the traditionally conceived autobiography *Ulises criollo* by José Vasconcelos and three examples of life writing by María Luisa Puga. Puga's works included here are the brief autobiography *El espacio de la escritura*, a collection of chronicles titled *Crónicas de una oriunda del kilómetro X en Michoacán* and *Diario del dolor*, a journal that explores the author's experience of living with the chronic pain of rheumatoid arthritis. Chapter 4 continues the discussion of diverse forms of life writing, now from a popular perspective with analyses of a testimonial autobiography, Benita Galeana's *Benita* and an ethnography in first-person form, *Juan Pérez Jolote* by Ricardo Pozas. In all of these books, the constitution of human subjectivity and the cultural construction of voice and life story are key concerns.

The chronicle is a genre of major importance in Mexican letters, and Chapters 5 and 6 are devoted to this manifestation of literary journalism. The crisis provoked by the Mexican government's violent reaction to the 1968 student movement, and the disaster caused by the 1985 Mexico City earthquake and by the government's ineffectual response to it, are the topics of numerous chronicles by the nation's best-known writers. Books such as Elena Poniatowska's *La noche de Tlatelolco* and *Nada, nadie*, and many of Carlos Monsivías's chronicles have been the objects of numerous critical studies. In the concluding chapters, I have chosen works that narrate and analyze crises in the form of two urban disasters (the gas explosions of 1984 and 1991 in Mexico City and Guadalajara, respectively), and a wide-ranging social and political movement, the Zapatista uprising. The primary texts studied in Chapter 5 are "San Juanico: Los hechos, las interpretaciones y las mitologías," Carlos Monsiváis's chronicle of the gas explosions in San Juan Ixhuatepec (popularly known as San Juanico), and Rossana Reguillo's mix of chronicle and anthropological study of the similar explosions in Guadalajara in her book *La construcción simbólica de la ciudad: Sociedad, desastre y comunicación*. In Chapter 6, writings by Elena Poniatowska, Carlos Monsiváis, Juan Villoro, and Alma Guillermoprieto offer four perspectives on the Zapatista rebellion and its leader Subcomandante Marcos.

Documents in Crisis claims a place at the center of literary studies for the theory and the practice of nonfiction narrative literature in Mexico in its diverse forms. I seek to complicate and enrich our reading of nonfiction by treating selected texts in the light of contemporary theories of historiography, subjectivity, narrativity, and genre. My analyses attend to the distinction of nonfiction by examining the interplay of conventions and expectations that inform the production and the reception of nonfictional narrative and that structure our reading of its particular relationship to material reality and human actions, past and present. By taking seriously the challenge that the theory and practice of nonfiction poses to our habits of reading, this book seeks to expand its prominence in the history and criticism of Mexican and Latin American literature.

1

The Distinction of Nonfiction

Toward a Theoretical Framework

> The chronicle illuminates with a different light than that of fiction: it puts its faith equally in reality and in textuality. The chronicler believes that the Word can go behind the scenes of real life and give a true testimony.
>
> —Dante Medina, "Patience and Urgency"

> Reportaje o novela sin ficción . . . este libro quiere ser el análisis detallado, minucioso, de un crimen ocurrido en la ciudad de México en octubre de 1978 . . . todos los datos consignados a lo largo del libro tienen un apoyo documental que se ha hecho público de algún modo o que de algún modo consta en escritos de diversa especie."
>
> —Vicente Leñero, preface to *Asesinato: El doble crimen de los Flores Muñoz*

Dorrit Cohn writes, in the preface to her book *The Distinction of Fiction* (1999), that she undertook to study the singularity of fictional narrative in part in response to a contemporary critical climate that has tended to disregard the distinctive differences between fiction and nonfiction, and to attribute fictionality to all types of discourse (vii). Deconstructive and postmodern theories and practices of literary writing are often said to blur the lines between genres and between fiction and nonfiction in the process of demonstrating how all verbal representations of the world are linguistic constructs. However, Cohn, like Phyllis Frus McCord to whom I referred in the introduction, refuses to accept that such blurring has made the problem disappear altogether. Cohn's work aims to show that fiction's unique claim on our attention lies in "its potential for crafting a self-enclosed universe ruled by formal patterns that are ruled out in all other orders of discourse" (vii). She develops her argument for limiting the category of fiction to nonreferential narrative by carrying out a systematic narratological comparison and contrast between various forms of history writing (biography, autobiography, historiography) and their fictional counterparts. In the present study, the focus is reversed to attend to the distinction of nonfiction by examining the interplay of conventions and expectations that inform the production and the reception of nonfictional narrative and that structure our perception of its particular relationship to material reality and human actions, past and present.

The two Mexican writers quoted above are well-known for their contributions to literary nonfiction, in particular the chronicle and, in the case of Leñero, the documentary or nonfiction novel and documentary theater as well. Their reflections that I have excerpted articulate the fundamental connection between nonfiction writing and real world events and identifiable people, and they introduce a number of concepts and terms that arise in any discussion of nonfictional narrative: reality, real life, testimony, datum, fact, and document are part of the essential vocabulary with which to talk about the texts brought together in this book. This lexicon, which must also include other terms such as evidence, plausibility, factual status, and factual adequacy, requires a rigorous interrogation and theorization that goes well beyond the limits of commonsense usage. In this chapter I have assembled critical resources provided by studies in history and literary and genre theory in order to formulate functional definitions for a core vocabulary, without negating the persistent ambiguities inherent in each concept.

Three distinct and competing conditions for writing and reading nonfiction inform my study, which acknowledges and seeks to explain the tensions at play among them. First, contemporary Western theories of language and representation posit the constructed, conventional nature of the discourses of both fact and fiction, and therefore destabilize the boundaries between them. Post-structuralist theorists working in many fields have challenged positivistic and humanistic assumptions about the status of the real and its linguistic referent in recognition of the irreducible role of language as constitutive and not merely reflective or expressive of human perception, memory, and communication. The contemporary interrogation of language and the overturning of the view of language as a transparent medium of representation have as one consequence an unveiling of the presumed, but false "naturalness" of certain commonsense notions that once anchored the study of literature. Roland Barthes's essay "From Work to Text," his book *S/Z*, and Michel Foucault's "What Is an Author?" are examples of seminal work that contributed to exposing the discourse-determined, historically situated nature of cultural phenomena such as the literary work, realism, and authorship. With regard specifically to writing that proposes to document the past, the most radical assertion of the materiality and the power of discourse, with a corresponding negation of the notion of a ready-made reality that precedes it, is found in Foucault's histories, such as those treating sexuality, prisons, and madness. In his books, the view of events understood as "what actually happened"[1] is displaced by the study of documents as events in and of themselves and a view of discourse in the service not of truth, but of power. As a result of the impact of the theories of post-structuralism and deconstruction, skepticism toward what we know about the world and how we know it increasingly pervades literary writing, historiography, journalism, anthropology, and ethnography, to mention the fields most central to my project.

Second, in the context of this skepticism and given the instability of textual categories, writers and readers nonetheless face epistemological and political imperatives to convey and acquire information and to create and control knowledge. On the one hand, the inadequacy of verbal representations to the presumed fullness and the elusive immediacy of experience, which is always already lost, opens an unbridgeable gap between event and story, and between the past and our knowledge about the past. On the other hand, and in spite of that gap, human subjects have an inescapable need to articulate and to negotiate the mode of knowledge that is created in narrative; a mode that permits us, however imperfectly, to make order and sense of experience, to preserve a memory of the past, and to resist oblivion. Throughout his many writings and interviews, Paul Ricoeur grapples with the nature of the relationships holding between human experience, the world, the linguistic sign and narrative. In "The Function of Fiction in Shaping Reality" and "Narrated Time," Ricoeur treats the issue of referentiality in both fictional and historical narratives. He asserts that fiction "refers to reality" and corresponds to entities in the world, but in a shaping, inventive, productive way and not in the sense of duplicating or re-presenting the real (*Ricoeur Reader* 120). Uniquely at work in historical narrative is the historian's "debt to the past, a debt of recognition to the dead" (*Ricoeur Reader* 347). The historian, and by extension the nonfiction writer in general, has recourse to the "traces of the past" that are the vestiges or the marks left by the passage of a human being through the world. In treating the trace as a present stand-in for an absent, irrecoverable past, interpretation is required, and the historian thus shapes reality in a way that recalls the inventive labor of fiction. Further, although Ricoeur maintains that the referent of narrative discourse is the order of human action, he complicates the matter significantly by stating that human action itself is charged with fictional entities, with stories and symbols. In his essay "Creativity in Language" he describes the power of stories succinctly: "Human action is always figured in signs, interpreted in terms of cultural traditions and norms" (*Ricoeur Reader* 469). All narrative therefore redefines what has already been defined, and its referent is not "raw or immediate reality but an action which has been symbolized and resymbolized over and over again" (469).

In the struggle for power that is the political imperative, narrative is an essential tool—or weapon—employed to a variety of ends. The exercise of power and privilege is defended and denounced, preserved and challenged through the stories that an individual or a community tells about its past. This is why silence is most often associated with powerlessness, in spite of its potential for a (limited) strategic value. Nonfiction writing, in particular, often functions as an instrument of advocacy or protest, and it is not disinterested or impartial regardless of claims it may make to truthfulness and accuracy.

Finally, many critics have observed that there is a positive correlation between experiences of crisis and trauma and the documentary impulse. In light of its capacity for meaning-making, it follows that narrative, and specifically nonfictional narrative, is a logical and necessary response to the threat and the opportunity of crisis. Holocaust literature, the North American New Journalism, Latin American testimonial literature, and the Mexican chronicle are examples of this phenomenon, which poses difficult questions of aesthetics and ethics for writers and readers alike. In their now-classic studies of the New Journalism both John Hollowell and John Hellmann analyze the new documentary forms of the 1960s as a response to the social and political upheaval of that era. Political assassinations, the civil rights movement and the violence directed against it, and the war in Vietnam seemed bewildering and chaotic to the North American public, who witnessed crisis after crisis more directly than ever before through the medium of television. The increase and transformation of nonfictional narrative is judged to be a critical and a creative response in the face of rapid and confusing change.[2] In Latin America, testimonial literature from the early writings of Rodolfo Walsh and Miguel Barnet to the many narratives produced during the dictatorships of the Southern Cone and the Central American civil wars in the 1970s and 80s demonstrate a wide range of narrative languages and techniques, but *testimonio* is also known for its correlation to individual and collective experiences of crisis and trauma.[3] This pattern appears in many but not all of the works included here, as the book's title commemorates. To varying degrees, Mexican nonfiction will always engage but not resolve the basic tensions at play in the conditions for writing and reading outlined above.

Attempts to define nonfiction literature typically begin by lamenting the fundamental negativity of the term nonfiction itself. To evoke an entity primarily by stating what it is not, admittedly seems to threaten foreclosure on establishing a positive identity in its own right. Such a gesture of exclusion may also be seen to be dismissive or marginalizing of the phenomenon so named. The literature of fact is the most commonly suggested alternative, but it has not gained general acceptance, and in this book I have chosen consistently to employ the terms nonfiction and nonfictional narrative. Dorrit Cohn, for purposes of distinguishing nonfiction from fiction, starts from the premise that referentiality is the key to their difference. Simply put, fiction is nonreferential narrative, while nonfiction is referential. As a consequence of its foundation in referentiality, nonfictional literature is subject to judgments about its truth or falsity through processes of verification, and it is in this way "constrained" and "incomplete" (Cohn 15–16). Other critics use phrases like "grounded in fact," "documentable subject matter," "factual content," and writing that concerns "real people in real places" to try to capture the core ontological status of nonfiction. All of these formulations contain problematical concepts and assumptions, but they point to a nearly universal recognition that one necessary condition of nonfiction is that it bear a visible link or "debt" to the lived world and that it further bear a kind of responsibility for accuracy or for truthfulness to that world.

Beyond positing a grounding in reality for nonfiction (and leaving aside for a moment what that might or might not mean), there is a general consensus that very little else separates nonfiction and fiction as verbal texts. All manner of linguistic registers, narrative structures, and rhetorical devices are common in all modes of storytelling. Most importantly, the story itself, whether it be characterized as historically based in nonfiction or hypothetical in fiction, is equally emplotted in both forms, and the strategies of emplotment construct a meaning that exists only in the narrative, and not, even for nonfiction, in some preexisting, original form that writing has somehow retrieved. Here is where the distinction threatens to blur. In the recognition that the plot of a nonfictional narrative shapes or composes its thematic "content" and does not simply transmit a meaning already contained in real life events, nonfiction seems to cut loose from its moorings to the referent and edge toward fiction.

Nevertheless, a crucial difference remains that characterizes the reading of nonfiction in Western cultures. Eric Heyne in his article "Toward a Theory of Literary Nonfiction" identifies *doubt* as the crux of the distinction between fiction and nonfiction (480). While it is pointless to doubt the accuracy of a fictional narrative—or, for that matter, to believe in it—nonfiction, by making a claim to facticity, invites doubt.[4] Doubt, in turn, may spur the reader to deploy his or her knowledge and competence in a process of verification of the narrative claim, as Cohn also suggests. Heyne offers two sides to this claim that prove to be useful in a critical reading of nonfiction. He says that it is the writer who determines whether a text is fact or fiction, and who endows it with what he calls "factual status." The reader, individually or in debate with others, determines the "factual adequacy" of the text, which is the degree to which it merits credibility (480). This determination may be made on the basis of a number of factors, including the degree of faith that one places in the writer, and the recourse to corroborating evidence found outside of the text. Heyne uses Truman Capote's *In Cold Blood* as a classic example of a book for which its author claimed factual status, but that some readers have found to be lacking in factual adequacy (481). In the context of Mexican literature, in a study that I have done of three chronicles of the 1985 Mexico City earthquake, I find that in contrast to works by Elena Poniatowska and Carlos Monsiváis, Cristina Pacheco's account proves to be factually "inadequate" under careful scrutiny, in spite of Pacheco's overt claim to factual status for her earthquake chronicle ("Matters of Fact" 84–85). Finally, I believe that the appeal of nonfiction writing is not only what it promises to tell us or the skill with which its story is told, but the invitation extended by doubt to undertake a journey outside of the text in search of other sources and other textual remains or traces of the facts on display. This investigation is always open-ended, and it soon reveals the vanishing point of knowledge in an infinite regress of documents. The reader's experience of the impossibility of reaching closure and of recovering the original, certain meaning of human actions and the marks they leave, and the confrontation with the constructed nature of those actions and their marks, are insights gained from taking nonfiction seriously as a distinctive mode of writing.

It follows from what has been said about the role of doubt in distinguishing nonfiction from fiction that nonfiction is fundamentally not only a mode of writing, but a mode of reading characterized by a combination of trust and skepticism. Philippe Lejeune proposes this very idea for autobiography in his highly influential studies of the genre. Lejeune's point of departure for his book *On Autobiography* is precisely that autobiography is a mode of reading and that it is a contractual genre. The contract or pact between reader and text in autobiography is based on the identity of the author, narrator and protagonist as revealed in the single name that designates all three functions (Lejeune 3–4). Lejeune also links autobiography to scientific and historical discourse in that they all entail a referential pact. Other forms of nonfiction entail a referential contract as well, and the narrative elements central to creating and sustaining the contractual relationship are numerous and varied. In my reading of the texts selected for this study, I pay attention to the presence and the significance of characteristic features of nonfiction that are signs of factual status and that influence the reader's determination of factual adequacy. The author's name, the making of an overt claim to present a fact-based account, the use of framing devices, and the visible traces of the real revealed in the incorporation of proper names, facts, documents, evidentiary procedures, photographs, and acts of witnessing are the primary supports of the contract that structures nonfiction as an activity of writing and reading.

Roland Barthes's polemical and widely-read essay "The Death of the Author" (1968) still casts a shadow on any discussion today of the role of the author's name in the reading of a text.[5] In declaring the absolute death of the "Author" as the originary authority or the sole creator of a text and its meaning, Barthes seems to be freeing the text from the tyranny of the author's person and life, and liberating or birthing the reader into the "multi-dimensional space" of writing. However, like E. L. Doctorow's previously quoted statement that "there's no more fiction or nonfiction now," Barthes's declaration is provocative but not performative. It certainly encourages readers to think differently about critical practices that were dominant throughout most of the twentieth century, but it does not, after all, abolish the name of the author or the function of authorship for the activities of publishing, cataloguing, and reading as they are commonly engaged.

With Barthes's provocation in mind, I find that Michel Foucault's analysis of the historically constituted role of the author is helpful in thinking about the category of nonfictional narratives. The essay "What Is an Author?" focuses on the "singular relationship that holds between an author and a text, the manner in which a text apparently points to this figure who is outside and precedes it" (*Language, Counter-memory* 115). While rejecting, like Barthes, a simple equivalence between an author and the "actual writer" of a text and also dismissing any ultimate authority to be granted to an author's originating consciousness, Foucault ascribes a series of positive and negative features to what he calls the "author-function." First, it is neither universal nor historically constant, but changes across time and across cultures and for distinct discourses. For example, he shows that the name of the author once mattered relatively more for scientific writing than for literature (epic poetry, folk tales), while that privilege is clearly reversed today. The author-function also operates to identify a form of property that is legally codified in the institution of the copyright. And, significantly for the study of nonfiction, Foucault mentions in passing that for scientific work the name of the author, while less important than once was true, can still serve to attest to the "reliability of the evidence" (*Language, Counter-memory* 126). Finally, in a very general way, the author's name functions to classify or group texts together as distinct from those grouped under another's name, and it characterizes the mode of existence of a text (121–127). For nonfictional narratives, the name of the author is a clue to, but not an absolute determinant or guarantee of the reliability of evidence and the understanding of the text's mode of existence, which are factors in the establishment of the reading contract. Within a given literary tradition, the association of an author's name with certain forms of writing (journalism, biography, historiography) and also in some cases his or her putative ties to the real-world referent of the narrative contribute to an acceptance of a particular text as nonfiction. This is not a judgment of how naive or how sophisticated such an association is, but a pragmatic statement about factors that inform reading and that are no less effective for being conventional and not "natural."

In addition to the author's name affixed to a book's cover, other immediately visible features may invite the reader to receive a text as a work of nonfiction. The title or subtitle often provides an obvious clue to factual status by incorporating recognizable proper names of persons or places, references to historical events, or terms that identify nonfictional genres (autobiography, memoir, history, etc.). Narrative frames are another device that signals an explicit connection between the text to be read and extratextual reality, and various forms of framing often play an essential structural role in distinguishing nonfiction from fiction. Acknowledgments, prefaces, or introductions are frequently used to explain many facets of a book's creation and shape a context for reading by making explicit the writer's debt to the real. The identification of archives and specific documents that have been consulted, correspondence with experts on the subject to be treated, interviews of the story's protagonist or of direct witnesses, the technologies used to record those interviews, the writer's own position inside or outside of the story to be told or his or her relationship to the human actors represented therein, all may be described in greater or lesser detail in order to make a promise of factuality and establish a contractual relationship with the reader. The inclusion of a simplified chronology of the events to be portrayed is another technique that confers qualities of historicity on the nonfictional narrative. At the end of a book, maps, charts, graphs and other appendices may offer data or documentation to supplement the narrative account; and glossaries and bibliographies also add the weight of scholarly authority to what has been written in the body of the text. Footnotes and photographs are conventional methods of documenting "the real" that may appear on the pages of the narrative itself and yet seem to stand apart from it in a position of secondary importance. The attention paid by the reader to these elements certainly varies, as the temptation exists to delve immediately into the "story itself" and skip over apparently extraneous or simply explanatory material, but the mere presence of these varied framing devices conditions our reading nonetheless.

In this regard, Jacques Derrida's critique of the commonsense view of the frame as ornamentation, adjunct, or "extra" element of a work of art in his essay "The Parergon" has relevance for the study of nonfiction. He states that traditionally the frame "is that which *should not* become, by distinguishing itself, the principal subject" (20). He goes on to challenge, or deconstruct, the notion of the frame as exterior and secondary to the work, by demonstrating the necessary connection between work and frame, which he describes as the frame's structural link to a lack within the work. The frame plays a cooperative and critical, even violent role vis-à-vis the production and the centrality of the work. "It is not incidental; it is connected to and cooperates in [the work's] operation from the outside" (20). In nonfiction, the narrative frames that frequently open and close the text fulfill many functions in establishing a pact with the reader, and they are a point of departure for determining the adequacy of the text to our expectations, but they do not, finally, provide either a determining orientation or a definitive closure to the reading process. On the contrary, the frame, with its double vision into and away from the narrative, may just as easily disrupt as consolidate the persuasive value of the many other elements that comprise the nonfiction narrative.

The assertion previously made that nonfiction is referential and brings the weight of fact to bear through its recourse to proper names, documents, and other evidence of reality, actually says very little that might be useful in an analysis of this literature. Each of the key terms deployed in that limited definition is complicated by a long and changing history of usage, and must be contextualized for the present study. To return to the notion of referentiality and the status of the referent, Linda Hutcheon's chapter on "The Problem of Reference" in her book *A Poetics of Postmodernism* offers a way to conceptualize the referent in light of contemporary theories of culture and literature. According to Hutcheon, who draws heavily on the work of historian Hayden White, as well as that of Jean-François Lyotard, modernist art, or high modernism, strove to distance itself from the language of representational realism, and in declaring its autonomy as art first and foremost, seemed to reject reference as a legitimate function of art (*Poetics* 141, 144). Postmodernism, in contrast, assumes the paradoxical position of creating narrative worlds that are both "resolutely fictive and undeniably historical;" a paradox that is somewhat resolved by positing that the historical or real-life referent is itself a *discursive entity*, not that which was lived, but that which is spoken (145). The past existed, but it is only known and available for acts of representation through the traces and the marks that it has left in the form of linguistic records and other cultural artifacts. The connection to an experience or an event is lost as soon as it is made, and while actions once occurred and continue to occur all around us, our only lasting access to them is through their textualized remains. Nonfiction is, therefore, referential, in the sense that it privileges not the "real" but the discursive traces of the past and asserts its own responsibility to a recorded, not a lived, reality.

The proper name is one of the primary traces of the real to which writers have recourse in reconstructing the past, and nonfiction generally endows the proper name with a stable identity. The attribution of concrete actions to the agency of an identifiable individual acting in an identifiable place and time, all of which are subject to verification by the reader, constitutes the core concern of nonfictional narrative. Beyond the proper name, nonfiction weaves a myriad of other facts into a persuasive and meaningful version of the past. Again, the primacy of language comes to the fore, as in Hayden White's definition of a fact as "an event under [verbal] description."[6] He goes on in his essay "The Real, the True and the Figurative in the Human Sciences" to say that "[e]vents must be constituted as 'facts' before they can be subjected to analysis and take up their place in the discourses of truth produced by the various human and social sciences" (15). The heroic notion of value-free facts, bare facts, plain facts, or "just the facts," if indeed anyone ever took such a notion seriously, has lost its currency not only in theory but in the popular imagination as well. White's view that events "are never given directly to perception but always come to the investigator in an already enfigured form" (15), goes far beyond a simple acknowledgment of a subjective element in the selection and presentation of facts. It points to a recognition that facts themselves are discourse-defined, to quote again from Linda Hutcheon, and all discourse is already interpretation. In this regard it is worthwhile to recall the etymology of the English word "fact." While in modern common usage a fact means something that actually exists, something known to have happened, or a truth known by observation or experience, its Latin root *factum* means something done or made and it signals an act of human agency and creativity. "Datum," in contrast, refers to something that is given, something that preexists our human agency and is waiting to be observed. In the Spanish language this distinction is readily available to its speakers even without any knowledge of Latin, due to the visible derivation of the nouns *hecho* (fact, deed) and *dato* (datum or information) from the verbs for to make/to do and to give, *hacer* and *dar*, respectively.

In reading nonfiction, one also encounters the use of evidentiary procedures and the presentation of evidence, which is a set of facts that have been deliberately assembled and placed into an interpretive context in the service of a claim. Evidence is part of an argument and it has a strong rhetorical dimension. An analysis of the status and the authority of the evidence that is used to defend a claim in a particular text must take into account a number of questions: the kinds of sources deemed valid for the specific field or genre in which the text participates, the reliability of witnesses and memory, the relative weight of competing and discrepant claims to truth, and the political dimension of the text's construction and reception, to start. The January 1996 issue of the *PMLA* was devoted to precisely this topic, the status of evidence, with an emphasis on evidence in literary studies. In her introduction to the volume, Heather Dubrow acknowledges the predominant skepticism of our time, without falling into a simplistic dismissal of the scholarship of the past as naively positivistic. She asserts that the problematical nature of all interpretations of evidence has long been debated, but what has certainly changed through time are our judgments of what counts as credible evidence. Yesterday's reliable source document may be called into question today, while the throw-away records of the past may be granted new value in a changing political, social, and intellectual environment (Dubrow 7–11).

James Wilkinson's essay in the same volume takes up this issue by looking at the changing status of evidence in the field of historiography in the twentieth century. "A Choice of Fictions: Historians, Memory and Evidence" defines its subject as the small subset of the vast remains of the past that historians use to write histories. Written documents produced by those in power and concerning political and military matters were once held to comprise the core of historical evidence. Now an expanded body of evidence includes scientific data, medical records, church and other institutional archives, folk tales, material culture, music, film, advertising, personal narratives, and a wealth of other individual and collective records (Wilkinson 80–81). Both Dubrow and Wilkinson address the tensions that exist between constructivist theories of evidence that deny its ultimate grounding in the real, and the need for reliable knowledge and for a ground upon which to recognize and judge it. Dubrow highlights the political aspect to this tension in the example of the reading of Holocaust literature and Latin American *testimonio*. Doubts about the (un)reliability of memory often come into conflict with a reluctance to challenge the testimony of witnesses to traumatic events, and the desire to respect the authority of experience when that experience has been so devastating, tends to overcome skepticism

(Dubrow 14). Wilkinson focuses on the tension between a historian's need for a standard against which to measure the truth claims made by a set of facts presented as evidence, and the impossibility of establishing a stable standard out of knowledge that is always constructed and partial (interested and incomplete), because it is generated from texts and interpretations of texts (85). Wilkinson cannot solve this conundrum, but he does explain how, in terms of practice, historians create a provisional working ground. Evidence, which is conventional and exists within a methodological and epistemological tradition, is endowed with validity by a community of scholars. Wherever the ground is located, be it in continually expanding stores of data, in memory, in official records or long-neglected archives or anecdotal information, it is bound to shift and it offers only a provisional foundation for constructing partial truths. In reading nonfiction literature, it is crucial to consider the status of its facts and its evidence with an eye toward discerning its internal standards for validity and the claim it makes to authority within a local and historical context.

A final term that requires attention is document. Inheriting from Latin the meaning of example or warning and the root meaning of a teaching, written documents afford our principal access to past and present realities that lie outside of our direct experience. They are the textualized remains of the past, and as such they are constructed in language and in relationship to other documents. There is neither immediacy nor transparency here, but a highly mediated reconstruction of irrecuperable events. Nonfiction literature, which is fact- and evidence-heavy, makes a commitment to verifiable documents, but this commitment may be more or less explicit in the text, and more or less consistently honored. Varying degrees of documentation will be noted in the examples of Mexican nonfiction chosen for this study, and our expectations for the presence of reliable, verifiable sources for a given genre will be examined.

References to historiography in the discussion of nonfiction literary writing and its employment of evidence and documents are virtually unavoidable. Like the forms of literature under study in this book, history writing has as its referent the proper name and the records of events occurring in a documentable time and place. Further, because historiography has been far more extensively theorized than nonfiction literature, it provides a wealth of critical approaches that can be productively employed in reading nonfiction. Theories and methods of writing history underwent significant, even radical, changes in the twentieth century, moving rapidly away from Leopold von Ranke's famous dictum, previously cited, that history properly done records the past "wie es eigentlich gewesen ist" (as it actually happened). This ideal, commonly held to be the essence of nineteenth-century "scientific history," in fact already came under question by some of Ranke's contemporaries, but in the twentieth century there is no doubt that the goal of capturing the past "as it really was" has been eclipsed by new concerns and new projects. Modern linguistics, structuralism and post-structuralism, and feminism and ethnic studies figure prominently among the fields that have prompted a radical rethinking of the historian's role in creating and not merely recording knowledge about the past.

In books and articles published since the 1970s, historian Hayden White has been a leading voice in opening up the field of history to the questions posed by contemporary literary theory and philosophy, and the imprint of his work can be seen in virtually all of the ground covered thus far in this chapter.[7] White provokes this opening through an interrogation of what he calls the "tropics of discourse," understood as the ways in which historiography is figurative, dependent on tropes, to the same degree as fictional narrative. Both history and fiction share the same narrative forms, and these forms shape or configure the story being told (*Tropics* 121–122). His chapter titles such as "The History Text as Literary Artifact" and "The Fictions of Factual Representation" have become catch phrases for his denial of a strict opposition of history to fiction, preferring to emphasize that historical narratives are "verbal fictions, the contents of which are as much *invented as found* and the forms of which have more in common with their counterparts in literature than they have with those in the sciences" (*Tropics* 82, emphasis in the original). In the critical vocabulary that White has made current for historians and literary critics alike, the term emplotment occupies a central position. Because "facts do not speak for themselves" and the meaning of events is not given but created in discourse, the historian (and the nonfiction writer) must engage in a process of organizing facts into a coherent totality, which is a poetic or fiction-making operation (*Tropics* 83). While he does distinguish historical *events* as those assigned to a specific time-place location and in principle observable, from imagined or hypothetical fictional *events*, White insists on the many formal and rhetorical features shared by historical and fictional narratives, and he defends the thesis that both discourses reconstruct rather than represent an image of reality. White also speaks of the standards of coherence and correspondence to which narratives are commonly subjected. Readers approach a historical text with the expectation of detecting evidence of a degree of correspondence between the narrative and the identified referent of which it speaks; and with the aim of discerning through the reading process a logical and/or aesthetic coherence to the text (*Tropics* 122).

In addition to taking up the textual and contextual features identified thus far, each chapter of textual analysis will introduce genre-specific criticism that complements the groundwork laid here toward a theory of nonfiction. In closing this chapter, I wish to summarize some of the key concerns that will guide my readings of Mexican nonfictional narrative. First, the nature of the facts and the evidence presented in a text and the privileged documents or other resources that are used to support a particular claim to truth are fundamental components that must be determined for each work studied. Published documents of many kinds, interview material, photographic images, personal notes and journals, and the workings of memory all serve as evidence for the agenda or the interests that an author consciously or unconsciously defends. Chapter 2 on "Writing the Mexican Revolution of 1910" foregrounds the ways in which multiple texts that treat what we usually recognize to be *the same subject* conceive of the documentary project and its basis in "facts" differently. Self-conscious and self-reflexive qualities are commonly found in narrative fiction, but they appear in nonfiction as well, and we must ask how such qualities affect factual status and the reader's sense of factual adequacy. The constructed, narrative nature of human identity and subjectivity is revealed in particular detail in autobiography, memoir, biography, diary, and testimony, but the chronicle and the historical essay also explore the complex contingencies of the human "I." Therefore, we must ask who speaks or writes and with what authority do the narrators under study claim the right to be heard and to be heeded through the conventions of factual discourse, and what roles do gender and social class play in this process. Finally, given that narrative is a meaning-making activity, it will be essential to examine the meanings that are created out of the remains of the past, and the extent to which an illusion of a manageable, ordered world is either conveyed or overturned in the narrative. By taking up an inquiry into these issues as they apply to a broad range of both well-known and marginalized examples of the literature of fact in twentieth-century Mexico, this book proposes to make a contribution to an appreciation of the art of nonfiction and its distinctive character, as well as to signal its role in creating the stories that construct the Mexican past and participate in creating its present.

2

Writing the Mexican Revolution of 1910

The standard literary histories have created an enduring and little-contested category in Mexican letters: the novel of the Revolution of 1910.[1] Although the most widely accepted definitions vary by establishing relatively more narrow or more expansive time limits within which the novel of the Revolution was produced, the central thematic unity provided by narrating the Revolution in its phases of armed struggle, consolidation of political power and legitimacy, and institution of socio-economic reforms is a given. Besides this obvious point of consensus, other common threads are frequently identified in the diverse group of texts that make up the canon: the presence of eye-witness narrators, who are often conflated in the criticism with the historical person of the writer; episodic structures of storytelling; a predominantly negative, pessimistic view of the Revolution as characterized by violent excess, internal divisions, lack of coherent direction, betrayal of ideals, opportunism, and failure to effect real change; the protagonism of either anonymous peasant soldiers or historically identifiable military leaders (Villa, Zapata, Carranza); reflections on the quest for national identity ("la mexicanidad"); and, significantly for the present study, the strongly documentary nature of these works of fiction. The documentary impulse—the desire to capture events both as they unfold and in retrospect, investing them time and again with renewed meaning—was a strong factor motivating Mexican intellectuals of the time to write about their experiences and observations of the extended period of Revolutionary upheaval. Novels such as Mariano Azuela's *Los de abajo*, Martín Luis Guzmán's *El águila y la serpiente*, and Nellie Campobello's *Cartucho* have therefore often been read for their "historical content," viewed as chronicles of verifiable events, or examined for autobiographical and biographical references.

John Rutherford, writing on the novel of the Mexican Revolution for the *Cambridge History of Latin American Literature* (1996), goes so far as to suggest that in a discussion of the narrative of the Revolution of 1910, the category of the novel must be expanded to include autobiographies, memoirs, and biographies provided that they "have any aesthetic pretences or qualities" (215).[2] Even María del Mar Paúl Arranz, who raises a rare dissenting voice in an article from 1999 by questioning the very existence of the novel of the Mexican Revolution as a coherent genre, comments on the generalized tendency to read these texts for their documentary value. According to Paúl Arranz, many readers, past and present, base their understanding of the Revolution of 1910 as a historical reality more on its novels than on Mexican historiography per se (50).

Matters of genre and canon aside, Mariano Azuela's novels written during the armed phase of the Revolution and the larger corpus of works produced in the 1920s and 1930s comprise a foundational literature for twentieth-century Mexican narrative. They set the agenda for later writers by modeling innovative narrative techniques and languages, and by creating compelling, enduring stories about the struggle for change and the struggle for power, idealism and opportunism, class conflict, individual and collective destinies, and national identity, all played out on the Revolutionary stage. Nonfictional accounts of the Revolution were also produced, including some written by well-known novelists. A study of selected nonfiction texts provides the opportunity to examine different factual versions of a single historical personage or series of events, and also to consider how the technology of photography became part of the documentary process and product in the early twentieth century. The figure of Francisco Villa has been endlessly created and recreated in the many official and popular discourses that narrate the Revolution of 1910: novels, histories, biographies, journalistic reporting, films, cartoons, corridos, and legends about him exist in abundance. Of the numerous literary writings about Pancho Villa, books by Martín Luis Guzmán and Nellie Campobello offer a promising site for a comparative reading, as each of them wrote both a novel and a nonfiction book about the famed "Centaur of the North." In *El águila y la serpiente* and *Memorias de Pancho Villa*, Guzmán creates contrasting versions of the "Pancho Villas" whom he knew first-hand and later researched in the archives; while Campobello wrote *Cartucho* and *Apuntes de la vida militar de Francisco Villa* to represent, respectively, her memories of the stories told about

Villa during her youth in the north of Mexico, and her adult efforts to vindicate the reputation of her childhood hero. Although *El águila y la serpiente* and *Cartucho* are nominally novels, while the *Memorias* and the *Apuntes* make an overt claim to factual status, these titles invite readings that go against the grain of generic classification, and the intersection of the conventions of fact and fiction in each work provides an ideal place to begin an inquiry into nonfiction literatures. *The Wind That Swept Mexico* by Anita Brenner, the second principal focus of this chapter, combines a concise narrative essay with an extensive photo gallery, and it casts the verbal and the visual in mutually supporting roles to build a case for the importance of a better understanding of the Mexican Revolution in the United States of the 1940s.

Versions of Pancho Villa

Martín Luis Guzmán's *El águila y la serpiente*, first published in Madrid in 1928, has defied classification in spite of the author's clarity in stating repeatedly that it is a novel. Even a cursory review of the existing criticism reveals stunning divergences of opinion over what to call the book. F. Rand Morton considers it to be neither novel nor history, but rather a kind of memoir that could be "best classified as a long conversation" (123, my translation). John Brushwood cites a "general critical agreement" that it is *not* a novel, but a kind of literary reporting that nonetheless contributed to the development of the novel in Mexico (200–203). Without any apparent irony, Adalbert Dessau calls it an autobiography and a memoir, albeit one that does not recount its author's life (340). Carlos Monsiváis has praised *El águila y la serpiente* as the finest chronicle of the Mexican Revolution, while others have referred to the book as a portrait gallery of Revolutionary characters, a document, a novelistic chronicle, and an example of the literature of fact. Manuel Pedro González sums up the prevailing confusion by declaring the text to be fundamentally unclassifiable, in that it combines elements of the novel, chronicle, reporting, memoir, diary, essay, and tale (256). Surely if González had written his essay today rather than over fifty years ago, he would have used the term hybridity in his discussion, as did Lanin Gyurko in his chapter on twentieth-century fiction for the 1994 book *Mexican Literature: A History*. In recent years, both Juan Bruce-Novoa and David William Foster have returned to Guzmán's own designation of the book as a novel in an effort to defend its status as imaginative literature in the face of the many documentary uses to which it has been put, seeing both the dominant readings and the initial English-language translations of the book as misguided in ignoring its literary qualities and its aesthetic coherence in favor of its historical value.[3]

It is not only the literary critic who has focused on the apparently documentary nature of *El águila y la serpiente*. The text aptly illustrates Paúl Arranz's observation that the reading public tends to approach the history of the Mexican Revolution through its novels, a tendency that affects the professional historian as well as the general reader. Histories of the Revolution of 1910 occasionally cite *El águila y la serpiente*, and more often refer to *Memorias de Pancho Villa*, as primary sources of information, particularly with regard to Francisco Villa, and in general Martín Luis Guzmán's writings are viewed as valuable first-hand accounts of many of the important events of 1913–1915, including Villa's military campaigns against the forces of Victoriano Huerta, the Aguascalientes Convention, and the short-lived presidency of Eulalio Gutiérrez. In some cases, the historian makes passing reference to the problems inherent in using these writings as source documents, but Guzmán's publications clearly must be reckoned with when reconstructing a history of the Revolution. For all of these reasons, Guzmán's "novel" provides a logical starting point for a selective overview of twentieth-century narratives that have been written and/or read in Mexico as literatures of fact. Most of the works that I will treat are, like *El águila y la serpiente*, hybrid compositions that combine the languages of fact and fiction in creative, subtle ways, and many similarly demonstrate the documentary impulse to impose order on the chaotic events of periods of social crisis through the meaning-making activities of storytelling. In my analysis of the book, I will discuss briefly the extratextual factors that influence an informed reader's willingness to attribute factual adequacy, at least provisionally, to a book that makes no overt claim to factual status. Then I will treat the textual markers of facticity that both attract and undermine our attempts to read the book as a document. The habits of reading that we associate with nonfiction, habits informed by doubt, intertextual inquiry, and questions about plausibility and accuracy, are triggered for many readers by those textual features of *El águila y la serpiente* that overlap with the conventions of autobiography and history writing. Martín Luis Guzmán's Ateneísta notion of what constitutes History, explained in an essay published in 1926 and titled "Un experto de la historia," is a further resource in which to ground an understanding of the contradictory demands that this novel makes on its readers. Finally, Guzmán's novelistic version of Pancho Villa will be explored as a point of comparison and contrast to his other monumental portrayal of the leader of the División del Norte in *Memorias de Pancho Villa*.

In a 1958 interview with Emmanuel Carballo that forms part of the lengthy entry on Guzmán in Carballo's book *Protagonistas de la literatura mexicana*, the writer says of *El águila y la serpiente*: "Yo la considero una novela, la novela de un joven que pasa de las aulas universitarias a pleno movimiento armado. Cuenta lo que él vio en la Revolución, tal cual lo vio . . . No es una obra histórica como algunos afirman; es, repito, una novela" (87). [I consider it a novel, the novel of a young man who went from the university lecture hall to a full-fledged armed movement. It tells what he saw in the Revolution, as he saw it . . . It is not a historical work as some affirm; it is, I repeat, a novel.] Guzmán's objections notwithstanding, his own defense of the book's status as a novel already introduces evidence that a reader might use to read it against the grain as memoir or as some other manifestation of the documentary impulse. Guzmán's participation in the Revolutionary movement is well known, and in 1913, when the novel opens, the future writer is that former university student who becomes involved with the Revolution and witnesses first-hand both armed combat and the political machinations of Mexico's Revolutionary leaders. After the "Decena Trágica" and the assassination of Francisco I. Madero, Guzmán fled Mexico, fearing possible persecution by Victoriano Huerta's new regime, and he later reentered the country across the northern border. In Mexico he met first with Venustiano Carranza and later with Villa, wishing to ally himself with the leadership that he judged would best serve the Revolutionary cause. This cause is defined by Guzmán as the creation of a liberal Mexican democracy based on the purity of impersonal ideas and a rejection of the historically prevailing "caudillaje" or strong-man leadership. During the period from mid-1913 to early 1915 Guzmán, trained in the law and experienced as a journalist, traveled with the Revolutionary troops and filled various administrative and diplomatic positions under the orders of Francisco Villa, whom he testifies he grew to know very well. He abandoned Villa and left Mexico again in 1915 when the General's ultimate defeat by Carranza and Obregón became an increasingly obvious certainty. The eye behind "lo que él vio" and the I-narrator of the book are therefore easily, almost unavoidably, identified with the historical Guzmán. This may explain the U.S. Library of Congress classification of the putative novel. In libraries in the United States, *El águila y la serpiente* is catalogued with the books on Mexican history, sharing a shelf with such sober nonfiction titles as *The Mexican Revolution*, *Venustiano Carranza's Nationalist Struggle* and *Mujeres y Revolución 1910–1917*, and far away from the Mexican literature section where Guzmán's political novel, *La sombra del caudillo* resides. Again, confusion over the book's disciplinary affiliation is common among professional scholars, here represented by bibliographers as specialists in the rules of classification, as well as among common readers.

The initial impression made by skimming the opening pages of *El águila y la serpiente* does not seem to support the long history of its documentary readings. The figurative title fails to establish a clear connection to historical events, but instead harkens back to Aztec myth. There is no subtitle claiming to present a true account of real events, and there are no prefatory comments attesting to the authenticity and accuracy of the narrative to follow. The book lacks any documentation of the kind to be expected in a history text: there are no footnotes, photographs, maps, appended documents or chronologies, and no bibliography. The index of chapter titles includes both fanciful phrases such as "La bella espía" and "La araña homicida" [The beautiful spy and The murderous buggy] alongside the names of historical persons and identifiable locations, and titles that evoke verifiable events. The openly subjective first-person narrative discourse, which is heavily invested with detailed descriptions, recreated dialogues, psychologically insightful portraits, and numerous metaphors, also allies itself more closely with the conventions of the novel than with those of historiography or documentary writing.

A closer look reveals the equally compelling presence of conventional markers of facticity. The first-person narrator-protagonist is named Martín Luis Guzmán, and this identity of the name of the character and that of the author is a crucial element in the "autobiographical pact" as defined by Philippe Lejeune.[4] The correspondence between the trajectory of the narrator's experiences and activities and what many readers could easily know about Guzmán's biography further strengthens the autobiographical contract and the mode of reading that it implies. If history is the "regime of the proper name," then the predominance of characters in *El águila y la serpiente* who bear the names of historical figures—Pancho Villa, Venustiano Carranza, Álvaro Obregón, Rodolfo Fierro, Felipe Ángeles, Alberto Pani, Miguel Alessio Robles and many more—clearly establishes the link to Mexican history that the book's title disguises. Place names are also carefully recorded in order to map the protagonist's movements within Mexico and outside of its borders in pursuit of his Revolutionary duties and in search of a truer revolutionary path. Finally, verifiable events—primarily military and political actions—are the ever-visible framework upon which the largely chronological narrative is structured. Victoriano Huerta's betrayal and assassination of Francisco I. Madero, the campaign against him led by Venustiano Carranza as "First Chief" and won by Villa, Obregón and other caudillos, the Aguascalientes Convention, Eulalio Gutiérrez's initial embrace and subsequent rejection of Villa's military support, and Villa's downturn in fortune in his struggle with Carranza and Obregón are all documented events of the Revolution of 1910. Even the showing of a Revolutionary newsreel in an improvised theater at the Convention has been documented.[5] All of these textual features may logically provoke the mixture of belief and doubt that is the hallmark of the reading of nonfiction. A reader focused on these elements might well weigh the accuracy of the book's account of the past, and might look to corroborating documents to support or to undo its apparent, although unspoken, claim to factual status.

A mere listing of the events and persons represented in the book, while it explains in part its documentary appeal, tells us very little about how Guzmán has selected and shaped the facts of the Revolution into an interpretation of the many conflicting developments and personalities that dominated Mexico's changing social and political order from 1913–1915. The language and the structure of the novel convey a meaningful image of the Revolutionary struggle, first against Huerta, and then over internal divisions among the Constitutionalist and Conventionist forces. This meaning, as we have seen, does not preexist the narrative in the form of an already coherent sequence of experiences, but rather it must be actively created out of the memories and the material traces of the past. Within the narrative as a whole, the representation of Pancho Villa is a central concern, and the Villa of *El águila y la serpiente* is one of the most memorable and widely known literary versions of the northern leader.

To start with the temporal organization of the events narrated in the novel, both linear sequence and circular return coexist, shaping a view of the Revolution that combines aspirations for progress and democratic change with a fear of the perennial return to authoritarianism. The book opens and closes with scenes of escape into exile: in the first chapters, the narrator recounts his passage by ship from Veracruz to Cuba and then to the United States, always under the fear of detection by spies of the newly installed Huerta government. The final chapters relate his escape from Mexico City and his overland trip to the United States, under the threat of detention by the Revolutionary authorities after he refuses an appointment as Minister of War. Huerta, the traitorous usurper of 1913; González Garza, the temporary executive after Eulalio Gutiérrez evacuates Mexico City in 1915; and Pancho Villa, the protagonist's one-time chief and protector, equally come to embody a potentially lethal threat to Guzmán's liberty and life. In the dilemma over whom to support as a worthy successor to Madero in the struggle for power on a national scale, there turn out to be no correct choices for the once-idealist intellectual who, in 1913 "llegaba a la Revolución libre de prejuicios en cuanto a personas" (*Águila* 36). [Came to the Revolution free of prejudice with regard to persons.][6]

Slicing through this cycle of exile, return, and exile revisited is the straight line of historical events, narrated in episodic fashion, and mapping out a series of dislocations and relocations across the Mexican landscape. The road or journey of the Revolution is a constant metaphor, and many chapter titles trace the narrator's continuous travel from town to town: "De Hermosillo a Guaymas;" "Una noche en Culiacán;" and "En el tren," for example. In his article "Martín Luis Guzmán: el viaje de la revolución," Horacio Legrás emphasizes the narrator's personal journey of self-discovery, in reading *El águila y la serpiente* as the story of an intellectual's efforts to understand his place *qua* intellectual "en una nueva configuración histórica dominada no por la palabra sino por el revólver, no por el abogado-político sino por el caudillo" (428–29). [In a new historical configuration dominated not by the word but by the gun, not by the lawyer-politician but by the military chief, (my translation).] Legrás interprets the ending of the novel as a representation of the intellectual's complete failure to recognize the voice of the masses, a voice that Guzmán as writer and historical personage cannot hear or represent, but can only silence with his own language (452–453). The structuring motif of travel can also be seen as an image of the chaotic movement of Revolutionary forces in an ever more divided political scenario that no one group is capable of comprehending in its totality. The reader sees the Revolution almost exclusively through the eyes of the narrator-witness, which provides the illusion of a very direct, clear view, but also a highly limited one. Traveling with Guzmán as he moves from town to town via nocturnal train rides, creates the sensation of a fragmented struggle in which no one can capture the full picture in a single, comprehensive vision. The narrator's acute powers of observation, recorded in the frequent use of the verb to see and its companions to look, to observe, to scrutinize, to perceive and to spy, result ironically in a kind of tunnel vision or even a blindness that prevents a global view. In combination with the increasingly negative trajectory of the individual episodes that lead from hope to triumph to defeat in the disintegration of the Conventionist government, the restricted sight lines of the narrator shape a pessimistic image of a revolution in which ideas and far-reaching programs inevitably succumb to individual and parochial interests. The narrator's own self-interest is clearly at stake in the closing chapters, when he seeks to escape the dangers of changing political fortunes and ensure his personal safety by betraying and abandoning the Conventionist cause and Pancho Villa himself.

Another feature of the novel's discourse that contributes to its nonfictional qualities is the occasional interruption of the narrative flow with essayistic passages of reflection on broad themes that preoccupy the narrator in his role as the writer's alter ego. These passages treat topics such as the differences that the narrator painfully perceives between the United States and Mexico, exemplified by the contrast between El Paso, Texas and Ciudad Juárez, Chihuahua; and also on Mexican identity, and the spiritual conditions that determine Mexican heroism, but that will also determine the failure of the Revolution. The narrator contemplates this last conundrum in the chapters "En el hospital militar" and "'¿Lo cree usted, señor presidente?'" [In the military hospital and Do you think so, Mr. President?]. He attributes to the Mexican people a deep faith in the strength of the spirit and the will to achieve any task—whether it be to organize a hospital or overthrow a dictatorship—in spite of apparently insurmountable obstacles. Recognizing that such a faith is both unrealistic and self-defeating, he nevertheless expresses pride and satisfaction in this insistence on the saving grace of the spirit over material reality. "Los mexicanos creemos, por ejemplo, que una fila de pechos heroicos es bastante a cerrarle el paso a una batería de cañones 42. ¿Quién negará que nos equivocamos? Pero, esto no obstante, es un hecho que nuestra creencia al fin y al postre, es lo único que nos salva" (137–138). [We Mexicans believe, for example, that a line of heroic chests is enough to block the way of a battery of 42-gauge cannons. Who can deny that we are wrong? But, it is a fact that our belief, when all is said and done, is the only thing that saves us.] In another famous passage, the narrator debates the relative dangers of entrusting the "truth of the revolution" to Carranza or to Villa, weighing the former's unbridled ambition against the latter's brutality. Guzmán's fear of perpetual *caudillismo*, represented by both Carranza and Obregón, is stronger than his distaste for Villa's ignorance and lack of moral conscience. A reader familiar with *La querella de México* and *A orillas del Hudson*, Guzmán's essays written from exile a decade before the publication of *El águila y la serpiente*, will recognize similar concerns over Mexico's attraction to authoritarianism and the need for the nation to find its spiritual and moral center as keys to Guzmán's thought. The connection between the ideology of the novel and the "real life" ideology of the writer is thus strengthened through intertextual explorations, and the nonfictional qualities of some passages of the novel may be enhanced as a result.

El águila y la serpiente has been described as a portrait gallery of Revolutionary characters, and Pancho Villa is without doubt the central picture in the exhibition. Villa is the protagonist in fourteen out of a total of sixty-two chapters, and these numbers alone give him a dominant position among the large cast of revolutionaries who come and go across the page. It has often been noted that Carranza and Obregón are portrayed as "farsantes" and "comediantes," actors reciting an empty rhetoric and relying on excessive pomp and circumstance in order to bolster their claim to authority. Pancho Villa, on the other hand, emerges under Guzmán's gaze as an authentic, if highly problematical personality. Often rash and mistaken in his decisions, frequently brutal in his treatment of his enemies, uneducated, uncultured, and prone to furious outbreaks of temper, there is nonetheless a kind of integrity and consistency of character in the man who is memorably associated with a mythic Mexican jaguar early in the novel, and less nobly with a wolf in the final chapters.

Villa's initial appearance occurs in the first part of the novel, Book Two, Chapter Three. "Primer vislumbre de Pancho Villa" [First glimpse of Pancho Villa] is one of the most frequently cited chapters of *El águila y la serpiente* due to the vivid image that it conveys. In relating his first impression of Villa during a nighttime meeting held in the General's tent, the narrator sketches the essential outline of Villa's physical and moral profile. Suspense is created by the detailed account of the long walk taken through Ciudad Juárez to find Villa and his bodyguard's reluctance to allow entry to the narrator and his two companions. Finally the three men make out Villa's reclining figure in the semidarkness: a long arm, an unblinking gaze, the flashing white of his eyes and his teeth contrasting with the coppery skin and reddish hair—details that function synecdochically as signs of the wild animal, the half-tamed jaguar that the Revolutionary intellectual approaches with cautious fascination. The description attests to the narrator-protagonist's presumed mental and moral superiority over Villa, but the power that Villa exerts over Guzmán is also revealed in a telling confession: "El calor de aquel lecho penetró mi ropa and me llegó a la carne" (47). [The heat emmanating from that bed penetrated my clothes and touched my skin.] Throughout the novel, interactions between the two characters are suffused with a dynamic tension arising from the narrator's recognition that he and his peers need Villa in order to achieve their "pure" revolutionary goals, while the alliance simultaneously poses a threat to their ideals and to their personal safety. Pancho Villa remains, until the end, "jaguar a quien pasábamos la mano acariciadora sobre el lomo, temblando de que nos tirara un zarpazo" (49). [A jaguar whose flank we caressed, while trembling with the fear that he would claw us.]

The narrator has sporadic contacts with Pancho Villa in the course of his activities as part of the anti-Huerta rebellion and later as a supporter of Eulalio Gutiérrez. The intellectual records his fascination, often turning into fascinated horror, at the former bandit's apparent lack of either a reliable moral compass or even a minimal degree of basic self-control. Based on his own direct observations and on stories told to him by others, the character Guzmán recounts acts of "revolutionary justice" carried out with the noose and the firing squad, as well as his own efforts to temper Villa's behavior through expressions of reason and appeals to military protocols. Interspersed with many acts of violence, are glimpses of Villa as an amusing conversationalist, a solicitous friend, and a commander who always looked after the welfare of his troops. At the end of the novel, the increasingly isolated Villa wins the reader's sympathy as we see him, through the narrator's eyes, abandoned by his former allies and threatened by the combined armies of Carranza and Obregón. The image of Pancho Villa in *El águila y la serpiente* is dominated by the savage, bestial face of the jaguar, but the silhouette of his humanity emerges from the shadows to complicate and complete a portrait that could have become a simple caricature.

It remains to return to the question in what sense Guzmán's representation of Pancho Villa can be read as a nonfictional account of a historical figure. The textual markers give mixed signals, and a review of the criticism suggests that the writer's extratextual status as an eyewitness to many of the events is a determining factor in reading the text as autobiography, memoir, and/or chronicle in defiance of Guzmán's own claims. Western culture bases its legal system on a privileging of eyewitness testimony and material evidence, the latter being a word whose root meaning denotes that which can be seen. Western historiography began in the early nineteenth century to privilege the use of eyewitness accounts in reconstructing the past, and the accurate dating of documents became an important factor in the authentication of source materials. In this context, the composition of *El águila y la serpiente* by a direct observer and participant just a little more than a decade after the events occurred tempts the reader to grant historical value to the narrative. However, the text simultaneously asserts and undermines the value of the eyewitness report. In spite of the constant references to acts of visual perception, the authority of the narrator's observations is problematized in a number of ways. Many significant scenes take place at night when a notorious lack of street lighting and poor interior illumination cast a shadow of a doubt on what the principal witness has seen. Through the accumulated references to half-glimpsed faces, indistinguishable figures, "luz furtiva," and "aspas de luz que mitigaban apenas la sombra," [furtive light; sparks of light that barely relieved the shadow] Guzmán renders Mexico as a nation that cannot be seen clearly. Even the testimony of an eyewitness is therefore not to be trusted.

Finally, Martín Luis Guzmán's own theory of history, which he outlined in "Un experto de la historia," an essay published in Paris in 1926, equally supports and challenges a reading of the novel as factual discourse. In the essay, Guzmán defends the "great men" tradition of historiography, and he defines the proper subject of Mexican history to be the deeds and personalities of individuals such as Cortés, Cuauhtémoc, Hidalgo, and Morelos. He therefore contributes to the nation-building project of history writing by creating a collage of great men in *El águila y la serpiente.* However, in the book's enactment of this model of history, a model that today competes with alternative constructions of the past, Guzmán vacillates between the value of the strictly verifiable and factual, and a broader concept of historical "truth" that includes legend in its embrace. *El águila y la serpiente* strives to be both history and literature in the Aristotelian sense, a double-life that is most obvious in Guzmán's appeal to popular legend as a legitimate source of truth about the Revolutionary experience. In one of the most vivid and most frequently anthologized chapters of the book, "La fiesta de balas," [Festival of bullets] Guzmán recounts a massacre of captive Federal soldiers by one of Villa's subordinates, the notorious Rodolfo Fierro. Here the narrator, following Aristotle, clearly distinguishes the "strictly historical" from the "legendary" exploits of the División del Norte, and he defends legend over history as a more worthy version of the true nature of historical figures and their deeds. The interest in an Aristotelian notion of truth ultimately outweighs the investment in accurately representing "what actually happened" in the past, thus adding yet another twist to a version of the Mexican Revolution that is both convincing and suspect as a nonfictional testimony. *El águila y la serpiente*, because it has been read across disciplines and across genres, provides an intriguing case for thinking about the definitions and functions of factual discourse as modes of writing and of reading in twentieth-century Mexico.

Las memorias de Pancho Villa is Martín Luis Guzmán's second, and very different, version of the exploits and the personality of Francisco Villa. The six-hundred densely packed pages of the 1991 Porrúa edition are organized into five books that cover the period from 1894, when Doroteo Arango took the name Francisco Villa and became an outlaw in his native state of Durango, until April 1915, when General Pancho Villa suffered a series of political and military setbacks in his fight against the growing ascendancy of Venustiano Carranza after the Aguascalientes Convention. The *Memorias* is clearly an unfinished work. Book Five, Chapter XXVIII abruptly and inconclusively ends with Villa's preparations for continuing to fight after his decisive defeat in the town of Celaya. This is neither a logical point at which to terminate his life story, nor even a sensible moment to make the transition from one book to another. The narrative simply and inexplicably stops. Guzmán published the first parts of *Las memorias de Pancho Villa* in 1938, and the "complete" edition of five books appeared in 1951. In later years he spoke of writing four additional volumes treating the years from mid-1915 to Villa's death in 1923, but at the time of the author's own death in 1976, only incomplete materials for the continuation were left behind.[7]

Although Guzmán stated in the 1958 interview with Emmanuel Carballo cited above that *Las memorias de Pancho Villa* was his best-selling title at the time, it is far from being the work that has attracted the most critical attention. On the contrary, very little analysis of the text can be found, and there are no in-depth studies of it. Any number of reasons may explain the dearth of critical interest, starting with the general indifference toward nonfiction as a mode of writing worthy of study. More specifically in this case, it is unsatisfying to read a long, detailed book about a figure such as Villa and find that the story breaks off midstream. In light of Guzmán's intentions to continue the work, the existing sections can perhaps be dismissed by arguing that they constitute only a fragment of a larger and more coherent design. In addition, Guzmán the acclaimed prose stylist is nowhere to be found in the monotonous, repetitive phrasing of the supposed memoir, and the reader cringes at the tiresome recurrence of certain expressions attributed to Villa's own voice. Nevertheless, the book does provoke a number of pertinent questions regarding nonfiction literature, and autobiography in particular, as well as offering a striking contrast to the recreation of Pancho Villa in *El águila y la serpiente*. My analysis will discuss the dominant, official image of Villa in Mexico against which Guzmán wrote; the claim made to factual status; the dubious validity of calling the book an autobiography or a memoir; and Guzmán's shaping of a relatively positive representation of the events of Pancho Villa's life and of his primary personality traits.

Pancho Villa was ultimately the loser in the power struggle waged by Gutiérrez, Obregón and, most importantly, Carranza in 1914 and 1915. Once the chief of the heralded División del Norte and then the commanding general of the Conventionist armies, by late 1915 Villa was a fugitive hiding out in Chihuahua and fighting a guerrilla war with a small band of men. Although he had some success against the Carrancista forces in 1916, in 1920 he surrendered to the federal authorities and retired to a hacienda in Durango. He was assassinated in July of 1923, arguably under orders of either Plutarco Elías Calles or Obregón. In the official histories of the Revolution of 1910, written from the point of view of the victors, Villa has been portrayed at best with ambivalence, and at worst with deep disdain. Miguel Alessio Robles's 1938 *Historia política de la Revolución* is highly favorable to Carranza and Obregón and, while it grants praise to the División del Norte's military feats in the war against Huerta, Villa's leadership role is downplayed and his troops are given the primary credit for the victories. In his confrontations with Carranza, Alessio Robles characterizes Villa as "furioso" and "frenético;" "una fiera y un niño," [furious; frenetic; a beast and a child] in the face of the Primer Jefe's "valor sereno y tranquilo" [serene and tranquil courage] (144). Jesús Silva Herzog accuses Villa of being a reactionary in his brief 1944 work *La Revolución Mexicana en crisis*, which is also admiring of Carranza. The negative, hegemonic view of Villa the outlaw and the murderer resurfaces as late as 1972 in Rodrigo Alonso Cortés's title *Francisco Villa, el quinto jinete del apocalipsis.*

In a context of proliferating anti-Villa histories, Martín Luis Guzmán began in the 1930s to write an alternative life story of the General. In undertaking a project of nonfiction, the author surely also had in mind the legendary or poetic truth that he had chosen to tell in *El águila y la serpiente*. One of the commons functions of fact-based discourse is as an instrument of advocacy or defense of an individual or group under threat. This tendency is at work in the *Memorias*, which seeks to provide a corrective, historically verifiable account in opposition to the official histories and to the popular legends, both positive and negative, surrounding Villa. The term "memoir" in the title immediately raises certain expectations, and Guzmán makes a strong claim to factual status for the book in his prologue. Here he establishes two real-life supports for what he has written: documents from the Villa archive, and his own Revolutionary experience and acquaintanceship with Villa. Guzmán carefully identifies a number of the pertinent archival materials, and he explains what parts of the book correspond most closely to them. The primary sources are: (1) a 40-page typewritten "Hoja de servicios de Francisco Villa" covering 1910 and 1911; (2) a collection of 103 handwritten sheets that treat the years 1894–1914, later referred to as the "Apuntes a lápiz;" and (3) a 242-page manuscript in "excellent calligraphy" titled "El General Pancho Villa, por Manuel Bauche Alcalde, 1914." Guzmán states that the "Hoja de servicios" and the "Apuntes" were evidently based on Villa's oral testimony, while the Bauche Alcalde manuscript rewrites the "Apuntes" and adds Bauche's own reflections on the Revolution. Roughly the first 150 pages of the *Memorias* utilize these documents as their principal sources, and Guzmán wrote the remaining 440 pages using (unidentified) historical documents and (unnamed) eyewitnesses with whom the author spoke. In 1958 he reiterated to Carballo: "En las *Memorias* no hay una sola palabra que no se base en un testimonio ocular y de primera mano o en un documento" (*Protagonistas* 90). [There isn't a single word in the *Memorias* that isn't based on an eye-witness testimony or a document.] These protestations aside, Guzmán's prologue makes a less-than-compelling case for the documentary basis and content of his book. Although it is in part firmly grounded in verifiable sources and in the author's experience, more than half of the memoir is attributable to documents and witnesses that remain unidentified by Guzmán and are therefore irrecuperable by the reader. By foreclosing on an intertextual reading, Guzmán undermines his claim to factual status in the eyes of the present-day reader, who might not be inclined to grant the writer blanket authority to make such a claim while suppressing key sources.

Turning to the memoir form, the prologue describes a writing process that entailed the editing of existing materials, filling in gaps by directly writing a wholly original narrative for the years starting with 1914, and subjecting the entire text to a remarkable sleight of tongue in order to inscribe (Guzmán's version of) Villa's own authentic voice on the page. According to Guzmán, the General's voice was obscured by the more educated style imposed by Bauche Alcalde on the texts that the latter edited. Guzmán explains his own qualifications for detecting the false notes in the source documents and for reproducing the exact tone of Villa's spoken language in the *Memorias*. Not only did he have personal dealings with the Revolutionary General during which he heard him tell numerous episodes of his life, but the future (auto)biographer also wrote down as faithfully as possible what Villa said. He makes this point in the prologue to the *Memorias* and again in the Carballo interview: "El germen de las *Memorias* data de las innumerables conversaciones que sostuve con él: Villa era un fabuloso conversador; yo, público entusiasta. Al finalizar éstas, trasladaba al papel, con fidelidad, lo que había escuchado" (90). [The seeds of the *Memorias* come from the innumerable conversations that I had with him; Villa was a fabulous conversationalist; I, an enthusiastic listener. After these conversations, I used to faithfully transfer onto paper what I had heard.] Ultimately, as a result of his meticulous research process and his own intimate knowledge and personal written record of Villa's voice, Guzmán claims to have created in the *Memorias*, "el verdadero Villa, no el deformado por las leyendas contradictorias difundidas por amigos o enemigos" (Carballo 90). [The true Villa, not the one deformed by the contradictory legends that were spread by his friends or enemies.]

The "true Villa" as written by Martín Luis Guzmán is a complex, contradictory subject whose life story traces a rising and then falling arc from youthful poverty and powerlessness to the height of national and international fame as the commanding general of the División del Norte, and finally the beginning of his descent into military and political irrelevance with Eulalio Gutiérrez's renunciation of their politico-military pact and the defeats at Celaya. The *Memorias* is a retrospective, autodiegetic text in which the narrator-protagonist, claiming to be Pancho

Villa himself, continually shifts between the equally dynamic roles of a remembering, speaking-I and a remembered, acting-I. In the analysis that follows, my strategy will be first to examine the meanings invested in the actions and the character of the protagonist Pancho Villa, and then to interrogate the status of the book as memoir. The postponement of a consideration of genre allows me to establish a clear contrast between the divergent images of Villa in Guzmán's writings and then to address the questions of genre and factual adequacy in more detail.

In its narrative structure and language *Las memorias de Pancho Villa* blends features of traditional historical discourse, traces of oral testimony or storytelling, and a marked tendency toward self-revelation. The referential orientation of history writing leads, as we have seen, to a discourse that is heavy in proper names and facts, both of which are linguistic constructs used to recall verifiable events that take place in identifiable locations at documented times. The retelling of the past in conventionally conceived Western histories preferably follows chronological order, an order that supports the determination of cause and effect in human affairs. The *Memorias* respects the chronological sequencing of the events of Pancho Villa's life, and it even highlights the orderly passage of time with a frequent accounting of dates. Book One, Chapter I opens with these lines that clearly locate the beginning of the narrative in time as well as place: "El 94, siendo un joven de dieciséis años, vivía yo en una hacienda que se nombraba Haciendo de Gogojito perteneciente a la municipalidad de Canatlán, Estado de Durango" (3). [In 1894 as a young man of sixteen years of age, I lived on an estate called Hacienda de Gogojito, in the township of Canatlán, Durango State.] A few lines farther on, the narrator identifies September 22, 1894 as a turning point in his life, the day when an act of violence that he committed in defense of his sister and his family's honor forced him to leave home and literally "head for the hills" to escape punishment. Within the first two pages, the narrative introduces key motifs that will be present until the end of Book Five: the narrator-protagonist as a victim of persecution (first by representatives of the Porfirian social order and later by his Revolutionary superiors); and his uncanny ability to fend for himself and to survive the odds heavily stacked against him. The twenty-three chapters of the first book recount Villa's life as an outlaw in the northern states of Durango and Chihuahua, his first meeting of Francisco I. Madero, and his beginnings as a Revolutionary chief in the fight to depose Porfirio Díaz and later to defend Madero's government during the Pascual Orozco rebellion. Intertwined with the story of his military victories and his growing prestige, is the recurring theme of persecution, no longer at the hands of the Porfirian police force, but by orders of Victoriano Huerta, Madero's commanding general and future traitor and assassin.

Books Two and Three trace the eighteen-month war against Huerta (February 1913 to June 1914), during which Villa leads the División del Norte and achieves a series of remarkable battlefield victories. Detailed descriptions of military campaigns and a wealth of very specific references to people, places, and actions dominate these books. This is a time of triumph for Villa, and it is equally a time of thwarted plans and ambitions due to his constant conflicts and his ultimately irreconcilable differences with the Primer Jefe Venustiano Carranza. Carranza has replaced Villa's enemy Huerta, who replaced the Porfirian "rurales" as the narrator's immediate tormentor, but persecution and conspiracy are constant complaints, as illustrated by these examples chosen from hundreds more: "Desde esa época no cesaron las persecuciones para mí" (4); "el Primer Jefe . . . por su impulso secreto, o por impulso de los que lo rodeaban, desconfiaba de mí y se mostraba inclinado a ponerme embarazos en el desarrollo de mi acción" (231); and "Me criminaban los periódicos de todo el mundo" (168). [From that time on the persecutions did not stop; the First Chief . . . because of his secret impulses or those of people around him, mistrusted me and he showed an inclination to place obstacles in my way; newspapers all around the world portrayed me as a criminal.]

The final two books tell of the chaotic period following the defeat of Huerta by the precariously united Revolutionary armies. The growing tensions and splits among the factions led by Carranza, Obregón, Zapata, and Villa, which explode into a continuation of outright civil war after the Aguascalientes Convention, eventually situate Villa on the losing side. The *Memorias* ends, as I have mentioned, with the dramatic reversal of Villa's military fortunes at Celaya. In addition to telling his battlefield exploits, the narrator-protagonist is preoccupied by his political maneuverings and his reflections on the goals of the Revolution during 1914 and 1915, as Villa compares his own loyalty toward the ideals of Maderista democracy and the cause of the poor to the authoritarianism and the greed that he attributes to Carranza and Obregón. Thus, although the *Memorias* is a drastically truncated version of Pancho Villa's life, its storyline suggests the familiar narrative pattern of the rise and fall of a great, but greatly misunderstood man.

In contrast to the snapshot portrayal that is focalized through Guzmán's eyes as the narrator in *El águila y la serpiente*, the autobiographical structure of the *Memorias* must by definition present its events, characters and locations through Villa's eye-witness testimony and self-revelation and, less frequently, through reports given directly to him by others. This results in an illusion of intimacy and direct access to the "transparent mind" of the protagonist.[8] *El águila*'s violently impulsive, fear-inspiring jaguar gives way to a wholly different persona characterized by a long list of positive virtues: generosity, honesty, loyalty, reason, obedience to his superiors, responsible leadership of his troops, and an idealistic sense of justice and concern for the poor. The episodes of anger turning to rage and leading to violence have by no means disappeared from this revised "self"-portrayal of Pancho Villa, but they are tempered in at least two ways. The narrator is disarmingly conscious of his own lethal temper and he records his efforts to control it; and the executions that he orders of innumerable "enemies" are placed in the context of military justice and the accepted code of warfare. At times Villa testifies that he allowed himself to be talked out of completing the orders for an execution, demonstrating a self-professed willingness to yield to reason. The emphasis on Villa as a reasonable and reasoning intellect defies his reputation as a murderous criminal. The I-narrator takes pains to deny charges of criminality and to defend his behavior in all circumstances with the justification that whatever he did, he did it to defend the Revolution and advance the cause of the poor. In these ways, the act of self-representation serves to counter the discourse of legendary violence propagated by Villa's foes during his lifetime and for many decades after his death.

Villa's dominant character traits are revealed in the narrated actions, the recreated dialogues and telegrams, and the instances of self-reflection in which the narrator engages. The alternation among these elements comprises a conventionally realistic narrative discourse in which events occur and are commented on in a predictable order. The language employed throughout is marked by the repetition of set phrases, a relative lack of figurative speech and simple syntactical structures. Among the clichés that appear and reappear at regular intervals are the following: "un hombre de mucha ley," "un hombre de muchas luces de inteligencia," "los dos de un solo parecer," "y como lo dije lo hice," "pensaba (reflexionaba) yo entre mí," "viva seguro de que," and, most notably, "se me revolvió toda la cólera de mi cuerpo" [a law-abiding man; a very intelligent man; the two of them in agreement; I thought (reflected) to myself;

rest assured that; my body churned with anger]. This limited range of expressions, a heavy dependence on the conjunction "and" to connect simple phrases and sentences, and the frequent use of rhetorical questions to express indignation constitute a restricted linguistic repertoire that Guzmán believed accurately represented the "pureza expresiva del habla que en Villa era habitual," (*Memorias* viii) [the expressive purity common to Villa's speech], but that has the contradictory effects of making the narrator-protagonist appear intellectually impoverished and provoking a kind of amused irritation in the reader.

To conclude the analysis of the *Memorias*, I return to its title and the matters of genre and the claim to factual status. Memoir is a form of autobiographical writing that typically focuses on the public life of the subject's mature years in its social and historical context. Like other forms of autobiography, it is generally classified as a nonfiction genre, although theories of autobiography raise many doubts about such a classification, citing the fragility and plasticity of memory, the fluid nature of subjectivity, the writer's self-interest, and the ways in which self-representation becomes self-reinvention as factors that weaken its documentary value. Like all putatively factual discourse, autobiography is necessarily informed by a process of selection and shaping that is not neutral but interested, and it is subject to the constraints imposed on that process by the limited repertoire of existing cultural plots available to the author. Looking at *Las memorias de Pancho Villa* it is not difficult to see how it places conflicting demands on the reader's expectations by appealing to and subverting the generic requirements of life writing. Philippe Lejeune established a fundamental definition of classic autobiography in his work of the 1970s and 80s: "Retrospective prose narrative written by a real person concerning his own existence, where the focus is his individual life, in particular the story of his personality" (*On Autobiography* 4). The *Memorias* conforms to this definition in all respects except one, and this proves to be a critical discrepancy. Lejeune expands on the notion of a real person writing about his own existence, when he states that the autobiographical pact, which is a contract for reading, is subject to an inviolable condition: the identity of name of the author, the narrator, and the protagonist. The social contract for reading is therefore irrevocably broken in the case under study by the nonidentity of the signature of the author, Martín Luis Guzmán, and the name of the person whose life story is being told, Pancho Villa. This opens up the text to a variety of possible approaches and even attacks. To start, textual statements such as "declaro yo, Pancho Villa," and "decía yo" [I, Pancho Villa, declare; I was saying] are fundamentally lies in the context of a book that appears to be Villa's autobiography (and not, for example, an autodiegetic novel), and yet bears the signature of Martín Luis Guzmán. Perhaps Guzmán is exploiting the powerful capacity of the linguistic sign to tell lies in order to tell the truth about Villa, as Lucille Kerr has said of Elena Poniatowska's role as author of *Hasta no verte, Jesús mío.*[9] Lying to tell the truth, in the sense of performing a literary transformation on materials gleaned from objective reality with the purpose of affirming the existence of that reality, may very well achieve an effect of convincing verisimilitude, but can a persuasive lie, a verisimilar fiction, be read as nonfiction?

Lejeune offers a variation on classic autobiography that might better fit the case of the *Memorias.* Under the rubric of "the autobiography of those who do not write," the theorist discusses the category of autodiegetic true-life stories that are produced through a collaboration between an autobiographical subject, or model, and a writer.[10] In the modern collaborative autobiography, which is frequently based on extensive taped interviews, the writer is "steeped in the spoken word of the model, imbued with his story" (*On Autobiography* 190). During the writing process, the author's own activity and language are assumed to be carefully erased in order faithfully to reproduce the voice of the model. Lejeune's groundbreaking work and more recent theories of autobiography and testimonial literature point out the many problems and obstacles inherent in a writer's efforts, however sincere, to absorb another's voice and convey it in an accurate, neutral fashion, but Guzmán claims to have done exactly this for Villa. Lejeune locates the origins of collaborative autobiography in an old tradition that Guzmán seems to have actualized: that of "secretaryship," in which famous men, especially politicians, used literary people to elaborate and improve their memoirs (186). It is quite possible that Pancho Villa cast Bauche Alcalde into the role of personal secretary when he dictated his life story to him, but he could not have anticipated or authorized Guzmán's subsequent intervention. There are many signs in the text of the act of oral testimony by Villa in the presence of another. I have already mentioned the frequent inclusion of verbs such as "I declare," "I affirm," and "I say" directed to an invisible interlocutor and not to a character present in the diegetic level of the narration. Pancho Villa as narrator also frequently evokes the present time of speaking in contrast to the past time of the retrospectively recounted life by using the terms "now," "today" and "up until now" in combination with verbs in the present tense in order to signal the present, timeless moment of remembering and testifying. It is logical to assume that these are the traces of the real past conversations between Pancho Villa and the person or persons to whom he dictated his service record and his life story, but it is also possible that Guzmán introduced them as markers of the orality that he deemed characteristic of the speech of a marginally literate man.

Several other points that have been elaborated in studies of testimonial literature help us to think critically about the claims that Guzmán makes for the *Memorias.* One is, again, the problem of the signature. Under the older model of secretaryship, the subject's name was affixed to the text as its sole author. Modern collaborative autobiographies and testimonies most often display two signatures. However, the *Memorias* is solely authored by Martín Luis Guzmán, while it offers itself as Villa's memoir. Pancho Villa owns the title, but not the title page. The name of Manuel Bauche Alcalde, for his part, is doubly erased. First, he may or may not be the implied, unnamed interlocutor whose presence in the text is rendered mute and invisible. Second, in his prologue Guzmán acknowledges the authorship of the source document "El General Francisco Villa" only to dismiss Bauche Alcalde as an unfaithful scribe who imposed too much of himself on Villa's language. The other witnesses whom Guzmán interviewed for the book are never identified at all. Guzmán the writer fully replaces the authors of his sources and he claims to restore the sole true voice of Pancho Villa by means of his personal powers of synthesis and his unique ear for speech.

Collaborative projects between two living, interacting human subjects are virtually always structured upon unequal power relations. Most commonly, either the model is a celebrity and enjoys superior status to the ghostwriter; or the model is a common person whose story is being taken by an elite-class writer and put to uses that are not under the model's control. Theories of testimonial literature struggle to lay bare the tensions inherent in how testimonies are produced and where and by whom they are read without foreclosing entirely on the ethical and political worth of such endeavors. In the case of the *Memorias*, a living writer appropriated the life story of a deceased person, perhaps rendering moot any concern over the dynamics of collaboration. However, the exercise of power—proper or improper—still comes into play. Christopher Domínguez articulates in his essay "Martín Luis Guzmán:

El teatro de la política" some of my own thoughts when I first read the book. He accuses Guzmán of acting as a ventriloquist and reducing Villa to the status of a puppet in a work that ultimately communicates Guzmán's own opinions about the Revolution and the Mexican "pueblo" through the mouth, if not the language, of Pancho Villa (29). In his wholesale repossession and repackaging of the source documents and his selling of the new product as the only authentic voice of the true Villa, Guzmán performs a gesture of authorship that seems especially heavy handed in today's literary environment. Nothing in the prologue or the later interviews indicates that he ever questioned his own authority in making these appropriations, which does not, however, prevent his readers from doing so.

Las memorias de Pancho Villa has been read as a work of nonfiction and it has been used as a primary source for other nonfictional accounts of the Mexican Revolution of 1910. Its facts can be checked for accuracy against other documents. For example, Friedrich Katz's stunning biography *The Life and Times of Pancho Villa* serves as a valuable reference against which to read Guzmán's text. Parting from Guzmán's open claim to factual status for his book, I have demonstrated some of the ways that it encourages and discourages the granting of factual adequacy by its readers. The writer's clear interest in fashioning an alternative, positive version of Villa in the context of official history and popular legend, the erasure of sources, and the suspect nature of the writer's claim to serve as a transparent vehicle for another's voice, must be weighed against the prominence of many of the markers of historical discourse in the work. It is not my aim to take the books included in this study and either lock them into or lock them out of a strongbox category called nonfiction. Rather, I am concerned to explore the ramifications of accepting at least provisionally a given work's invitation to be read as such. *Las memorias de Pancho Villa*, in ways that set it significantly apart from *El águila y la serpiente*, equally stretches our commonsense understanding of the meanings and the functions of nonfiction literature.

The narrative works of Nellie Campobello, like those by her friend Martín Luis Guzmán, have provoked a variety of critical responses. Her long-neglected masterpieces *Cartucho* (1931/1940) and *Las manos de mamá* (1937) have been equally often treated as nonfiction (autobiography, memoir, or testimony) and as fiction (novel or montage of stories or vignettes) in the scholarly literature that has grown up since her rediscovery in the 1970s; while her biographical work *Apuntes sobre la vida militar de Francisco Villa* (1940) is still generally ignored. Campobello's writing offers an interesting case for this study in part because the very ground upon which her readers might base an autobiographical interpretation of her works, has turned out to be shaky indeed. In the studies of *Cartucho* and *Las manos de mamá* published earlier than the late 1990s, Campobello's accepted birthdate of 1909 was a critical factor in identifying the child narrator with the real-life child Nellie Campobello.[11] These narratives cover the period from 1915 to 1919, when the future writer would have been between five and nine years old. The narrator's name, Nellie, corresponds to the name of the author, in autobiographical fashion, and her mother's name Rafaela is also invoked. These points help to explain and justify the degree of veracity, spontaneity, and faithfulness to memory that many readers have perceived in Campobello's texts.[12] Nevertheless, the elemental facts of Campobello's life that were once used to support autobiographical interpretations of her work, have been revealed by her biographer Irene Matthews's careful investigation to be "false," in the sense of inaccurate and unverifiable, as shown below.

In the analysis of *Las memorias de Pancho Villa*, I have already touched upon the ways in which contemporary theory puts into doubt the factual accuracy of memoir, autobiography, and testimony, doubts which form part of the overall interrogation of referentiality that was addressed in Chapter 1. In the case of autobiography, in particular, it is important to keep in mind that, as Paul Ricoeur succinctly put it, "The *subject* is never given at the beginning. Or, if it were so given, it would run the risk of reducing itself to a narcissistic ego, self-centred and avaricious—and it is just this from which literature can liberate us."[13] That is, the autobiographical subject writes him- or herself into existence through a complex interplay of remembering, revealing, and inventing the self, and not simply by recording the facts of a life or capturing a self that had been already given beforehand. Nellie Campobello adds a further dimension to autobiographical creativity by illustrating how self-invention is not limited to acts of writing, but are central to the way an individual lives in the real world, the way he or she lives the very life that autobiography is supposed truthfully to recount. It is well known that Nellie Campobello was baptized María Francisca Luna, and she took the name that now identifies her when she was a young adult. In a 1960 interview with Emmanuel Carballo she also states that her given names are Nellie Francisca Ernestina (*Protagonistas* 409). Later, she used the assumed or adopted name of Nellie for her narrative (self) creation in *Cartucho* and *Las manos de mamá.* Irene Matthews, who has written the only biography to date of Campobello, *Nellie Campobello: La centaura del norte* (1997), located her baptismal records in a church in the town of Villa Ocampo, and this document states that the child María Francisca Luna was born on November 7, 1900. This date of birth, nine years earlier than the date that Campobello preferred to claim for herself, places Francisca as an adolescent and not as a child during the years of Pancho Villa's guerrilla campaign against the Carranza government. Matthews further discovered that Campobello mothered a child who died before the age of two; a child disguised in *Las manos de mamá* as Rafaela Luna's youngest son and poignantly described as an "angelote rubio" [a blonde angel]. These "facts," these alternative, documented descriptions of the events of the writer's life significantly undermine the autobiographical status of her two narratives.

Authorial support for documentary readings of *Cartucho* is found in Campobello's extratextual commentaries on her work. In 1960 her collected works were published in the volume *Mis libros*, for which she wrote a lengthy prologue. The prologue, characterized by some as a memoir, contains several references to the fundamental truth-value of the stories told in *Cartucho.* A love of truth and a hatred for the "mundo de mentiras en que vivía" (*Mis libros* 13) [the world of lies in which I lived] inspired Campobello to take up the challenge of writing about the Revolution in the north and her childhood hero Pancho Villa at a time when speaking out in his defense was not a politically astute move. In fact, the initial reception of *Cartucho* in the nation's capital was largely hostile. However, the author states that a moral obligation to tell the truth prevailed: "Latente la inquietud de mi espíritu, amante de la verdad y de la justicia, humanamente hablando, me vi en la necesidad de escribir" (12). [Given the latent disquiet of my spirit, lover of truth and justice, humanly speaking, I was compelled to write.] Later in the essay, she seems to contradict her own epigraph to *Cartucho*, written years earlier, in which she had stated that the novel is composed of "cuentos verdaderos" [true stories] that her mother gifted to her. The structure of the novel reiterates this claim by introducing many of the vignettes as stories that she heard from her mother. However, thirty years later, perhaps in an effort to bolster the book's claim to historical accuracy, Campobello states that "[l]as narraciones de *Cartucho* . . . son verdad histórica, son hechos trágicos vistos por mis ojos de niña" (17).

[*Cartucho*'s narratives . . . are historical truth, tragic events seen by my own eyes as a child.] At roughly the same time, the writer attests to Emmanuel Carballo: "Escribí en este libro lo que me consta del villismo, no lo que me han contado" (472), [I wrote what I know myself about Villismo, not what they have told me], further identifying the "relatos" as her own eye-witness account and not as stories told by others.

Gustavo Faverón Patriau subjects the entire web of statements about *Cartucho* and the contradictions between Nellie Campobello's self-representation throughout her life and the telling details that surfaced during Matthews's meticulous research to a thorough-going critical examination in his article "La rebelión de la memoria: Testimonio y escritura de la realidad en *Cartucho* de Nellie Campobello" (2003). Faverón Patriau starts with Paul de Man's premise that all autobiography is a form of fiction in which a character, not a person, speaks. Faverón Patriau does not, however, deny the capacity of fiction to say something about extratextual reality, including about the reality of the past. The question that he poses is how one can read *Cartucho* critically as part of a study of the Revolution of 1910, while not reading it naively as history. His conclusion is that *Cartucho* is not the "memorias de una niña traumatizada por la guerra" (69) [the memoir of a child traumatized by war], and it should not be read as autobiography according to the definition given by Lejeune. Nevertheless, it is a highly valuable text if read as a virtually unique source for a feminine perspective on the Revolution and a subversive rewriting of history which suggests that, in addition to the risks suffered, women enjoy certain freedoms from patriarchal control during times of war.

Faverón Patriau's analysis leaves open the potential for reading a kind of truth-value in *Cartucho* that does not hinge upon factual accuracy and adequacy. As we saw in the study of *El águila y la serpiente*, the preoccupation with truth in the poetic sense trumps the concern for facticity. These texts can be seen, then, as true stories, but not as nonfiction. The truths of *Cartucho* are strongly partisan and were consciously constructed as part of Nellie Campobello's personal campaign to rehabilitate the name of Pancho Villa and right the wrongs committed by the Carrancista histories of the Revolution. A corrective version of the General can be gleaned from his appearance in thirteen of the fifty-six stories that comprise *Cartucho*, although readers who expect to find a detailed description of Pancho Villa or a coherent account of his military feats from 1915 to 1919 will be disappointed. Whether cast as the protagonist or placed in a secondary role in roughly one-quarter of the book's very brief sketches, the representation of Villa is profoundly shaped by the work's fragmented structure and elliptical style. Its fifty-six separate anecdotes introduce an almost equal number of characters, and favor the brief lives and the violent deaths of Villista partisans, most of whom appear and disappear from one page to the next. Metonymy and synecdoche are the favored tropes, as in the way a pair of green eyes, loose-fitting trousers, broad hands, or a long, blonde mustache evoke the figures of the soldiers and endow them with their individual significance: physical beauty, proximity to death, strength, or elegance. Villa, whose repeated presence supplies a measure of continuity, acquires a fuller range of meanings through the gradual accumulation of isolated traits from one chapter to another. In the section "La camisa gris" [the gray shirt], the General is all-knowing and never forgets a betrayal. In "Los tres meses de Gloriecita" [little Gloria's three months], Villa is the defender of the town of Parral and can count on the support of the townspeople, while, in an inversion of the dominant discourse in Mexico at the time of the book's publication, the Federal troops fighting against him are branded as "bandidos" and pillagers. Pancho Villa is also a father figure, shown to love and to mourn his favorites as if they were sons and to guard the welfare of all of his troops. Villa's voice is the most important synecdochical reference to his person. As pure sound—loud and resonant across great distances—his voice commands obedience and respect and unifies the people. As a vehicle for language, his speaking voice reveals the General's understanding of other men's fears and his mastery of a kind of psychological warfare waged through wit and a sense of irony that veil the very real threat that he poses to his enemies.

The book's frequent violation of chronological sequencing, another dominant narrative device, achieves its peak semantic potential in permitting Villa to survive and even to triumph over his own narrative death, as he has survived death in the popular imagination and the official histories. Fragment forty "El cigarro de Samuel" [Samuel's cigar] commemorates in an unusually understated and sidelong fashion Villa's assassination in 1923: "Un día Samuel, aquel muchacho tímido, se quedó dormido en un automóvil, Villa y Trillo también se quedaron allí; dormidos para siempre" (111). [One day Samuel, that shy boy, fell asleep in an automobile, Villa and Trillo fell asleep too, asleep forever.] The focus of the episode is the shy boy Samuel, and Villa's death appears as an incidental sidebar to the main topic. Villa reappears numerous times in the remaining sixteen episodes, and the book ends anachronistically by recounting the battle plans and strategies of one of Villa's victories over General Francisco Murguía. In a final reversal of the language of official history, Murguía's troops are characterized as "salvajes" [savages], and their defeat by Villa is greeted with enthusiastic gratitude by the common people of the north, whose corrective memory the book recuperates.

Nellie Campobello's campaign to rehabilitate the name of Francisco Villa began in 1930 with the publication of a magazine article and the first edition of *Cartucho*. Ten years later, she completed the public phase of that effort by publishing the expanded and final version of *Cartucho* and the biographical chronicle *Apuntes de la vida militar de Francisco Villa*. I use the term biographical chronicle to describe the book's particular approach to the writing of a person's life. The *Apuntes* distills Villa's personality, his human relations, and his life story from youth to death into an account that admits only of his activities as a military leader. By defining Villa almost exclusively as a warrior, it is narrower in scope than many biographies, but it is nonetheless biographical. Additionally, it shares with the journalistic chronicle the presence of a personal narrator, the concern for the recent past, and the careful locating of events in time. It contrasts sharply with *Cartucho*, where the precise spatio-visual coordinates of home, window frame, doorway, street, and plaza occupy the primary narrative plane, and time is registered only vaguely on the narrator's consciousness. In *Apuntes de la vida militar de Francisco Villa*, the exact dates and the duration in hours and days of each battle are meticulously recorded, and the chronological sequence is rarely interrupted by narrative anachronisms. Told retrospectively, the story marks time from one battle to the next according to the measured rhythm of marching armies.

My reading of *Apuntes de la vida militar de Francisco Villa* finds it to be a highly partisan but solidly nonfictional piece of writing about Pancho Villa. The no-nonsense title suggests a documentary approach to its subject, and the author's "Nota preliminar" explains both the documentary writing process and the advocacy role that is assumed by the narrator in the body of the work. First, Campobello identifies her sources of information: conversations with Villa's widow Austreberta Rentería de Villa; the Villa written archives (presumably the same ones used by Martín Luis Guzmán); interviews with two of his "Dorados" and correspondence with a third soldier (all of whom she names); consultations with Guzmán; and personal visits to the scenes of some of Villa's battles.

This documentary basis is visible throughout the narrative to follow. In the same preliminary notes, Campobello gives her interpretation of the essential truth of Francisco Villa, and she alludes to her motivation in researching and writing about him. She identifies the life of the warrior as the *only* life proper to "Francisco Villa, conductor de hombres de guerra; en otro aspecto no existe. La verdad de sus batallas es la verdad de su vida" (10). [Francisco Villa, leader of warriors; he has no other existence. The truth of his battles is the truth of his life.] Her motivation is to represent Villa as a true and unique military genius, "uno de los más grandes de la historia" [one of the greatest in history] and to defend him from "tantas historias falsas y leyendas ridículas" (10) [so many false histories and ridiculous legends].

The *Apuntes* devotes one brief chapter to Villa's life on the margins of society prior to 1910, a life that the narrator characterizes as that of a rebel and not an outlaw. In this telling, as early as 1893 he embarks on a struggle to right the wrongs of an oppressive social structure and to experience the freedom denied to hacienda peons of the Porfiriato. However, Villa is not truly born until 1910 when he takes up arms on behalf of Madero's revolution, and the book traces his ten-year fight first to win the war for Madero and later to defend the Revolution from the autocratic designs of Huerta, Carranza, and Obregón. Short chapters are grouped into sections that cover each year of his military campaigns, 1910–1919, with a few final pages treating Carranza's death in 1920 and Villa's subsequent return to civilian life. Although the book carries Villa's life story farther than did Guzmán's incomplete memoir, Campobello also stops short of recreating the General's retirement years and his assassination. Perhaps for a man who only truly existed as a warrior, the laying down of arms itself must be seen as a premature death.

The primary features of the narrative discourse are the representation of time, the configuration of the narrative voice, the alternation between the narrative retelling of actions engaged in by Villa and evaluative or summary statements posed by the narrator, and a scant recourse to figurative language. There is no dialogue in the *Apuntes* and no revelations of the private thoughts and feelings of the protagonist. The representation of Pancho Villa focuses on the exterior dimension of actions and their quantifiable parameters: dates, places, name and rank of individual participants, numbers of troops, kinds and number of arms, and the toll of the dead, wounded, and imprisoned on both sides of the conflict. Time is linear in the *Apuntes*, and it is viewed retrospectively from the present moment of narrating. The use of the past tenses is unremarkable in its ordinariness, and the historical present is only occasionally employed with the effect of giving immediacy to an action. Although few in number, the anachronisms that disturb the orderly progression of events from 1910 to 1920 have a significant role to play. Twice the narrator creates a pause in the story by recounting an anecdote out of sequence and attributing it to a named informant. These embedded testimonies serve to give additional detail, and they lend evidentiary support to the narrator's overall interpretation of Villa's action, character, and motives.

A second type of interruption in the temporal scheme is seen in the references scattered throughout the book to the present time of narrating. This slippage between the past time of the story and the unspecified present of the storytelling is revealed by the adverbs "ahora" [now] and "hoy" [today], by phrases such as "conviene advertir" [it is worth noting] and "ya en estos momentos" [at this time], and the verbs "digo" [I say] "afirmo" [I affirm], and "aclaro" [I clarify]. They are all textual markers that reveal the presence of the narrating-I lurking behind the scenes, but very much in control. Such markers consistently appear in the context of passages that defend Villa and justify his actions, refer to his future vindication, or excoriate his enemies. In the *Apuntes* the narrator thus openly assumes the dual role of advocate for Villa and virulent detractor of his foes (Carranza first among them). This is quite different from the fictitious autobiographical-I of Pancho Villa in Guzmán's *Memorias*, where the narrator-protagonist is seen to be constantly defending himself against attack and protesting his own good revolutionary intentions. Guzmán's ambitious ventriloquism, which ultimately falsifies the voice that it claims to authenticate for Pancho Villa, is replaced in the *Apuntes* by a more modest combination of conventional "third-person" or heterodiegetic narration and intradiegetic interventions by the narrator, who takes responsibility for the evaluative and idealizing interpretation of the main character. It is worth noting that the usually invisible narrator is most vocal and present in the chapter that tells of the battle of Celaya, which is almost universally considered to be a decisive defeat for Villa and a turning point in his military career. In order to shape the facts of the battle into evidence of a Villa victory, the narrator assumes a visible and actively persuasive stance. "Puedo asegurar" [I can assure you], "aclaro también" [I also clarify], "es mi deseo explicar" [I wish to explain], and "me refiero" [I refer] are signs of the narrator's efforts to represent Villa's retreat as a victory and the enemy's gain of territory as a trivial consequence of Villa's successful, strategic withdrawal. The narrator's line of reasoning rests on the premise that Villa retreated only due to a lack of ammunition and not due to a lack of strength, courage, military skill, or moral advantage. Therefore, the battle was a true triumph for Villa and a hollow victory for the Federal army, who had once again failed to overcome Villa in a legitimate contest. The only admissible "defeat" was a political one, in that the U.S. government had decided to back Carranza and thus denied to Villa needed supplies of arms. This interpretation strains logic, and the narrator's voice also strains to make the case to her reading public.

Finally, in addition to the claim to factual status that Campobello makes for the *Apuntes* in the "Nota preliminar," the narrative is peppered with references to the kinds of primary sources that historians prize in their research: legal documents, telegrams, verbatim transcriptions of eye-witness testimonies, and the text of various agreements, treaties, and manifestos in which Villa participated. Although explicit documentation is limited to about a dozen instances in the book's two hundred pages, it is enough to remind the reader of the documentary basis for the work and to open up a process of intertextual cross-checking. For example, I was curious to compare the "Manifiesto al pueblo mexicano" [Manifesto to the Mexican people] issued from Chihuahua in 1914 as it appears in the *Apuntes*, to the same document that is quoted in Guzmán's *Memorias*. This manifesto denounces Carranza's wielding of power in his position as Primer Jefe and it defends the decision of the generals of the División del Norte to fight against him. Although I was able to match the two documents, both of which are presented as transcriptions of what one assumes is a single original text, what I found were two quite different versions of the "same" manifesto. The presentation of the "facts" follows a similar path and arrives at a like conclusion, but the language is so dissimilar that they cannot be taken as two copies of one source. If one wished, one could try to sort out the disparate versions through archival research, but that lies outside of the scope and the interest of this study. I will conclude simply by highlighting the curious blend in *Apuntes de la vida militar de Francisco Villa* of nonfiction procedures with the apparent manipulation of primary sources and a strikingly partisan optic as a manifestation of the shaping, inventing, and creative activity of all writers of nonfiction and of all verbal representations of the irrecuperable real.

The final example of a text that writes a nonfictional version of the Mexican Revolution is Anita Brenner's *The Wind That Swept Mexico* (1943). Brenner was born in Aguascalientes in 1905 to a family of Latvian Jewish immigrants who had first settled in the United States in the late 1880s and after some years moved to Mexico. They became successful dairy and fruit farmers and were well established in their community by 1910, but they briefly left Mexico in 1912 and 1914, and then moved permanently to Texas in 1916 due to the danger to foreigners created by the ever-changing political and social climate of the Revolution. Anita Brenner spent twenty-five years of her life in the United States, where she earned a doctorate in anthropology from Columbia University, married and began her career as a writer. She pursued advanced university studies in Mexico City from 1923–27, and she again moved to Mexico in 1944, where she remained until her death in 1974. Brenner's daughter Susannah Joel Glusker has written a biography of her mother in which she uses Brenner's diaries, letters, published writings, and her own extensive archival research and interviews with Brenner's Mexican and American friends and acquaintances to create a portrait of a talented and fiercely independent intellectual who lived within and between two cultures. As can be seen in *The Wind That Swept Mexico*, Brenner used her unique vantage point to interpret and represent Mexican art, culture, and history to a U.S. audience, offering a point of view that is always sympathetic to her native country and often highly critical of her second homeland to the north.[14]

Brenner's work is little studied by scholars of Mexican literature in spite of her birth and her long residency in Mexico, her passionate promotion of Mexican art and artists, and the Mexican themes of her two major books, *Idols Behind Altars* and *The Wind That Swept Mexico*. She was an intellectual "border-crosser" long before the borderland became a prominent site of cultural theory and production, and the publication in English of her books and many of her articles sets her apart from most standard definitions of Mexican letters. However, her writing merits a fresh look by scholars south of the Río Bravo and north of the Rio Grande who are interested in nonfictional, bicultural representations of Mexican society in the early to mid-twentieth century.

The Wind That Swept Mexico: The History of the Mexican Revolution of 1910–1942 was written over the course of nine years starting in 1934. It had its origins that year in a series of articles that Brenner wrote for the *New York Post*. These pieces aroused the anger of the Knights of

Columbus and the U.S. Catholic Church hierarchy due to their portrayal of Mexican anticlericalism, the political role of the Church in Mexico, and the presence of fascist sympathizers known as the "Camisas Doradas" [gold shirts] among other controversial topics (Glusker 202). An article on the Mexican Revolution titled "The Wind That Swept Mexico," published in *Harper's* in 1942, was another clear precursor to the book that Harper and Row would issue a year later. Glusker documents both positive and negative reactions to the work, opinions usually motivated by the extent to which the reviewer identified with a pro-Revolution stance or with a more conservative, Catholic perspective on events in Mexico since 1910 (Glusker 207–208). No one, however, questions the factual and documentary basis of the book, whose structure and language conform to the standards of journalistic discourse of the time.

The Wind That Swept Mexico is a two-part history of the Mexican Revolution: the first part is a 100-page narrative essay covering events, personages, and social, political and economic conditions in Mexico from 1910 to 1942; the second is a 184-page photographic "history" of the same period. There is a clear formal division between the essay written by Brenner and the photo gallery assembled by George R. Leighton, but in reading the book, both parts are perceived to be mutually supportive and mutually dependent in conveying an overall interpretation of the Revolution of 1910. Aspects of the verbal and the visual representations can be examined separately, but ultimately their interconnections stimulate a more suggestive line of inquiry. Word and photograph have a complex relationship based on the different referential, explanatory, and evidentiary powers of text and image vis-à-vis the past.

Brenner's essay is comprised of a brief introduction dated 1943 and titled "Winds Sweeping the World," and three longer chapters, "Fall of a Dictator," "Upheaval," and "Mexico for the Mexicans." These treat the final months of the Porfiriato, the armed phase of the Revolution and the period from the early 1920s until 1942, respectively. All of the chapters combine a chronological account of historical events with passages that address the key social, political, and economic factors at play in Mexican society and frequent discussions of the relationship between Mexico and the United States. The style of writing is fast paced and concise, so that the essay manages to be comprehensive in scope and limited in length to a few hours' read. The ironic use of rhetorical questions and capital letters for common nouns, mild parodies of the languages of power, short quotes of direct speech, and the use of comic or telling details to caricature well-known figures lighten the weighty load of proper names, dates, and statistics, and convey the impression that the narrator maintains a sense of humor in the face of largely discouraging facts.

In the first line of the introduction, Brenner lays her cards on the table to make a case for the importance of the work to follow: "We are not safe in the United States now and henceforth, without taking Mexico into account; nor is Mexico safe disregarding us" (3). The narrator, who will soon disappear from the page by occupying a position external to the history being told, assumes the first-person plural voice to identify herself as an American living in the United States and therefore a member of the book's intended audience. The strategic appeal to shared national interests will contrast sharply with the book's later critique of American influence in Mexico, and it functions here to make an appeal to the reader to venture across the border into unknown territory in the company of a fellow citizen. The book is, above all, an urgent invitation to Americans to consider the emerging reality of their neighbor at a time of worldwide conflict and upheaval, and an assertion of the importance of information and knowledge in a democratic society where all citizens may participate in critical decisions: "[T]he Mexican Revolution . . . puts questions to us our government will have to meet . . . questions which the American people cannot leave safely to deals and power barters and accident and intrigue" (5–6).

In addition to staking out its readership through its choice of narrative voice, the language just quoted reveals what some readers might call a persistent bias, and others a "preferential option," for the poor that informs the entire book. Anita Brenner tells the story of the Mexican Revolution and its aftermath not only to represent the importance of Mexico for the United States, but also to defend the role and the aspirations of the poor, the disenfranchised, the underdog in a society that preserved, twenty-three years after the Revolution was "won," a drastically hierarchical and exploitative political and economic structure. Brenner is writing on behalf of those who are not the dealers and the power brokers on either side of the border, but rather those who fought a revolution for "land and liberty" and yet remained dispossessed in 1942. The critique of power and the advocacy of the poor's claim to justice are the ideological underpinnings of the history that Brenner shapes with words and images.

The most effective verbal ploy in *The Wind That Swept Mexico* is the way in which Brenner's narrator engages various cultural languages in order to express critical or sympathetic or more neutral points of view toward her subject. The first chapter, "The Fall of a Dictator," illustrates the critical potential of a parody of official discourse in its political and religious manifestations. Adopting the language of the "Científico" politicians and the Catholic Church, whom she aims to skewer, the narrator entertains the reader while carrying out a serious critique of the Porfirian status quo. She supports her critique by incorporating a variety of quantifiable and therefore seemingly objective data into the chapter. References to the regime's values of thrift, stability, business, science, order, and "music in the plazas in the evenings" are voiced in mock reverential tones. Brenner's representation of the Mexican elite's anti-democratic and racist attitudes toward the nation's "dominantly Indian, racially inferior" "practically subhuman" population (10) appear absurdly debased in the context of a presumed belief in democracy and liberty on the part of the text's target audience in the United States. Parodies of religious language, in particular when used to describe the operations of government, also seem designed to touch a nerve in the far more secular United States: "At [Díaz's] right hand . . . hovered Don José Ives Limantour, primate of the holy of holies, Secretary of the Treasury. Respectfully close to the chair there knelt, bringing gifts and testimonials, a select little group of men of affairs named the Circle of Friends of Porfirio Díaz" (8).

In contrast, when the narrative voice adopts the point of view of the peasants and takes on the features of oral discourse, the tone is sympathetic and not critical, and it endows their worldview with a kind of ingenuous dignity. This is apparent early in the first chapter when there is an abrupt cut from the foregoing description of the "cozy little status quo" (18) to a passage that recounts the peasants' awestruck memories of Halley's Comet in 1910 and their nostalgic evocation of more distant times "before Porfirio." "In those days there had been much corn, and prices had been half of what things cost now . . . people had had real silver money and could buy in the market, instead of getting everything out of a book at the hacienda store. . . . But engineers had come and measured them, and it had been ruled that all the earths for which there was not the right paper must belong to the haciendas" (19). Although the passage shows the peasants to be naive and unschooled, it portrays their vague intimations of the injustices done to them with a language that recalls oral storytelling and respects the authenticity of popular, collective memory.

The essay portion of *The Wind That Swept Mexico* carries the story of the Revolution up to 1942, demonstrating a conviction that the process of social change initiated in 1910 acquired a powerful momentum from the energy released when millions of former hacienda peons and exploited laborers had reason to believe in the promise of "Mexico for the Mexicans." While acknowledging the reactionary forces still at play, the self-interested economic role played by generals-turned-businessmen and the enervating effect of pervasive corruption, the last and longest chapter offers a cautiously optimistic assessment of thirty-two years of revolution in Mexico. Insofar as the rhetorical force of language is foregrounded in the essay genre, the textual portion of *The Wind That Swept Mexico* argues persuasively for its thesis regarding the critical need for mutual understanding and respect between Anita Brenner's two homelands. The almost two hundred photographs that comprise the second part of the book also participate in the powers of persuasion employed by Brenner.

Roland Barthes is well known for works of literary and cultural theory that challenge conventionally conceived claims for the transparency of language or the directly referential nature of the linguistic sign. He again raises the problem of referentiality when writing on the meaning of the photographic image in his book *Camera Lucida: Reflections on Photography*. Here, in a passage meant to demonstrate the unique relationship that holds between the photograph and the "necessarily real thing which has been placed before the lens" (76), Barthes contrasts the image with the fundamental fictionality of language. In this context, he makes a passing comment, almost a throw-away remark, on nonfiction writing, saying that "any attempt to render language nonfictional requires an enormous apparatus of measurements" (87). That "apparatus" is not Barthes's concern in the essay on photography. However, as we have seen, it is comprised by the myriad conventions of documentation and intertextuality that function to bend the linguistic fiction to the uses of the real in nonfiction literature. Photographs are another "authenticating" device, to use Barthes's term, that can accompany a verbal text in support of its claim to factual status.[15] *The Wind That Swept Mexico* invites our further reflection on the relationship between verbal narrative and photographic representation in the practice of history writing.

Barthes is only one of many theorists who affirm that "reference is the founding order of photography," and the photograph "compels us to believe that its referent has existed" (*Camera* 76–77). In the book *On Photography*, published three years before *Camera Lucida*, Susan Sontag makes a similar distinction to that proposed by Barthes. "What is written about a person or an event is frankly an interpretation. . . . Photographed images do not seem to be statements about the world so much as pieces of it" (Sontag 4). The phrase "do not seem to be" is a warning that Sontag will soon problematize the status of the photographic "pieces of the world," which she does by discussing the interpretative and transformative effects of scale, exposure, and color. Nevertheless, she does not let go completely of the assumptions behind our conventional way of thinking about photographs as furnishing evidence that a given thing has existed or has happened. "The picture may distort, but there is always a presumption that something exists, or did exist, which is like what's in the picture" (5). Sontag's own way of looking at photographs is anything but conventional or automatic, but I believe that what she says about the prevailing, commonsense view is pertinent to Anita Brenner's use of the photographic archive of the Mexican Revolution in her book. Andy Grundberg, too, while discussing the "crisis of the real" in his analysis of photography and postmodernism, pays tribute to an older way of seeing that is implicit in *The Wind That Swept Mexico*. "Photography's distinction has always been its connection to the world outside the imagination, and it traditionally has been practiced not in the artist's garret but on the streets or battlefields or mountaintops. A photograph traces something real" (*Crisis of the Real* 172).

In the 1970s Susan Sontag wrote about how our photo-saturated culture creates image-junkies who need to have reality confirmed by photographs. Thirty years later, photographs are far more pervasive, even intrusive, in our everyday experience of the world. Perhaps it is not surprising, then, that when I first picked up *The Wind That Swept Mexico*, I opened it immediately to the "Photographic History of the Mexican Revolution," and I began avidly to view and to consume the frozen, often somewhat blurred black-and-white images of people, places, and events that I had long read about. Here were not the two or three photos stingily reproduced in a typical history text, but a wealth of visual pieces of the world displayed for my perusal at any pace and in any order that I wished. Beginning with the stiff, formal portraits of Porfirio Díaz and his ministers, resplendent in gold-embroidered uniforms and expensive suits, and ending 184 images later with that of an anonymous man, perhaps a worker or a peasant, gazing seriously into my eyes, I saw the "proof" of the stories that I had been told, their thousand or ten-thousand words condensed into "the best photographs of the time."[16]

Principles of inclusiveness and completeness seem to have guided Brenner and George Leighton in their selection of images from the vast photographic archive available to them. The subjects are arranged in chronological order, tracing the sequence of the narrative text that precedes them. First appear seven photographs of the major figures of the Porfirian regime and the lavish splendor of the National Palace. Images number eight to seventeen, still representing the "Paz porfiriana," achieve an ironic effect in showing scenes of the poverty and desolation of the vast "peaceful" rural landscape of the time. Photographs of banks, railroads, mines, men in top hats, and the fashionable avenues of Mexico City return us to signs of the prosperity achieved under Díaz's pro-business government. The year 1910 is generously represented by pictures of the Centennial celebration and Halley's Comet, and Francisco I. Madero and the early bands of men who would turn his call for "Sufragio efectivo, no reelección" [effective suffrage, no reelection] into an armed revolution. The middle one-third of the images portrays the Revolutionary chieftains and their armies, and a very few scenes of battles and daily life in war. The remaining one-third covers the years from 1924–1942, showing key political leaders, signs of modernization, labor and agrarian organizations, the swastika on the German consulate, and, finally, our anonymous peasant or laborer.

The summary that I have provided, without its being particularly complete, points to an enormous amount of information to be gleaned from the photo display. The photographic promise of access to things far away or long disappeared seems to be fully realized in this extensive gallery of the visual remains of the past. Nevertheless, I could not have made the foregoing list of subjects, nor located them in time or space, based on my viewing of the photos alone, nor do I recall having spent more than a minute or two looking at them before my eyes searched out the words, the accompanying verbal captions which identify, date, situate, and ultimately interpret the images. My quest for knowledge and understanding soon ran full-bore into the limits posed by the mute, nameless photograph, and so I looked and read, and looked again in an effort to make the reception of image and word into a single, coherent cognitive experience.

The limitations of the photographic fact and the interdependence of photo and text are described by the same critics whom I have already quoted making the case for photography's direct relationship to the world and its provision of visual data. Andy Grundberg in his review of Susan

Meisalas's photo-essay *Nicaragua*, concludes that "the photographs are completely ambiguous. The book separates the pictures from their captions, which are lumped in the back. This has an unsettling consequence: looking at the photographs alone, it is impossible to tell who is fighting whom, or why . . . Such pictures suggest that without language, the meaning of a photograph is inherently ambiguous" (*Crisis of the Real* 182). Susan Sontag similarly argues that: "Strictly speaking, one never understands anything from a photograph . . . Only that which narrates can make us understand" (23). She goes on to say that words speak louder than pictures, and captions—even if false—tend to override the visual evidence. She concedes a limit to captions as well, pointing out that the "missing voice" of a photograph constitutes only one possible interpretation of it (108). Max Kozloff, also addressing the needs of understanding, finds that: "The picture does so very much on its own but then stops short of delivering, not its particulars, but their significance. It supplies an enormous amount of what we may need—visual data—but finally denies us what we want—the import of its message" (*Privileged Eye* 13).

A photograph standing alone has limited analytical or explanatory power. It allows us to see something that is absent and it certifies its existence, but viewed in isolation it cannot identify its subject, show cause and effect, recall the before and after of the one dissociated moment that it captures, or otherwise convey meaning. An individual image is cut off from temporal sequence, and therefore cut off from history understood as a narrative of events occurring in time. The title for the second part of Brenner's book, "Photographic History of the Mexican Revolution," therefore achieves its validity insofar as the author has included captions to supply the means for reading and understanding the images as history.

Just as a narrative frame, which appears to stand outside of the work itself, is an integral part of it, so also the two distinct sections of *The Wind That Swept Mexico* are interconnected, and the interpenetration of one by the other ultimately generates its meaning. Most obviously, the captions that accompany the photos are taken directly from the essay and redeployed as abbreviated references to the history that has already been narrated in the book. Sontag suggests that the use of photographs to awaken conscience—surely a central goal of this essay's persuasive energy—must be linked to a given historical situation that the images in and of themselves cannot explain. One who has read Brenner's essay and then turns to the "photographic history" will experience the pleasure of rereading familiar passages of text now linked to visual data that certify the existence of Revolutionary people and events. The captions, however, do not exhaust the potential interpretations of the photographs. The viewer may decode elements of light and dark, framing, distance of the shot, posture and expression of the human subjects, and a hundred other compositional and topical details in order to read additional significance into the image. He or she may also bring information acquired from other sources to bear on the viewing, information that can supplement or challenge the meaning assigned by the caption. Photo eighty-six shows Pancho Villa galloping on horseback directly toward the camera through a dusty, blurred rural landscape. In the background, an indeterminate number of out-of-focus horsemen follow him. The simple words "Villa was taking one town after another from the Huerta garrisons" accompany the image, but they clearly do not begin to limit how a viewer is likely to see this one picture of such a storied figure. Outlaw, cattle rustler, guerrilla fighter, avenger of Madero, popular hero, ruthless foe, cold-blooded killer, military genius, defender of the poor, unpredictable savage are among the many meanings that a reader might imagine to be certified in the frozen instant of his rush forward.

It is also the case that the images inform and shape the narrative essay in ways that are not necessarily obvious to us when we read histories and see photographs as authenticating illustrations of what has been written. Brenner, like Martín Luis Guzmán, sketches brief verbal portraits of leading figures from Porfirio Díaz to Lázaro Cárdenas, and she favors the device of using a telling detail to define a whole personality. Some of these details could be based on Brenner's direct observations and visual memory, as in the case of the leaders whom she saw arrive for the Aguascalientes Convention in 1914. Other textual passages, however, appear to describe not an observed reality but a photograph, in a gesture that suggests how image and text, visual data, and narrative interpretation create each other in a reciprocal shaping of the facts, rather than seeing the photos as merely following and illustrating the essay. Photographs two and three are examples of images that may have prompted Brenner's verbal characterizations, in this instance her descriptions of Porfirio Díaz's advisors. Number two is a group portrait with Díaz seated in the center, symmetrically flanked by four seated and four standing men. Their identical dark suits and ties, the uniformly white hair, the nine matching mustaches and the hands all held in a similar pose could well have inspired Brenner's account of these reliably obedient actors in the Díaz administration as the "group of courtly elderly men," the "cherubim and seraphim," and the "constellation of grayed experts" (7–9). Illustration three shows José Ives Limantour seated in a wicker chair, his body angled somewhat toward the viewer's right but his head turned straight at us. His exquisite suit, the precise inch of snow-white shirt cuff visible below the jacket sleeve, the starched collar supporting his delicate head and his slender, straight-backed frame make Brenner's choice of words visually over-determined: "At his right hand—pale, scrupulous and faultless as a tailor's dream—hovered Don José Ives Limantour" (8). I cannot document the process through which the essay and the photo gallery might have been thus constituted as mutually influential and interdependent representations of the Mexican Revolution, but as a reader, my reception of the text performs that relationship in response to its internal organization.

The conventions of history writing and other nonfiction genres mattered in important ways to Martín Luis Guzmán, Nellie Campobello, and Anita Brenner, and their separate efforts to write the Revolution of 1910 in documentary forms reflect significant historical attitudes toward the status of factual discourse and narrative authority. Writing at different times and for different audiences, they shared a common desire to make the Mexican Revolution better understood by others and a common sense of the rhetorical potential of the literature of facts to serve a given set of interests. Guzmán and Campobello wrote within the "great men" tradition of historiography that privileges military actions and politics as properly historical events, although thematically they wrote counter to Mexican official histories by striving to vindicate the marginalized figure of Francisco Villa. In *El águila y la serpiente*, *Las memorias de Pancho Villa*, and *Cartucho*, they also share an Aristotelian orientation toward the truth-value of legend in recapturing the past. Brenner's narrative essay and photo gallery represent the top political and military leaders of the period, while also focusing on the role of farmers and laborers in the Revolution and in the hoped-for refashioning of Mexican society. Her version of the Revolution of 1910 can be seen to have been shaped by a diverse array of influences: an anthropologist's interest in the broad spectrum of society; her experiences conducting research in rural Mexico; and U.S. ideals of participatory democracy across social classes; and the imperative to justify seeing Mexico as a valuable partner with the United States in a world enmeshed in violent conflict. The analyses that form the basis of the chapters that follow will show how the assumptions and presuppositions that shape the work of Guzmán, Campobello, and Brenner are duplicated, challenged, and transformed by the ongoing production of nonfiction literatures in Mexico in response to crises throughout the twentieth century.

3

Living Stories, Telling Lives

Autobiographical Writings of José Vasconcelos and María Luisa Puga

. . . the subject is never given at the beginning.

—Paul Ricoeur, "Life: A Story in Search of a Narrator"

Autobiography studies began to claim a central place in literary criticism and theory in Europe and the United States with the dissemination of the work of Georges Gusdorf, Philippe Lejeune, William Spengemann, and James Olney in the 1970s and early 1980s.[1] These theorists created a canon of texts and a definition of the genre that dominated the debate over autobiography for at least a decade. Their canon located its origins in St. Augustine's *Confessions* and it unanimously privileged the well-known and influential life stories of Jean-Jacques Rousseau, Benjamin Franklin, Johann Wolfgang von Goethe, and John Stuart Mills, among others. According to the prevailing readings, these texts had in common the representation of the exceptional life and personality of a unique and highly individualized self, who embodied Enlightenment values of autonomy, originality, agency, and a stable, essential identity. That the autobiographical subject was Western, white, usually middle-class, and male went without saying. In terms of establishing formal criteria for including and excluding titles from the canon, Philippe Lejeune's concept of autobiography as a contractual genre and his oft-quoted definition of the form seemed to be beyond appeal: "Retrospective prose narrative written by a real person concerning his own existence, where the focus is his individual life, in particular the story of his personality" (*On*

Autobiography 4). Nevertheless, it didn't take very long before these premises of autobiography and the concept of a coherent, unitary autobiographical "I" were challenged by critical readers who expanded the canon and deconstructed its founding theories through an interrogation of the central notions of subjectivity, genre formation, representation, referentiality, and narrativity. The diverse contributions and directions for critical debate that are associated with post-structuralism, psychoanalysis, deconstruction, and feminism in all of their manifestations informed the work of a number of critics who began to publish on autobiography in the 1980s and whose work continued through the 1990s and into the new century. Sidonie Smith, Domna Stanton, Liz Stanley, Carolyn Kay Steedman, and Paul John Eakin are among those who have accomplished ground-breaking work in autobiography studies by bringing a rigorous knowledge of contemporary literary and cultural theory to bear on the analysis of issues such as the construction of gender, race, ethnicity, and class in autobiographical projects; the dialectic of the autonomous and the relational selves; and the narrative quality of lived experience. In the process of their discussions, the terms *personal narrative* and *life writing* began to be used in order to signal a move toward a more expansive body of texts than that which was once located under the sign of autobiography. I will return shortly to these critics in order to establish a theoretical framework for the study of four examples of twentieth-century life writing by two members of Mexico's intellectual elite.

In Mexican literature, as in other Spanish-American national traditions, autobiographies that conform to conventional definitions and alternative forms of personal narrative have been widely produced and read since the colonial period. However, critical studies have lagged far behind the creative output. Sylvia Molloy's 1991 book *At Face Value: Autobiographical Writing in Spanish America* is widely acknowledged to be the first comprehensive study of the genre across the region. For the colonial period, Molloy views the chronicles, letters, and diaries of the exploration and conquest, certain confessions given to the Inquisition, and selected works of Sor Juana Inés de la Cruz as forms of self-writing that function as precursors to autobiography per se. "True" autobiography, deliberately and primarily conceived as an expression of a unique self, emerged as a literary response to the ideological crisis of nineteenth-century independence, according to Molloy. After independence and in the absence of colonial authorities and institutions to whom to direct one's personal narrative, the nineteenth-century autobiographer sought new justifications for writing and often found validation in didactic projects tied to nation building (3–4). Molloy's choices of individual texts for her ten chapters of analysis reflect the expanded notion of autobiography that feminist theorists, in particular, had been promoting since 1980. She includes a slave narrative, numerous texts by women, and Domingo F. Sarmiento's hybrid work *Recuerdos de provincia*, as well as titles more usually associated with the genre. Molloy's central focus is on intertextuality in the works studied, and her interest points to what some theorists regard as the fundamentally narrative nature of human selfhood, a concept that I will develop further in what follows.

Sylvia Molloy's final chapter examines José Vasconcelos's *Ulises criollo* under the rubric "First Memories, First Myths." Vasconcelos is the only Mexican writer treated in her study of nineteenth- and twentieth-century autobiography, and by choosing the first volume of his massive four-part life story she remains well within the canon of Mexican literature. Looking more closely at literary studies that treat Mexico, there is a pronounced scarcity of critical work on autobiography. The most comprehensive effort undertaken by a Mexicanist to account for the genre consists of two lengthy bibliographical studies completed by Richard Donovan Woods. In 1988 Greenwood Press published his bilingual *Mexican Autobiography/La autobiografía mexicana*. The book provides a very brief introduction to autobiography in Mexico that primarily serves to define the variety of forms of life writing that Woods includes in the annotated listing. These include autobiography "proper," memoir, oral autobiography of a collaborative nature, letters, autobiographical novel, autobiographical essay, and interview-based autobiographies of cultural celebrities. The over two-hundred-page bibliography identifies three hundred and thirty-two texts written between 1800 and 1986, with eight titles dating from the late seventeenth and eighteenth centuries. Again, as in Molloy's book, autobiography is an inclusive rather than an exclusive category into which a wide variety of personal narratives are admitted. In 1994 Woods published a follow-up article in *Hispania* to cite an additional three hundred and forty-seven examples, most of which had appeared since 1980. Woods's exhaustive research clearly establishes the existence of a vigorous tradition of autobiographical writing in Mexico, a tradition which, like other forms of nonfiction literature, has been commonly relegated to the margins of literary history and criticism. In this chapter and the next, I examine diverse examples of life writing in light of recent theories of self-representation and personal narrative. I start with a study of texts written by two elite authors: José Vasconcelos's *Ulises criollo* (1935), and three books by María Luisa Puga published between 1990 and 2004. In Chapter 4 I examine two personal narratives produced by members of the popular sector.

Autobiographical writing in the West commonly makes a claim not only to factual status, but to a special quality of truthfulness that recalls the genre's roots in an act of confession before the Christian God. In autobiography's early manifestations the moral weight of confession, in which one's eternal salvation was in play, committed the autobiographer to truth telling, and the gravity of this obligation established an expectation for later, more secular versions of the genre. In order to tie autobiographical truth firmly to the lived experience of a real person, Philippe Lejeune insists on identity and not mere resemblance among author, narrator, and protagonist as a necessary condition of autobiography. The proper name shared by the writer and the subject of the life-story is a trace of the world-beyond-the-text, and it positions a real person standing behind the text and guaranteeing narrative sincerity, authenticity, and accuracy (Lejeune 11, 19–20). These premises seem to lay a solid ground on which to read and judge autobiography, and they cast the reader in the role of a detective who submits the text to a "test of verification" (22). The reader might ultimately determine that the autobiographical-I has lied rather than telling the truth, but the primary referent remains indisputedly a real life lived in a verifiable world, and this relationship constitutes in large part the appeal of autobiography, which addresses our desire to know, as well as our enjoyment in playing the voyeur. However, Lejeune's own work begins to complicate the definition that I have summarized above, as when, for example, he questions the difference between accuracy of information and fidelity of meaning (23). Going well beyond Lejeune's glimpse into the slippery nature of narrative truth, the theorists who are most central to my readings largely reject the emphasis on "real persons" and lived experiences truthfully revealed as the essential core of personal narrative. Just as the historical event is no longer viewed as a stable and recuperable entity that preexists historical discourse, but rather it is seen to exist as a product of that discourse, so the autobiographical subject is seen as being constituted in the very process of narrating and cannot be usefully traced back to or measured against an original, pre-narrative self. The degree of correspondence between the story told by the autobiographical-I and the life of its author, or between the textual subject and the subjectivity of the writing-I is largely closed to scrutiny for a variety of reasons that recent theories of life writing are concerned to explain.[2] A brief consideration of the concepts of subjectivity, narrativity, and intertextuality as they pertain to the study of personal narrative will lay the groundwork for the textual analyses in this chapter and the next.

It is a widely shared idea that the writing of autobiography is an act of self-invention or self-creation in which individual experience and psychology, an imperfect memory, and the demands of the present time of writing dynamically interact with linguistic, literary, and social conventions and scripts in order to shape a narrative version of a self and a life. The meaning and status of the I of autobiography is a central concern of readers, as is demonstrated in the titles of many seminal studies: *The Auto/Biographical I*, "Autogynography: Is the Subject Different?," *Subjectivity, Identity and the Body*, and "Historians of the Self," to give just a few examples.[3] It follows that some form of a theory of subjectivity must underlie all such inquiries, whether it is explicitly addressed and defined, or simply taken for granted and left unspoken.

Paul B. Smith's challenging engagement with twentieth-century theories of subjectivity in his book *Discerning the Subject* (1988) offers a useful starting point for a discussion of the status of the autobiographical-I. Smith begins with a creative parsing of the verbs "to cern" (to accept an inheritance) and "to cerne" (to encircle or enclose) in order to explain the purpose and the scope of his project. Through an interrogation of post-Marxism, deconstruction, Lacanian psychoanalytical theory, anthropology, and feminism, he sets out to "dis-cern(e)" the subject, meaning to disinherit the concept from its humanist legacy as a unified, coherent, autonomous bearer of consciousness, and equally to release it from the Marxist legacy of the dominating or "enclosing" force of social formations. Smith proposes a theory of subjectivity that accounts not only for the ways in which the person is determined by the shaping power of discourse and acts out ideological roles, but is also an agent of resistance, a *discerning* reader of received scripts and an active negotiator of multiple and contradictory subject positions.

At the center of his study, then, is a notion of the person as a determined subject and a determining agent, neither wholly subjected to ideological pressures, nor wholly free to choose and self-realize. Smith's human subject acts in and on the world, accepts and refuses its demands, acquiesces in and subverts social formations and hegemonic practices. The critic identifies a number of keys to the contradictory and therefore dynamic nature of the human subject. The role of language is crucial in that it mediates self-other relationships and shapes consciousness, but it is a system that is heterogeneous and always in flux, and therefore it is open to change rather than fixed and closed. The common notion that ideology, while powerful, is not monolithic, coherent, and totalizing allows Smith to affirm that the subject is empowered to resist its pressures because he or she is only imperfectly and provisionally cerned (enclosed) by them. Furthermore, the recognition that each individual occupies multiple and contradictory subject positions at every moment of life, and that these positions change over time, also contributes to the potential for agency, due to the inherent instability of such a fluid construct and the constant need for the individual actively to negotiate the competing demands of conflicting roles and changing conditions of existence. For Smith, human agency and capacity for resistance and refusal are limited and tempered by the dominant ideology, but they nonetheless exert their own innovating pressure on the world. This theory of how the human subject is constituted and how it pushes back on the forces that determine and restrain its intervention in the world will figure into my reading of selected works of life writing in Mexico.

In the realm of autobiography studies, Sidonie Smith is one of a number of critics who view subjectivity in a manner similar to Paul Smith and whose work foregrounds the role of gender in the practices of self-writing. In scrutinizing the early attempts to theorize women's autobiographies and account for their difference from male-authored texts, Smith argues that the initial findings of thematic and formal distinctions have ultimately proved to be of limited value for reading women's personal narratives. Early studies of women's autobiography identified an emphasis on the private sphere, the predominance of fragmentary, discontinuous forms, and the expression of women's preoccupation with relationship over autonomy as shared characteristics of female-authored texts. In doing so, these theories tended to essentialize women's experience, overlook factors of race, class, and age, and make assumptions about the transparent readability and unproblematical representation of experience through language, notions that Sidonie Smith rejects (*Poetics* 17–18).[4] She further grapples with the double bind that is created by theories that posit that all language and all writing practices produced in patriarchal societies are inflexibly gendered male and therefore necessarily silence the female. Smith challenges the assumption that if women speak and write, they enter discourse irremediably subdued and alienated. Alternatively, if they remain silent, they forego any possible entry, limited though it may be, into the process of history.[5] In response to these reservations about prior work on autobiography and in an attempt to understand women's achievements within a context of constraints, Smith looks at three central problems in her study of the Anglo-American tradition of formal autobiography: how a woman's gendered position inflects her autobiographical project; the autobiographer's strategies to establish the authority to interpret herself publicly; and the relationship between the woman autobiographer's literary authority and her sexuality (45).

Here I wish to return to the quote with which I opened the chapter. The post-structuralist rejection of the concept of a coherent, whole, stable I that preexists our acts of speaking and writing and the view of subjectivity as a continually negotiated and changing construct are elegantly captured in Paul Ricoeur's spare formulation that "the subject is never given at the beginning." Nor, one might add, is it given at the end, either. The context for this statement is his essay "Life: A Story in Search of a Narrator," in which he asserts the importance of fiction and narrativity for human life and for a person's sense of self. Although he does not address the formal genre of autobiography in the essay, his assessment of the role that stories play in the living and the interpreting of human action sheds light on the strong presence of intertextuality in life writing, a characteristic that we will particularly observe in the autobiography of José Vasconcelos. Ricoeur holds that human beings are capable of purposive action and not mere movement, because we understand the meaning of project, goal, means, and circumstance both through language and through the stories that we acquire and wield (131). That is, our actions are charged with fictional entities in the form of the plots and scripts that we assimilate, imitate, and transform in the process of our living always "entangled in the stories" that happen to us (130). Ricoeur calls this the "narrative identity which constitutes us" as a way of emphasizing the dynamic nature of the human being's relationship with "the intrigues we received from our culture, and our capacity of thus experimenting with the various roles that the favorite *personae* assume in the stories we love best" (131). I would suggest that intertextuality in autobiography is a visible manifestation of the pervasive but usually unseen, unexamined process of living stories and telling lives in which the subject is constantly engaged. The autobiographical texts that I have chosen enact the dynamic constitution of subjectivity and the subject's entanglement with cultural narratives in ways that reveal much about the multiple positions of the autobiographical-I and his or her invention of self in the act of self-narration.

José Vasconcelos's four-volume, two-thousand-page *Memorias* belongs squarely to the tradition of classic autobiography as defined by Gusdorf, Olney, and Lejeune. Here is a prime example of the Western, male, middle-class, well-educated subject writing the story of his own personal development with an emphasis on his individuality and originality, his intellectual formation and his public achievements, as well as ample treatment of his family life and his intimate relationships. Vasconcelos began writing his life story in 1931, a time of personal crisis. At the age of forty-nine, he found himself in exile in Spain after his bitter defeat in the 1929 Mexican presidential elections, and his autobiography represents a response to this crisis of subjectivity. The entire work covers his life from infancy until the early 1930s, and although the writer lived to the age of seventy-seven, he never completed his autobiographical project beyond the initial volumes that were published between 1935 and 1939.[6]

Ulises criollo, published in 1935, is the first and most widely-read volume of the autobiography, and it treats the period from the subject's very early childhood (1885) until the assassination of President Francisco I. Madero in 1913. The full title of the book, *Ulises criollo: Vida del autor escrita por él mismo* [Creole Ulysses: life of the author written by himself], establishes the foundation for the autobiographical pact, which is further cemented by the requisite identity of the name of the author and that of the first-person narrator-protagonist. The representation of Vasconcelos's childhood, his education from primary school through the university and law school, his early career as an attorney, and his role in Francisco I. Madero's election campaign and his government follows an overall trajectory from youthful optimism and idealism toward decline and increasing pessimism. The positive, self-confident image of the childhood experiences that he lived under the protection of parents and teachers, gives way to the increasingly negative scenario of revolutionary Mexico that was dominated, according to Vasconcelos, by unrestrained violence and the many acts of treachery committed by Madero's enemies. Throughout the entire first volume, the enormity of Vasconcelos's ego, what some critics diplomatically call the "force of his personality," and the tenacious strength of his animosities toward his political rivals, are constants within the representation of an ever-changing social context and an ever-evolving sense of self.

The immediate popular and critical success of *Ulises criollo* is well documented in the numerous book reviews that started to appear in the Mexican press within a month of its June 1935 publication. The book was an instant best seller, quickly running through a first printing of two thousand copies and reaching sales of eight thousand within a few months. By 1949 it had been reprinted ten times in runs of two to three thousand copies, according to Rafael Oleas Franco in his study of the book (778). Claude Fell's critical edition of *Ulises criollo* (Fondo de Cultura Económica, 2000) brings together a wealth of resources for readers of the text, including a carefully annotated edition of the primary text and reprints of critical studies and of more than a dozen book reviews published between 1935 and 1937 in such periodicals as *El Universal*, *Excélsior*, and *El Ilustrado*. A survey of the reviews reveals a wide range of responses and opinions contemporary to its publication, although most of them share a common tendency to use the autobiography as a basis to judge Vasconcelos as a man, a politician, and a historian, while few of the early readers address matters of literary concern. The life, rather than the writing, is the focus of attention, and condemnation is as prevalent as praise. Conflicting voices characterize Vasconcelos alternately as a mystic or a megalomaniac, a creole or a mestizo (used as racial terms), a conservative descendent of the Spanish conquerors or a visionary with the soul of an Aztec, and a slave of his passions or an idealist. Fifty years later, a critic would still ask, "¿Quién no tiene, en México, una opinión sobre José Vasconcelos?" [Who in Mexico doesn't have an opinion of José Vasconcelos?].[7] Nevertheless, even those contemporaries who were critical of Vasconcelos, his many personal indiscretions and his pessimistic view of recent Mexican history acknowledged the qualities of passion, sincerity, and honesty in his autobiography. In fact, the reviews are virtually unanimous in attributing "sincerity" to Vasconcelos's self-portrait, usually equating sincerity with his willingness to expose the details of his many sexual adventures, a feature that made the book a *succès de scandale* among Mexican readers of the time. One reviewer, however, a self-proclaimed defender of "el gran presidente" Porfirio Díaz, reviles Vasconcelos for his hatred of the former dictator (Teodoro Torres in *Ulises* 831); while a self-proclaimed impartial reader praises the writer's bold truthfulness ("Fígaro" in *Ulises* 824); and one of two women who review the book protests against his unjust, insulting, and self-centered representation of women and motherhood (A. Izquierdo Albiñana in *Ulises* 841). As is true of any critical and argumentative writing, the book reviews of the mid-1930s say as much about the reading habits and the cultural expectations of the reviewers as they do about the book under consideration. At a time when the changes brought about by the Revolution of 1910 and the Constitution of 1917 were still being consolidated (or betrayed), and the nation was undergoing a transition from the years under Plutarco Elías Calles's control to the presidency of Lázaro Cárdenas, the defeated, exiled candidate of 1929 was a fascinating and controversial figure in Mexican society. It is logical that the historical value of the book and its portrayal of an exceptional personality should occupy the attention of its readers. It is also to be expected that the language of contemporary assumptions about race and gender roles in Mexico should come into play in the reviews, and an in-depth study of the reviews themselves would shed light on the predominant ideologies of the period.[8]

Quite apart from the matter of its initial reception in Mexico, *Ulises criollo* continues to invite a variety of readings due to the complexity of both the individual life story and the collective, national history that it interprets, and also due to the wealth of literary devices and cultural discourses that it employs. As an outstanding example of life writing in twentieth-century Mexico, it has been the object of numerous critical studies to date, and I will place the focus of my own analysis in the context of significant existing work on the text. To begin, a useful general evaluation of the themes and the structure of *Ulises criollo* is offered by Noé Jitrik in his 1988 article "Lectura de Vasconcelos." In addition to identifying the book's predominant themes to be recent Mexican history, the relationship between intellectuals and politics, the Revolution of 1910, readings of literature, and experiences of loyalty and betrayal, Jitrik makes the important observation that in writing his autobiography José Vasconcelos was concerned to represent the past in accordance with his present needs and circumstances. Writing from exile, he wanted to show that he was correct in his opposition to Carranza and Calles, and correct in believing that the Revolution had been betrayed by all of the successors to Madero (Jitik 268–69). In fact, Carranza and Calles are evoked surprisingly frequently in the first volume of the *Memorias*, whose story ends a number of years before their rise to power. The names of Carranza and Calles surface anachronistically like a repressed memory of the future, and they appear in the life story long before they entered the chronology of Vasconcelos's lived experiences.

Sylvia Molloy, in the book chapter already mentioned, has carried out the most careful and insightful analysis of an intriguing dimension of the autobiography: the centrality of the figure of Vasconcelos's mother and the mother-son bond in *Ulises criollo*. Molloy studies the significance of the mother as the primary purveyor to the child of identity, culture, and memory, and she characterizes Carmen Calderón as the first champion of her son's singularity. Molloy also explores the implications of the autobiographical subject's Oedipal desire for the mother, highlighting the many scenes that portray an exclusive relationship between mother and son and that manifest a pronounced intimacy. The mother is both a reader of the stories that significantly mold the child's sense of self and an enduring object of his desire. The recurring reflection on episodes of union, separation, and reunion with the mother is a constant theme that persists long after her death.

Finally, two articles that appear in the Claude Fell critical edition of *Ulises ciollo* treat the book from a historian's perspective. In "Tres asedios a Vasconcelos" Javier Garciadiego establishes the necessary historical context to elucidate three key moments in the life story: José Vasconcelos's membership in the Ateneo de la Juventud, his participation in the Maderista movement, and his role in Madero's short-lived government. Garciadiego's thesis is that Vasconcelos's actions show him to be a lukewarm supporter of Madero, in sharp contrast to the self-image in the autobiography of a loyal, fervent, and even reverential follower of Mexico's "Apostle of Democracy." The contrast between the historical record as interpreted by Garciadiego and the version of the past that Vasconcelos's autobiographical-I reconstructs suggests the extent to which the present narrating-I shapes the past in response to the exigencies of current circumstance, that is his exile in Spain and his disillusionment with the direction of the Revolution. In the same volume, Víctor Díaz Arciniega's essay "La voz: el eco. Vasconcelos: Lección de historia y vida" affirms the documentary value of the book which, in spite of the overwhelming presence of José Vasconcelos as its central subject, allows the historical and social context to emerge. In this regard, the ever-present invective against Carranza and Calles is a remarkable and telling element of the author's personal obsessions within the context of a narrative whose story ends in 1913.

My analysis of *Ulises criollo* focuses on two pillars of autobiography: memory, and intertextuality, or the signs of narrative identity. Recent theories of life writing radically question the reliability of memory and seek to understand the inventive and creative function that it serves in the autobiographical act, rather than its merely recording or preserving function. Paul John Eakin draws on developments in cognitive science and neurobiology as well as theories of narrativity and narrativization in his study of the role of memory in the dynamic process of "making selves" and telling lives (*How Our Lives Become Stories* x). Referring to a variety of scientific work, Eakin advances a notion of memory as consisting not of a set of fixed images that are stored away for later retrieval, but as a series of ever-new perceptions that occur in the present (19). The brain continually binds together the multiple inputs produced in the interface between self and environment into single perceptions, making perception itself a creative, shaping activity and not a passive mirroring of the environment. Memory is constructed and not given, and acts of remembering reinvent and transform what is remembered and do not simply recall a set image of the past. It is contingent upon the complex interplay between the human organism, understood as the indivisible union of mind and body, and the ever-changing context or environment in which it lives. Self and memory are therefore emergent and evolving, because they are generated out of the body and its experience of limits, and out of the dynamic system of language and all of the signifying practices of culture (19–21). Autobiographical memory, which entails the enduring, sequenced memory of significant events in one's own life, is inventive and unstable and not invariant. It is ever modified by the new inputs supplied by the environment, by interpersonal relations and by culture (106–8). Let us not overlook, either, the lesson of Jorge Luis Borges's story "Funes el memorioso," which teaches that forgetting has an essential role to play in meaningful, creative acts of memory.

In *Ulises criollo* the autobiographical-I occasionally employs the phrase "recuerdo" [I remember] in order to signal a personal recollection of something directly experienced in the past. "I remember" or its variant "I haven't forgotten" refer to the seemingly unproblematical and conventional sense of the act of remembering, which is the *sine qua non* of autobiographical narration. This "I remember" is usually left unstated in autobiography, but it is assumed to underpin every evocation of the past life and self. The temporal gap between the present tense of "recuerdo" and the past tense of the verbs used to reconstruct the remembered event is a sign of the distance that separates the re-creative work of memory from the irrevocably lost past. In an autobiography of two-thousand pages, the author's capacity for remembering people, events, places, ideas, physical sensations, emotions, and all the minutiae of daily life presents itself as seemingly unlimited. The sheer bulk of the *Memorias* speaks to a powerful memory, and this is indeed the case for Vasconcelos if memory is understood as the creative reconstruction and reinvention of the past from the vantage point of the present and not as the accurate, objective recall of "what really happened." What is interesting in *Ulises criollo* is that within the forceful, ever-advancing trajectory of the narrative, the narrating-I sometimes pauses to reflect deliberately and consciously on the nature of memory itself, putting into question the meaning of his acts of remembering and forgetting. These instances of self-reflection and scrutiny express a notion of memory that is very close to that which Eakin employs in his studies of autobiography.

The opening lines of the book are frequently quoted: "Mis primeros recuerdos emergen de una sensación acariciante y melodiosa. Era yo un retozo en el regazo materno. Sentíame prolongación física, porción apenas seccionada de una presencia tibia y protectora, casi divina" (4). [My first memories emerge from a sensation that is caressing and harmonious. I was a playful movement in my mother's lap. I felt myself to be a physical extension of her, not yet cut off from a warm, protecting and almost divine presence.][9] Sylvia Molloy, among other readers, interprets the passage as an image of physical union and protection that is soon undermined in the text by references to radical separation and loss in the Biblical story that the mother reads of Moses, the baby abandoned in the rushes. The juxtaposition of the two circumstances, union and separation, establishes a patterning structure that holds for much of the first volume of Vasconcelos's *Memorias* (Molloy 195–96). Molloy further points out that the first pages of the book with their mythical overtones should not be seen as a representation of a "spontaneous" recollection, but as a carefully polished "set piece" designed to serve the heroic self-image of José Vasconcelos that is soon to emerge (196–97). This self-image, I would emphasize, responds to the reality of 1931 and not to that of his birth year, 1885. I would also suggest that the initial passage commemorates, albeit intuitively and not consciously, the centrality of the body in the creation of memories and the construction of self. Human identity formation is a life-long process in which the body and its boundaries play a central role. Without denying the critical importance of language and narrative in structuring our social selves, the body and its responses to the environment are equally a core component in the human sense of self-awareness. Paul John Eakin takes this idea from the work of the neurobiologist Antonio Damasio, and he integrates it with theories of narrative identity in order to account for the complexity of the autobiographical self in his article "What Are We Reading When We Read Autobiography?" (125–26). If, following

Damasio, we consider that the narrative of the self is biological as well as linguistic because it exists in part in wordless stories about what happens to the body and is processed by the brain, then the first memories of José Vasconcelos can be seen as an artistic representation of the idea of the self as being of and about the body.

Numerous passages found primarily in the first one-hundred pages of *Ulises criollo* directly address the problem of memory. Given that these reflections are attributed to the present moment of narrating and do not claim to refer to thoughts that he had as a child, the meditations on memory often also include allusions to the problem of identity and the difference between the I of the remembered child and the I of the remembering adult. Thus memory and identity are shown to be intertwined. The first overt reference to memory occurs early in the first chapter when the narrator makes a distinction between objective memory and emotional memory: "En vano trato de representarme cómo era el pueblo del Sásabe primitivo. La memoria objetiva nunca me ha sido fiel. En cambio, la memoria emocional me revive fácilmente. La emoción del desierto me envolvía" (6). [I try in vain to recall what the primitive town of Sásabe was like. Objective memory has never served me well. In contrast, emotional memory easily comes back to life for me. The emotion of the desert enveloped me.] The emotion so easily recalled is that of the vastness of the desert landscape and the way the desert diminishes or even obliterates the human figure. The phrase "me revive fácilmente" is semantically rich because it invites two interpretations: emotional memory easily comes back to life for me or, easily brings me back to life. In the first, memory is seen as something that happens or returns to the remembering self; while in the second it is the very life force that revives the I, suggesting that the past self is reborn in memory. "Memoria emocional" can also be a reference to the memory of emotionally charged events, explaining the frequent attribution of "passion" in its broad sense to Vasconcelos's autobiography. A later reference to the difficulty of remembering what is merely routine and repetitious reaffirms this privileging of the emotional peaks of existence.

Twice in the book Vasconcelos compares memory to the movies, using the power of modern technology to reveal the limits of memory. In the first instance, the narrator likens memory to a defective movie reel that stops and interrupts the steady flow of images that the film would deliver. The broken film is an apt metaphor for the incomplete recollection of routine, easily forgotten events, and "días sin relieve"

(70), [days of little note]. In the second cinematic metaphor, memory is contrasted to the intact, smoothly running movie reel that reliably preserves and endlessly projects all that the camera has shot. Unlike the well-oiled machine, Vasconcelos compares unreliable human memory to the sudden, unpredictable and fleeting bursts of fireworks that appear in the surrounding night without order or motive, and that return again to darkness, suggesting that forgetfulness is the other side of the coin of memory and is essential to its brilliance.

A second metaphor has mythical rather than technological overtones. Memory, which is not linear and objective like film, but fluid and amorphous, appears as an underground river or as a pool of deep, dark waters. Memories flow and feed the currents of the life story, but they cannot be perfectly controlled and they often do their work of reinventing the past well out of sight. The river of memory becomes confused with the thread of personality in this passage from the first chapter of the book: "Nada más descubro de este período. El hilo tenue de la personalidad se va rompiendo sin que logre reanudarlo la memoria; sin embargo, algo aflora del río subterráneo de repente" (9). [I can't uncover anything else from this period. The fragile thread of my personality breaks off without memory's being able to mend it; nevertheless, something suddenly surfaces out of the subterranean river.] Self and memory emerge, inseparable, from the same fluid source. The discontinuities that characterize the self are similarly evoked much later while remembering his life as a young bureaucrat in the town of Durango: "Lo cierto es que cuando pasan los años, y meditamos, las cosas se nos presentan amparadas en imágenes más o menos vivas, pero lo que es más nuestro, la esencia de lo que fuimos: ¿Qué era yo que ni yo mismo recuerdo? ¿A dónde se fue quien vivió aquellos días de mi destierro durangueño? (279). [It is true that as the years pass and we think back, things come into view aided by more or less vivid images, but what is most ours, the essence of what we were: What was I that not even I myself can remember? Where did he go, the one who lived through those days of my Durango exile?] In his reflections on memory and self, made from the perspective of the present, timeless moment of narrating, the autobiographical-I perceives the disconnects and the blind spots, the ebb and the flow of the twin phenomena of memory and identity. Far from achieving the ideal of a stable, coherent, essential I that was supposed to stand firm at the center of the traditional autobiography, Vasconcelos's self-representation grapples with the fluid, unstable, and incomplete nature of a self-in-process in close alignment with the concept of subjectivity as it has been developed and widely accepted forty or fifty years after the publication of *Ulises criollo*. Literature has a long history of prefiguring changes in ways of thought that eventually emerge and are developed systematically in other discourses.

In the chapter of Paul John Eakin's book *How Our Lives Become Stories* titled "Storied Selves," the critic continues his examination of the ways in which selves and stories are intimately linked in the writing of a life and, just as importantly, in the very living of life. As we have also seen in Paul Ricoeur's work, narrative is not simply *about* the self, but is one constituent part of the self (Eakin 101). While most of us most of the time experience our daily lives largely unaware of the structuring role of narrative in our sense of personal and collective identity, "run[ning] as it were, on automatic narrative pilot" (Eakin 124), the act of writing an autobiography seems to highlight the "storied selves" of the autobiographical-I. The pronounced intertextuality of some examples of the genre is a clear manifestation of the connection between narrativity and personhood, in that it makes visible the influential stories that have shaped one individual's identity. In an observation that perfectly fits the opening chapter of *Ulises criollo*, Eakin says that one of the great themes of autobiography is "the child's awakening to the call of stories as they are performed within the family circle and the larger community" (118). In "El comienzo" [the beginning] Vasconcelos extracts from the vague, blurred workings of his early childhood memory "una visión imborrable. Mi madre retiene sobre las rodillas el tomo de la Historia Sagrada. Comenta la lectura y cómo el Señor hizo el mundo de la nada" (7–8). [one indelible image. My mother holds the tome of the Sacred History on her knees. She comments on the reading and how God made the world out of nothing.] Vasconcelos's "awakening to the call of stories" is thus commemorated in a scene that will repeat itself not only as long as his mother is alive to instruct and mold him through her storytelling, but in his own well-documented program of reading the canonical literature of his culture.

The title *Ulises criollo* is an obvious, perhaps too obvious, homage to the extent to which Vasconcelos's memories of the past, his sense of self and the language of his life story are shaped by literary models assimilated over the course of many years. It also points to the fact that these models are drawn from the most privileged stories of Western myth and literature: the Bible, Homer's *Odyssey*, Virgil's *Aeneid*, and

St. Augustine's *Confessions*, chief among them. In his foreword to the book, the writer justifies the analogy that he draws between his own life and destiny and that of the Greek hero: "Un destino cometa, que de pronto refulge, luego se apaga en largos trechos de sombra" (4). [A comet-like destiny that suddenly shines bright and then is extinguished in long periods of shadow.] Experiences of war, exile, and return lend some support to his claim on the self-aggrandizing comparison, although Sylvia Molloy, among others, has noted Vasconcelos's greater resemblance to Telemachus than to Ulysses. At least in the first volume of the autobiography, the centrality of the mother-son bond suggests the Penelope-Telemachus dyad over the singular figure of the wanderer journeying home (Molloy 201).

Given his mother's fervent Christian faith and the family's regular attendance at the Catholic Mass and their daily reciting of the rosary, it stands to reason that biblical stories and role models exert an even greater influence on the formation of Vasconcelos's identity and his aspirations for himself and for Mexico than the ancient Greek myths that he encountered as a child in school. For all that he chose to call himself the Creole Ulysses, the story of Moses holds a more highly honored place in the autobiography. On the second page of the book, there is a reference to an illustration that shows the baby Moses floating on the river in his basket woven of reeds. The familiar story of the child whose mother seeks to save him by abandoning him, and who is indeed saved by a stranger and ultimately becomes a champion for his mother's faith and people, takes on special significance for a family living in a frontier town in northern Mexico in the mid-1880s. In the autobiography Vasconcelos's mother tells him the story of Moses more than once to serve as an example of how he must survive and thrive if he is ever kidnapped by the Apaches living in the region. "Si vienen los apaches y te llevan consigo, tú nada temas, vive con ellos y sírvelos, aprende su lengua y háblales de Nuestro Señor Jesucristo, que murió por nosotros y por ellos, y por todos los hombres" (8). [If the Apaches come and take you away, don't be afraid. Live with them, serve them, learn their language and speak to them of our Lord Jesus Christ, who died for us and for them, for all men.] In casting her son as a new Moses chosen not only to survive as an individual but to spread God's word and lead his people out of the wilderness, she entrusts him with a civilizing mission that has resonances throughout the text. This is particularly striking in the way that the autobiography represents Vasconcelos's admiration for

Francisco I. Madero and his support for Madero's campaign and presidency. He unambiguously recreates Madero as a latter-day composite of Moses and Jesus Christ, who will fulfill the mission of leading Mexico out of the wilderness of tyranny into the promised land of democracy and also serve as a model of forgiveness and peace. Ancient Mexican culture similarly provides stories to endow modern lives with meaning, and Madero becomes "Quetzalcoatl Madero" after the white-bearded god who tried to abolish blood sacrifice, was duly exiled, and whose promised return would bring salvation. Quetzalcoatl's association with the origins of music and the arts has a further echo in the portrayal of Madero in *Ulises criollo.* Vasconcelos repeatedly contrasts Madero's civilized manners to the violent savagery of the other Revolutionary caudillos, citing not only his refusal to turn military victories into opportunities to massacre captured enemy troops, but also his support of the arts and his rejection of bullfighting as evidence of his superior nature. In the conflict between Madero and his enemies Huerta and Calles, Vasconcelos's new Quetzalcoatl is tragically defeated by Huichilobos, but he lives on as a hope of future redemption in *Ulises criollo.*

The most sustained and complex intertextual relationship informing Vasconcelos's life story is the one that holds between his autobiography and St. Augustine's *Confessions.* The parallels between *Ulises criollo* and the text that is often classified as the first true autobiography in the West are numerous, and they take the form of direct references and more subtle signs of its influence. It is clear that Vasconcelos "remembers" and patterns many episodes of his life story after those that he read in the *Confessions.* The earliest autobiographical memories evoked by St. Augustine are the involuntary smiles and random movements of an infant, activities that the adult narrating-I has observed in other infants and then adopts to describe his own pre-verbal self. The dependency of the infant on adult caregivers and the intimate bond between them are similarly reimagined by Vasconcelos in his opening lines, but he less easily relinquishes the attachment to his mother, as we have seen. The figure of the mother as first teacher and her crucial role in raising her son within the Church are important themes in both autobiographies, and they afford the opportunity for Vasconcelos to draw explicit connections between his own life and that of the Christian saint. For example, creative memories of his family's daily reciting of the rosary bring to Vasconcelos's adult consciousness thoughts of St. Augustine and his encounter with an angel on the shores of North Africa (*Ulises*

48). In another passage, Vasconcelos's mother plays St. Monica to her grown son's Augustine on the eve of his return to the university and his separation from the family: "a imitación de la Santa Mónica, extremaba el fervor de sus oraciones para sostenerme en la prueba. Exaltándose, a ratos me veía como un nuevo Agustín que ha de conocer el mal para mejor vencerlo" (139). [in imitation of St. Monica, she increased the fervor of her prayers in order to sustain me in my trials. Agitated, at times she saw me as a new Augustine who must know evil in order better to conquer it.] Besides the evocation of the mother as a guardian and spiritual guide, other predominant themes of *Ulises criollo* connect this highly confessional autobiography to the Augustinian model. The detailed accounts of the protagonist's education, the youthful embrace of sensuality and pleasure, a marked ambivalence toward marriage, the son's intense reaction to his mother's death, reflections on the nature of memory and language, and the emphasis on books and on interpreting one's life through books all strongly recall the fourth-century foundational text. The study of intertextuality in autobiography illuminates the dynamic process of living stories and telling lives in writing the self. It also helps us realize how highly fictionalized an autobiographical text can be without the reader's rejecting it as a true-life story. An overtly metaliterary text like *Ulises criollo* fits within the flexible boundaries of nonfiction narrative because human memory and subjectivity are constructed and reconstructed out of the stories that our bodies and our minds continually capture, process, and reinvent.

Returning briefly to the context in which José Vasconcelos wrote *Ulises criollo*, there are many ways in which his treatment of the Revolution of 1910 and post-revolutionary Mexico poses a challenge to hegemonic versions of the national history. By writing as an ardent supporter of Madero, as a defeated presidential candidate and, later, as an ever more conservative thinker, Vasconcelos contradicts the heroic idealization of the Revolution as a popular uprising against oppression as it is portrayed in the work of the muralists whom he sponsored while he was Minister of Education. He also contradicts the version promoted by the party and the regime of his victorious opponent in 1929, Pascual Ortiz Rubio. However, in so far as Vasconcelos writes as a member of Mexico's cultural and economic elite and masterfully uses the language of high culture to tell his life story, he is also speaking from well within the circle of power and authority. His autobiography is therefore oppositional, but it is an attack aimed horizontally from one elite to another, and it does not fundamentally threaten the hierarchy of power. In contrast, the first text considered in the next chapter, Benita Galeana's *Benita*, articulates the need to overturn the existing structures of power from a position "below" or at the margins of authority, and it uses the languages of oral history, conventional social roles, and popular political discourse to tell the story of the need for radical change. However, before leaving the arena of elite autobiography, I will explore a different kind of challenge to Vasconcelos's heroic concept of the self and his model of storytelling as it is posed by the work of a woman writer two generations removed from the Mexican Ulysses's influence, María Luisa Puga.

María Luisa Puga: Life-Writing Against the Grain

While José Vasconcelos's *Ulises criollo* fits readily within the tradition of elite male-authored autobiography as defined by Gusdorf, Olney, and Lejeune, three autobiographical texts by María Luisa Puga stretch the limits of that definition and expand our consideration of life writing in this chapter. Puga (1944–2004) is perhaps best known for her first book *Las posibilidades del odio* [The possibilities of hatred], a collection of short fiction published in 1978. These narratives, which are set in postcolonial Kenya and are peopled by characters from across the racial, ethnic, and class spectrum of Kenyan society, identified Puga as an up-and-coming young writer with an uncommon perspective on her nation and its literary traditions. The six stories are often read as a commentary on Mexico as mediated through Puga's observations of Kenya, where she lived for a year and half in 1976 and 1977. *Las posibilidades del odio* treats Kenyan history, the difficult formation of national and individual identity in a colonized country, racism, poverty, class divisions, and the experience of seeing one's own nation in a new way from outside of its borders. These preoccupations and the generational and gender conflicts that are also explored in the book recur throughout Puga's work, which further expresses an intense interest in human relationships and advocates the value of writing as a tool to realize our human potential.[10] In the twenty-five years following the publication of *Las posibilidades del odio*, Puga devoted herself full time to writing and she produced a steady stream of novels, short stories, essays, chronicles, and children's literature. The novels *Cuando el aire es azul* (1980, When the air is blue), *Pánico o peligro*, winner of the Xavier Villarrutia Prize (1983,

Panic or danger), *Antonia* (1989) and *La reina* (1995, The beauty queen); four volumes of short stories; and the essay collection *Lo que le pasa al lector* (1991, What happens to the reader) are a few of her more than two dozen titles.

Puga's fiction is notable for its strong female protagonists, and she once said in an interview with Gabriela de Beer that her particular contribution to Mexican narrative was the creation of "a voice of the independent woman" (de Beer 41). This characterization applies equally to her fictional characters and her autobiograpical self-representations. Her narratives emphasize the inner lives of complex characters over the telling of anecdotes or the description of their physical appearance and their external environment. In one notable exception, the rooms that her characters occupy and the places that they observe through ever-present window frames, are regularly, almost obsessively described, as I will discuss. Reflections within her fiction on the act of writing develop a metaliterary dimension for her novels, in which the narrators often keep journals or write novels themselves. In these ways, the image of the human being as fundamentally an observing and writing subject is predominant, and an overarching thematic and structuring device seen in her work is the perspective of the outsider who looks in on the world while paradoxically being positioned within an interior space looking out. In her nonfictional life writing, this doubly "inside out" perspective is one of the tensions to be explored by the reader.

A striking aspect of the existing criticism and analysis of Puga's narrative fiction is the tendency to identify and discuss its autobiographical elements. This is particularly true for studies of *Las posibilidades del odio*, *Pánico o peligro*, *Antonia*, and *Las razones del lago* (1991, The lake's reasons). Reading women's fictional narratives as autobiography is a strain of criticism that was once pervasive in literary studies, but it is an approach that many women writers have rejected as simplistic and even condescending. It can, and often did imply that women are lacking in creative imagination and can only write about themselves, in contrast to the male author's putative talent for originality and invention. Without engaging here in that debate, I would point out that Puga seems quite comfortable in her interviews in acknowledging the transformed presence of her own life experiences in her novels, and she doesn't hesitate to draw direct connections between herself and her characters.[11] My project, however, does not examine Puga's fiction, but rather it studies the author's deliberate acts of self-representation and autobiographical reflection utilizing the languages and the forms of nonfiction literature. Three of her books are examples of life writing: *De cuerpo entero: El espacio de la escritura* (1990, Full-length view: the space of writing), *Crónicas de una oriunda del kilómetro X en Michoacán* (1995, Chronicles of a native of kilometer X in Michoacán) and *Diario del dolor* (2004, Diary of pain). Puga creatively employs three genres, autobiography, chronicle, and diary, in order to explore four primary concerns of her own life experience: the dynamic nature of identity; attachments to place and experiences of dislocation; the activity of writing; and confrontations with physical pain.

The very brief autobiography *El espacio de la escritura* serves as a point of departure for examining the chronicles and the diary. It is one of a series of autobiographies by contemporary Mexican authors that were invited and published by Silvia Molina under the common title of "De cuerpo entero." The series comprises roughly fifty titles, most published from 1990 to 1992. Vicente Leñero, Luis Zapata, Brianda Domecq, Ethel Krauze, and María Luisa Mendoza are among the writers who have participated in this ambitious project. Puga's text is a scant forty-five pages long, and it recounts episodes from her childhood and her ten-year sojourn abroad (England, Italy, Spain, France, Kenya), which lasted from 1968 until her return to Mexico and the publication of her first book in 1978. It complies with Lejeune's definition of autobiography by offering traces of the narrator-protagonist's "real-life" identity through the inclusion of photos captioned with her name and a dedication to her sister Patricia, who is a character in the early chapters. The narrating-I is anonymous in that she does not explicitly state her own name in the body of the text, but the framing elements just mentioned serve to establish identity between author and narrator-protagonist and not mere resemblance, as Lejeune requires.

The title *El espacio de la escritura* makes transparent the two defining terms of María Luisa Puga's autobiography, in which the process of becoming a writer is structured as an itinerary through space. The autobiographical subject documents her frequent moves from city to city over a period of more than twenty years, and in each temporary destination she settles into a room that serves as the locus of her writing. In this narrative mapping of her life, movement along an ever-evolving itinerary signifies both escape from and encounter with the self and the other, and the space of the room is experienced as enclosed or bounded and also open to the world outside. In his article "Narratives in Space and Time: Beyond 'Backdrop' Accounts of Narrative Orientation," Mike Baynham looks at spatial orientation in oral storytelling and its function in the production of narrative action and agency. Although Baynham analyzes oral narratives, his study of stories of migration and resettlement of Moroccan workers in Europe is a useful starting point for considering how space is invoked in Puga's text. In rejecting a static "backdrop" or "stage setting" view of space, Baynham emphasizes social space, that is, space shaped and inhabited by social relations, and he examines the ways in which social space creates opportunities and constructs identities for narrated selves (358). As is true for Baynham's Moroccan immigrants, Puga's autobiographical-I traces a process of location, dislocation, and relocation occurring over an extended period of time, and she experiences the movement from center to periphery and back on a variety of levels, both personal and geopolitical. The geographical itinerary from city to city, the private space of the rooms occupied by the protagonist, and her relationship to the "space of writing," ultimately understood to be language, are the constitutive elements of the narrative action through which the autobiographical-I invents herself as a writer.

The title of the first chapter of *El espacio de la escritura* is "Acapulco" and all of the subsequent chapter headings similarly designate the autobiographer's cities of residence: Mazatlán, Mexico City, London, Paris, and the many others that comprise a pattern of dislocations and relocations, first within Mexico, and then abroad. Acapulco was her birthplace and her first home, and it is significant that the move from Acapulco to Mazatlán was made necessary by the early death of her mother and her father's prompt remarriage. This loss initiates a string of moves, those decided by her father during her childhood, and those prompted by her own decision at age twenty-four to leave Mexico for England. Future changes of residence are equally associated with experiences of loss, as when the end of a relationship or the loss of employment motivate later moves within Europe. The life story takes shape as a journey across a geography of loss in search of an ever-moving target that one might provisionally call "home." If loss is the "push" factor that uproots the protagonist, the prospect of a certain kind of gain is what pulls or attracts her to new destinations. When she chooses England, she is drawn by her fondness for English literature, her knowledge of the language, a desire to see the world in a different light, and the determination to become a writer. From there the pushes and pulls of life steer her to Rome, Greece, Paris, Madrid, again Rome, Cuernavaca (very briefly), Nairobi, and Oxford before her definitive resettlement in Mexico in 1978. Curiously, her travel story is not characterized by a wealth of reflections on her encounters with other cultures. The observations of European societies contained in the book rarely go beyond a repetition of cultural stereotypes, such as bicycle-riding Oxford dons, the charm of Parisian cafes, and the noisy sociability of the Italians. This superficiality cedes to a deeper engagement with the local culture and history in Nairobi, where Kenya's colonial past and impoverished, racially divided present cause her to see Mexico with new clarity. Here the aspiring but frustrated writer undertakes the research and reflection that produce her first successful novel, her "African" novel. At the most distant point in her journey she has arrived home, and now the search for home is revealed to be the search for her identity as a writer. The narrative tracing of a geographical itinerary has shaped and been shaped by the story of becoming a writer.

The activity of writing is the constant that orients and grounds Puga's autobiographical-I in every city where she takes up residence beginning in her childhood. The privileging of location, as seen in the chapter titles, and the faithful description of each room occupied by the protagonist are the distinguishing features of this very brief, and in some ways schematic autobiography. As Baynham shows, space is much more than backdrop to narrative. In *El espacio de la escritura*, the space of the room, in particular, is intimately linked to writing and it is therefore an integral factor in the formation of the writer. The room further plays a complementary role to that of an ever-shifting geography. Against the movement and exposure to the world signified by the travel between cities, the room represents a stable, enclosed space within which the writer can engage in her self-defining, self-creating work, no matter where she is located.

In a profile of the author that was published in 1996, George Szanto quotes Puga describing her relationship to the rooms she has inhabited: "I have to feel the space around me. To remember different places I have written—I don't know why but it is something tremendously agreeable to me. I remember the room in Nairobi, and the room in Oxford. I remember more the room than the life I was leading" ("Civil Societies" 5). In these comments and in the attention paid to the "room" over the "life" in *El espacio de la escritura*, Puga acknowledges but goes far beyond the obvious allusion to the woman writer's need for a room of her own that Virginia Woolf memorably portrayed.

Privacy and uninterrupted time to work are, of course, prerequisites to the writing life and Puga was famously devoted to defending both the time and space to write, but in the autobiography the preoccupation with the room is foregrounded to an unusual degree. Given that the text is only forty-fives pages long and it covers thirteen intercity moves, the rented rooms are not described in detail, but rather the same essential elements are aways documented: the desk, the door, and the window. The desk with its functional surface, the door that ensures privacy, and the window that allows a view of the world outside create the minimum conditions for the aspiring writer to enact her identity.

The multiple roles played by ever-present windows particularly illustrate how space creates opportunities and shapes action. At the simplest level, windows cast light onto the scene of writing, and certain qualities of light establish a mood. London's melancholy gloom offers a rest from the "arrebatado sol de México" (20) [Mexico's glaring sun], while the orange light of Rome provides comforting warmth after Paris and Madrid's wintry gray. Equally important for the developing writer is the way that windows allow reflective observation by opening up a view to the outside and simultaneously shaping and containing that view within the limits of their frames. The window extends an invitation to the viewer to enter the world, but it simultaneously excludes her, because the glass is both transparency and barrier. In this play of access and exclusion, the writing-I is located inside the room looking out, and is also positioned as an outsider looking in at a world to which she does not wholly belong. In what follows, I will show how the problem of insuperable outsiderhood, alluded to in *El espacio de la escritura*, centrally informs Puga's second autobiographical book *Crónicas de una oriunda del kilómetro X en Michoacán*.

To conclude the examination of *El espacio de la escritura*, the autobiographical-I not only writes within a room in a literal sense, but she refers to language and to the act of writing in spatial terms. Her first attempt to write a story requires coming to terms with the room that secludes her from the larger world and with the demands of the "severe," "hermetic" desk covered in books (18). At first, writing is a "manoteo a ciegas" (17) [a blind groping], which, when accomplished removes the defining boundaries that separate self and other, and empties the writer "porque algo propio ha trasladado su existencia a otra parte" (19) [because something of one's own has transferred its existence to another place]. Puga variously installs herself in a dialogue with language, and enfigures language as a door, her room as a periscope, and the Spanish idiom as a space of her own, "mi propio islote" (24) [my own little island]. She observes that language "occupies us" through its power to dictate our convictions and make things happen (35–36). Consciousness is described somewhat statically as a wardrobe or an attic where images are stored until they are pulled out and written (49). Stories themselves unfold in space rather than in time: "se extienden hacia atrás, hacia adelante, a los lados" (55) [they stretch backwards, forwards, to the sides], and her notebooks offer room to practice and room to breathe. The centrality of place as the literal space of writing and the metaphorical characterization of language in spatial terms in *El espacio de la escritura* can perhaps be interpreted as an attempt to compensate for a profound feeling of displacement caused by the death of her mother when the protagonist is nine years old. The loss of the mother may be evoked metonymically by the depiction of place and displacement: the first home with its shared bedroom, the loss of that home, and the passage through a series of houses and cities within Mexico and abroad. The radical separation caused by death forces an early exile from the maternal, and the father's reorganization of his life through remarriage further uproots the child, who seeks to recover a sense of wholeness and of being at home by recording the details of each new dwelling in the absence of the centering figure of the mother. The young protagonist and her sister even invent a game to substitute for the missing mother: a language game of novel-writing that inscribes an imaginary place of origin, a magical Acapulco where mothers never die (13).

Puga's gradual realization that she is fundamentally an outsider no matter where she lives extends a conceptual bridge between *El espacio de la escritura* and her second work of nonfictional life writing, *Crónicas de una oriunda del kilómetro X en Michoacán*. Her awareness that as a writer she observes reality without fully taking part in it, and the conceptualization of the act of writing as a space that she inhabits and yet must also continually travel to reach are insights that are presented in the final pages of *De cuerpo entero* and more fully explored in the chronicles of Puga's life in the town of Zirahuén, Michoacán. On the next-to-last page of the autobiography she admits that "El escritor es siempre un fuereño" (55) [the writer is always an outsider]; and she closes the book with the observation that "el espacio de la escritura está en uno. Para propiciarlo a veces es preciso recorrer mucho kilometraje" (56). [The space of writing is inside of you. To gain access to it, sometimes you need to cover a lot of distance.] Her use of the word "fuereño" establishes the central problematic of her exploration of human identity in many of her subsequent works, and most particularly in the *Crónicas*.

María Luisa Puga ultimately found her "space of writing" by traveling many miles from Mexico City to the small town of Zirahuén in Michoacán, and she reflects on the meaning of that geographical displacement in the hybrid text *Crónicas de una oriunda del kilómetro X en Michoacán*.[12] The book's title, the name of the series to which it belongs, and the site of its cataloguing in U.S. libraries suggest three distinct generic classifications for *Crónicas*, none of which quite hits the mark. In libraries, presumably because of the words "oriunda" and "Michoacán" in the title, it is stunningly mis-shelved with books about the history of Mexico's indigenous peoples. Next, it is part of the series "Cuadernos de viaje" [travel notebooks] published by the Consejo Nacional para la Cultura y las Artes and conceived to "retratar a un México múltiple y evocador" (4) [portray a multiple and evocative Mexico], through diaries and other travel accounts. However, Puga's contribution to the series is highly untypical of travel writing, in the sense that it reflects on one person's experience of taking up permanent residence in a town within her own country of birth. Finally, the chronicle genre is also a problematical fit. The chronicle is the subject of Chapters 5 and 6 of this book, and a more developed definition can be found there. To summarize very briefly, the contemporary Mexican chronicle is a form of literary journalism that combines elements of the essay, the short story and news reporting to represent social, political, and cultural events, people (both well-known and unknown), places, customs, and ways of life. The focus is primarily on the urban milieu, and the chronicler often assumes the role of a *flanêur*. The most widely-read and highly-regarded chronicles of the past fifty years offer a critical perspective on the Mexican government and a counter-version to official history. Puga's *Crónicas* conform to some of these criteria in that they treat present-day, local reality from the point of view of an observer who is also a participant in events, and they have a clear documentary basis. They are untypical in their treatment of small-town life and their pronounced autobiographical dimension. Finally, they are untypical of Mexican letters in general and its oft-noted obsession with national identity in the way in which they reflect not on what it means to be Mexican, but what it means to be fundamentally an outsider to Mexico while living as a citizen within the national territory.

Crónicas contains roughly twenty short pieces written over a period of nine years for the newspaper *El Economista* and the magazine *México Desconocido*. They are organized into two sections: "La fuereñez experimentada" and "La fuereñez presenciada" [outsiderhood experienced and outsiderhood witnessed, respectively]. In her fiction writing and in the numerous interviews that she has given, Puga frequently constructs her characters and herself as outsiders. The narrator of the novel *Antonia* is a young Mexican woman residing in London, one character in *Las posibilidades del odio* is a Kenyan living in Italy, and the autobiographical Puga in *El espacio de la escritura* spends a decade abroad and on the move. However, the feeling of being an outsider transcends the experience of geographical and cultural displacement across national borders. As previously quoted from the final pages of the autobiography, "the writer is always an outsider" (55), an idea that Puga repeats in other contexts. Speaking with George Szanto in 1996 about her life in Zirahuén, she commented that, "There is the urban identity, the rural identity and the *fuereño* identity. We are *fuereños*. . . . It may sound pretentious but I think for us the most authentic identity is the *fuereño*" (10). As late as an interview with Emily Hind published in 2001, Puga reiterated "yo desde hace mucho, estoy instalada en una tierra que se llama la fuereñez" (175). [For a long time I have been settled into a land called outsiderhood,] *Crónicas de una oriunda del kilómetro X en Michoacán* is the example of Puga's life writing that most closely examines this experience within the concrete conditions of the writer's daily routine in Zirahuén.

María Luisa Puga's use of the terms outsider and outsiderhood is consistent across a number of her books and in her interviews, and it is important to note that she never refers to herself as an exile. Exile has been a common experience of dissident intellectuals, artists, and writers since ancient times, and a great deal of excellent theory and analysis of the literatures of exiles has been produced in many cultural contexts.[13] Nevertheless, Puga is resolutely an outsider and not an exile, and not even Paul Ilie's persuasive theory of the inner exile, who might seem to resemble Puga's internal outsider, accounts for the specificity of her meaning. I do, however, see a certain resonance between Puga's *fuereño* and the "dissident intellectual" of Julia Kristeva's well-known 1977 essay.[14] Kristeva uses the term exile to denote the process of becoming a stranger to one's own country, language, sex, and identity which is a necessary precondition to writing. This estrangement permits one to "avoid sinking into the mire of common sense" (298) and to engage in a ceaseless "dismanteling of the workings of discourse, thought and existence" (299). As a woman and as a writer who challenges the conventional limits of national and gender identity in Mexico and who questions the conventional notions of center and periphery in Mexican culture, María Luisa Puga has much in common with Kristeva's dissident intellectual, although her writing does not approach the radical experimentation of the authors whom Kristeva privileges.[15]

The first part of the *Crónicas*, "Outsiderhood experienced," contains fifteen very short pieces that narrate a series of everyday events and special occasions in the life of a resident outsider in a small Mexican town. The routine of an ordinary day, a wedding, a funeral, local politics, a vacation trip to the coast, a hardware store, and a rainstorm are the concrete realities that ground the narrator's reflections on identity and on her relationships with others, with place, and with writing. Many details can readily be correlated to Puga's "real-life" experiences in Zirahuén, but the representation of the main character, the *fuereño*, and the play of narrative voices complicate an autobiographical reading and introduce irony into the text. The ironic take on the identity of self and/as other and the questioning of our reliance on ready-made ideas and commonplace uses of language show the chronicler catching herself sinking into the "mire of common sense," as Kristeva warns, and resisting its pull. She portrays herself over time as moving from a position of distance and separation from the community toward experiences of encounter on common ground, without ever losing the unique identity of outsider.

The fundamental inner tension that characterizes Puga's outsider is that between belonging and not belonging to a place and a community. "Quiere ser parte, pero quiere vivir en paz;" "está sin estar, detenido en la frontera misma de la realidad" (14). [He wants to belong, but he wants to live in peace; he is there without being there, held up at the very border of reality.] This borderline, in-between identity is further described in negative terms: he is not a tourist because he doesn't leave; he is not a foreigner because he is a Mexican citizen; he lives next to but not in the town to which he does and does not wish to belong. The most intriguing textual markers of this tension are the fluctuation in the use of grammatical person to evoke the outsider, and the predominant assignment of masculine gender to him. The narrator speaks of the protagonist in the third person "he" in the first chronicle; for example, but switches to "you" ("usted es un fuereño") (16) in the second; then uses the first-person plural "we" in the fourth; and openly self-identifies as an I narrator-protagonist-*fuereño* for the first time in the seventh of the fifteen pieces. This alternation continues until the end of "La fuereñez experimentada," albeit with a growing preference for claiming the first-person voice and an eventual nod to the feminine gender of the I, a writer whose husband owns a hardware store (58).

The shifting among personal pronouns connects in a direct way with the overarching problem of how to live in a community without belonging to it, how to be an observer and yet be part of the scene observed, and how to be a citizen from a position of voluntary marginality within the nation. The varying degrees of distance implicit in constructing the self as he, one, you, we, and I (inflected as feminine) express the range of relationships of separation and proximity from her neighbors and from her own experiences that the chronicler records in her daily life. The fact that there is a rough trend toward first-person forms (singular and plural) as the text progresses, but without abandoning references to herself as he or you, signifies a move toward reconciliation with the self and with choices made. However, the split subject of the chronicles never achieves an absolute wholeness, but rather he/she remains in a position of outsiderhood, embracing multiple subject positions. The final sentence of the fifteenth chronicle condenses this entire dynamic into a few phrases that seamlessly flow from I to he to one to we: "[M]e digo oyendo el silencio: el fuereño tiene siempre un pie puesto aquí y otro allí. Y no se está tan mal. Es vivir como vivimos todos: de la mano del azar" (65). [Listening to the silence, I tell myself: the outsider always has one foot here and one over there. And it's not so bad like that. It means living as we all live: grabbing chance by the hand.]

The dual and duplicitous nature of the outsider is illustrated in several of the passages already quoted from the *Crónicas*, as well as in the play of personal pronouns. In her exploration of what it means to live as an ousider in one's own country, María Luisa Puga the chronicler is aware of the contradictions inherent in her character's identity—her own identity—and as a result, as a narrator she remains somewhat detached or distanced from her literary creation. This distance permits moments of criticism and self-criticism, as well as self-revelation. The reader, in turn, perceives the variable relationship of identity and difference between the narrator and the character inscribed in the shifting use of pronouns. This structural feature, in combination with explicit reflections on the duality of belonging and not belonging, activates an ironic reading of the text. In his classic analysis of irony in Spanish-American narrative, Jonathan Tittler posits two necessary conditions for irony: the fundamental duplicity of all words and actions; and an act of perception or conscious awareness of a discrepancy or a contradiction in an event or a verbal act (18–20). Both the narrator and the reader of the *Crónicas* apprehend the ironic potential of the contradictory nature of the outsider and the situations in which he finds himself. For the narrator, this leads to a playful acceptance of her borderline, neither-here-nor-there identity as given by the epithet "fuereño irredento" (incorrigible outsider), which is repeated in more than one piece.

In "Una boda en el pueblo" [a town wedding], the *fuereño*'s participation in the religious and secular rituals that celebrate a young couple's marriage brings him surprisingly close to a sense of real belonging, almost a state of grace. The narrator carefully sets up the conditions for a happy ending to this anecdote of unexpected *convivencia* [coexistence], but the spell is broken when the outsider sinks into "the mire of common sense" and answers a simple question with a banal, ready-made reply: "¿Y qué le parece nuestro pueblo? . . .—Muy bonito" (19). [And what do you think of our town? . . . Very pretty.] The narrator adds in conclusion: "Usted es un fuereño irredento" (19). The irony of the narrator's perception of her character's (her own) failure to say something original and meaningful in a moment of connection with the other is a commentary on the traps that language and habit set for us; while the readers, with our dashed expectations, are the victims of the ironic turn of events. In the following chronicles the outsider will again feel herself to be part of the town when attending a funeral and when working in the hardware store that serves the practical needs of the local residents and provides a meeting place for neighbors. Nevertheless, the awareness of living always on the edge of town and being always somehow different from the others persists throughout the book, as does the stance of ironical (self) reflection and criticism.

María Luisa Puga's final publication before her death in December 2004, *Diario del dolor* [Diary of pain], is her third excursion into life writing in a nonfictional mode. In the tradition of much journal writing, the *Diario* is a response to personal crisis and to a perceived threat to the writer's sense of self. As Puga explained in a public presentation of the book, "para un escritor uno de los motores para escribir es algo que de alguna manera está invadiendo su existencia. . . . En mi caso fue el dolor."[16] [for a writer one of the driving forces for writing is something that is invading his existence. . . . In my case it was pain.] Puga lived for a number of years with the invasive presence of chronic pain throughout her body and a gradual but profound loss of strength and mobility caused by rheumatoid arthritis. A variety of medical treatments and adaptive devices, some of the latter custom-made by her husband, made it possible for her to continue living in their shared home in Zirahuén and to continue writing, and it is striking that in an interview conducted as late as January 2002 the question of the writer's illness and disability is not raised.[17] However, the *Diario* records an intense struggle to understand and accept the shattering impact that unremitting pain had on Puga's body and on her identity. As readers of Holocaust diaries have shown, this genre can be of special importance when subjectivity is under threat and when there is an urgent need to preserve memory and self in the face of that threat. Journals of illness, on the other hand, often engage in a dialogue with the body in order to name amorphous fears and restore a degree of control over one's life.[18] While Puga was not confronting death through genocide or fatal illness, her experience of living with disabling and incurable physical pain prompted the writing of a diary that examines issues of the self's integrity and survival in the form of a dialogue with her body's constant companion, *Dolor*.

Contrary to convention, the entries in *Diario del dolor* are not dated, but are simply numbered in sequence from one to one hundred and given a short title that links directly to each fragment's opening sentence. Scattered references to the passing of time suggest that the diary was written over the course of about a year, but the entries begin *in medias res* without a contextualizing introduction or start date. The ending of the diary, still undated, does commemorate a life turning point. Entry number ninety-nine attests to the growing importance of the personal computer in Puga's life and how it has displaced pain as her primary interlocutor. The conversation with pain has run its course. Entry number one hundred is brief and conclusive, and it plays effectively with the double meaning of *diario* as daily and diary: "100. En fin/Así es esto del dolor diario" (92). [In conclusion, that's how it is with daily pain (or with the diary of pain).] In the analysis that follows, I will pay particular attention to the relationship between the diarist and her pain and the fear of the loss of self under the stress of pain, as manifested in the construction of the narrative voice and the personification of Dolor.

The reader looking for textual evidence to grant factual adequacy to Puga's *Diario* might initially be skeptical of its status as a work of nonfiction. The fictional novel in diary form is a common enough narrative subgenre that the work's title alone is not necessarily persuasive. In this case, the diarist remains anonymous until one-third of the way through the book, so that the first thirty-three fragments lack the identity of name between author and narrator-protagonist that is a hallmark of life writing. The absence of dates contributes to the impression that this is not a "real" diary but an invented one. In contrast, an early claim to factual status is made by the dedication to a Dr. J. Gabriel Herejón Cervantes, in so far as the proper name is a trace of the real and invites verification. The autobiographical dimension of this unusual diary is clearly given in fragment number thirty-four when the narrator, who is waiting for her name to be called in a hospital says: "Seré yo cuando digan María Luisa Puga" (33). [That will be me when they say María Luisa Puga.] The diagnosis of rheumatoid arthritis, and references to trips to Mexico City, the house in Zirahuén, her husband's hardware store, writing workshops, a cat named Gato, a writer's conference in Monterrey, and other identifying details connect the diarist with the author, but the moment of self-naming is the defining act in the autobiographical performance.

G. Thomas Couser, one of the foremost scholars of disability life writing in the United States, discusses the prominence of the body in narratives that are conceived in response to bodily dysfunction. His general observations about stories of illness and disability identify key thematic concerns found in *Diario del dolor*: a heightened consciousness of self and one's own contingency, the disruption of one's life plot, and the threat that pain poses to identity (*Recovering Bodies* 5). Lucy Bending focuses her essay "Approximation, Suggestion, and Analogy: Translating Pain into Language" on the notion that although pain resists language it does not silence it, and pain can be effectively translated into linguistic representation through analogy and narrative.[19] In comments that could have been written directly about Puga's *Diario*, Bending says that pain and illness change the familiar body into one that is unrecognizable, and it creates a fissure between the idea of the self and the new self that has taken its place (132). Puga expresses anxiety about this fissure in several of her journal entries.

The construction of narrative voice and narrative personae in *Diario del dolor* are the formal manifestations of all of the issues identified by Couser and Bending. As per convention, the diarist herself occupies the position of the first-person narrator and protagonist of the anecdotes and meditations that comprise the entries. Her protagonism is foregrounded to the virtual exclusion of other human characters, although Puga's husband, always evoked as "el HOMBRE" [the MAN], makes an occasional appearance in an auxiliary role. The entire text is a one-sided conversation between the diarist and pain/her pain/herself in pain, during which Dolor, her mute but eloquent interlocutor, shifts between being a distant third-person "he" and a more intimate "you." In this way Puga represents the split between mind and body, self and other, that chronic pain causes. Pain and the stress of living with its unpredictable and debilitating companionship destroy any illusion of the integrity and coherence of the self, creating, as Couser notes, a heightened consciousness of one's own contingency. Puga, in recording her year-long struggle to understand, accept, and survive the constant invasion of her body by physical pain, textually splits off what she resistantly identifies as her "self" from her alien body-in-pain and she structures a variably hostile and intimate relationship of I-he-you around her own threatened, divided subjectivity. As early as the second fragment she captures the paradox of a self-and-other, self-as-other identity: "Entendemos, mi cuerpo y yo, que el espacio ya no es nuestro; tampoco es del dolor, es de los dos. Y hay que aprender a compartirlo" (10). [We understand, my body and I, that space no longer belongs to us nor to pain, it belongs to both. And you have to learn to share.] The plural "we" broken down into my body and I represents a divided subject confronting a common enemy, an intimate enemy with whom she must share the entire space of her existence.

Some of the most poignant moments in the *Diario* are those that express the loss of a familiar self and the familiar body that the self once inhabited; a body now transformed into an alien figure. "Ahí estás Dolor, no sé por dónde te vas a aparecer nunca, pero me estarás dando jalones más o menos apremiantes todo el día, todos los días. Antes yo no era así y a veces me extraño" (10). [There you are, Pain, I don't ever know where you're going to appear, but you'll be giving me sharp little pokes all day, every day. I didn't used to be like this and at times I miss myself.] Later she repeats her nostalgia for her former self and expresses her sorrow over the stranger that she has become, as in entry eleven where she reflects on the loss of her self and attributes this loss to "his" invasion of her territory, again evoking the image of an alien intruder into what was familiar territory. "Perdí mi imagen. Esa que tanto tiempo he pasado en construir, que es tan frágil porque cualquier cosa la distorsiona. De repente capto una imagen en el espejo y no la identifico conmigo. . . . Soy algo huidizo, indefinible, algo que se está evaporando. Y es cuando lo siento a él, Dolor, engordar a mi costa" (14). [I lost my self-image. The one that took me so long to make and was so fragile that anything distorts it. Suddenly I catch a reflection in the mirror and I don't identify it with me. . . . I'm elusive, indefinable, something that is evaporating. And that's when I feel him, Pain, getting fat at my expense.]

In the course of a year of writing the diary, Puga records a process of imperfect reconciliation between her self and her pain. Having lost past and future, memory and hope, she lives in the present and imagines herself more and more as one half of a couple, joined in a love-hate relationship that is only partially mitigated by doses of humor and irony. The diarist's ironical view of all of the incongruities occasioned by pain and disability reinforces the distancing effect achieved by the split subject of narration, who is simultaneously and yet incompatibly I-he-you, self and other. Considered with some degree of detachment, pain has admirable and even humorous qualities as well as deeply negative ones. He is all of a piece, impossible to distract, constant, attentive, patient, composed, and straightforward, among other worthy attributes. What makes it possible for the writer to achieve distance and detachment vis-à-vis her own physical suffering is the very act of writing about pain, and throughout the diary, writing becomes a third character whose presence slowly supplants the antagonism of pain. Without ever evoking the widely accepted idea that writing, and especially journal writing can serve as an effective therapy for trauma, Puga successfully translates traumatic experience into written language in a process of self-knowledge and understanding of the other that leads to growth and change. The diary reaches its logical conclusion when the writer has learned all that she can by recreating her story of pain in the form of a conversation with Dolor, and by journal entry ninety-five she is ready to move on. "Me quiero ir a otras zonas de la existencia y tengo que cerrar este diario. . . . Puedes no irte de mí nunca, pero de mi escritura sí te vas a tener que ir porque ya terminamos contigo" (89). [I want to go to other spheres of existence and I have to end this diary. . . . You might not ever leave me, but you are going to have to leave my writing, because she and I are finished with you.]

The personification of pain, Dolor with a capital "D," is a second, highly distinctive and effective element of the narrative discourse in the *Diario*. The figure of the intimate enemy is vividly evoked by endowing pain with a multitude of human attributes and by addressing him directly as a conversational partner and constant companion. There is nothing abstract or vague about pain. He is a material presence whose individuality and vitality fill the space and the body that he and the narrator share. His human form is that of an older man, unattractive, thin in a sickly way, balding, and suffering from dandruff. The use of personification both distances the sufferer from her pain and grants him an independence and an initiative over which she has no control. He is part of her, but he is autonomous, an intruder who has settled in for the duration, an unwelcome, unappealing guest who refuses to leave.

The complexity of the relationship between the diarist and pain drives the rich and varied vocabulary employed to create his human persona. Pain is capable of a full range of emotions and activities and he has both physical and psychological traits. He appears and disappears, takes up space, watches, speaks and remains silent, laughs, jokes, becomes frightened, sits, stands, walks, eats, sunbathes, wades in the ocean, gets bored, dances, and has opinions, to offer just a few examples. The diarist consistently addresses him as a human companion in informal terms—"mi cuate," "mano" [my pal, bro]—and she frequently refers to his shoulders, arms, head, and legs. Throughout the one hundred entries there is a marked tension between the depiction of the aggressive, cruel nature of pain and his power to transform the writer's life and identity, and her resistant power to make fun of him and diminish his stature through her control of language. In creating Dolor as a human character, sometimes she treats him like a child or a pet dog. She scolds him, takes pity on him, teases him about his appearance, and whispers behind his back, opening the door to humor in the context of suffering and loss. Humor is a common coping mechanism, and Puga primarily exploits the comic potential of the personification of pain in her descriptions of his physical appearance. She imagines Dolor as a stooped old man whose thin shoulders are covered in dandruff and whose skinny legs and yellowed skin evoke pity for his vulnerability rather than fear, thus cutting him down to a manageable size.

In María Luisa Puga's *Diario del dolor* pain is simultaneously a threatening, powerful presence that invades, torments, and ambushes the writer, and he is also an object of derision and a clownish, squalid figure. Puga's creative use of the diary form to inscribe her singular relationship with the chronic pain of rheumatoid arthritis yields a document that transforms crisis and the threat of annihilation into a fascinating and un-self-pitying story of survival and begrudging acceptance of loss. In order to push back against the destructive, impersonal power of pain, she embodies pain as a human companion with whom she can struggle and coexist. Far from presenting an image of a coherent, stable self triumphing over adversity, *Diario del dolor* holds up brokenness and suffering to scrutiny and allows the reader to witness a particularly elegant and ironic "translation" of pain into the language of personal narrative.

The four texts studied in this chapter tell the storied lives of their authors, and each work manifests the impulse to respond to a personal crisis or life question in a nonfictional form of writing: autobiography, chronicle, and diary. The predominant element of intertexuality in José Vasconcelos's lengthy and wide-ranging *Ulises criollo* depicts a life remembered and reconstructed according to highly privileged cultural narratives assimilated by the writing subject over the course of a lifetime. The narrative nature of human selfhood is clearly illustrated by this classic example of Mexican autobiography. In María Luisa Puga's life writing, conceived in short, fragmentary texts, she examines specific experiences that are critical to her self-understanding, rather than attempting a totalizing view of the past self. The aspiring author in search of her identity in *El espacio de la escritura*, the outsider in the *Crónicas* and the subject-in-pain in *Diario del dolor* are all single facets of a complex subject who is both remembered and newly invented in the process of writing. Vasconcelos's heroic concept of the self contrasts sharply with Puga's decidedly antiheroic and ironic portrayal of her struggles to write, to belong, and to live with chronic pain, but both writers' work demonstrates that in fact, "the subject is never given at the beginning." The human activity of narration creates a dynamic representation of the unstable, contingent nature of subjectivity. In the following chapter, two examples of life writing by working-class, marginally literate or agraphic subjects will demonstrate that all members of a society are formed within the cultural narratives of their time and place, and that formal education and reading are not the only means of access to the shared stories that build our narrative identities.

4

Life Writing from a Popular Perspective

> [W]e would not restrict autobiography to any age or sex, creed, class, or color. . . . Let him be ever so obscure or humble, it needs but the sincere relation of what he has been and done and felt and thought to give him a place in *this most democratic province of the republic of letters.*
>
> —William Dean Howells (emphasis mine)

The access of subaltern voices to "this most democratic province of the republic of letters" is a question that Latin American writers, intellectuals, and grassroots activists began to engage in a sustained fashion in the second half of the twentieth century through the production and the study of testimonial literature and the rediscovery of slave narratives. The question of authorship and authority to speak resonates throughout much of the theory and criticism of Latin American testimonial literature, as producers of *testimonio* and scholarly readers alike continually grapple with the problem of the relationship between elite writers and subaltern subjects and with the question of who speaks in mediated testimonies.[1] Or, as Elena Poniatowska suggestively asked when speaking about her "novela-testimonio" *Hasta no verte, Jesús mío*, "¿Qué hubiera sucedido si Jesusa Palancares [Josefina Bórquez] escribe ELLA su propia historia y no soy yo la autora de *Hasta no verte, Jesús mío*?" [What would have happened if Jesusa Palancares wrote her own story and I were not the author of *Hasta no verte, Jesús mío*?][2] Although some very early readings attributed a kind of naive transparency to the "voice of the voiceless" that is presumably captured in *testimonio*, most studies reject any illusion of an uncomplicated immediacy in testimonial narrating. The work accomplished by the writer-editor of a collaborative text in selecting and organizing the material provided through oral interviews is a significant, although often nearly invisible shaping force that does not "belong" to the testimonial subject. Just as importantly, like all subjects, the speaking-I of *testimonio* is a storied self whose experiences and memories are inextricably entangled with multiple preexisting cultural narratives and are not free of their enabling constraints. This chapter examines two texts that tell the storied lives of subaltern subjects in twentieth-century Mexico, *Benita* by Benita Galeana and *Juan Pérez Jolote* by Ricardo Pozas.

Elena Poniatowska's hypothetical and seemingly unlikely scenario of a subaltern member of society who *directly* authors his or her autobiography, was realized as early as 1940 in Mexico. *Benita* by Benita Galeana, a long-time Mexican Communist Party militant, recounts Galeana's life story from the age of three or four to about thirty-six years old. Galeana was born in rural Guerrero in 1904[3] and was raised in poverty by her older sister.[4] Early in adolescence she moved to Acapulco to live with another sister, and she eventually made her way to Mexico City, arriving in the early 1920s. She spent most of the rest of her long life in the nation's capital, where she died in the spring of 1995. *Benita* is still relatively little known and little studied in spite of new editions in Mexico in 1974, 1979, and 1990, and an English translation that appeared in the United States in 1994. The interest in Latin American *testimonio* and autobiography, in particular their appeal as vehicles for the expression of women's lives, has thus far largely overlooked this life story of a working-class Mexican woman of peasant origin. In the analysis that follows, I will examine *Benita* as an early example of testimonial life writing and I will focus on the inherent intertextuality of popular as well as elite discourse.

In Mexico, Carlos Monsiváis paid tribute to the historical Galeana and to her autobiography in a newspaper article from 1975, and he later included the article in his book *Amor perdido* (1977). Monsiváis emphasizes Galeana's political militancy, which he interprets as a continuation of the energy of the Mexican Revolution of 1910 and its promise of social transformation. He also acknowledges the critical perspective that Galeana brings to her generally celebratory representation of the inner workings of the Mexican Communist Party (Partido Comunista de México, PCM).[5] Two other published essays analyze *Benita* within the context of writing by Mexican women. Martha Robles includes Benita Galeana in her book *La sombra fugitiva: Escritoras en la cultura nacional* (1985). Robles offers *Benita* as an alternative to the predominant trends in writing by middle-class women, seeing Galeana as both an exceptional individual and a representative of the masses of poor Mexican women. She seems to advance the idea of testimonial transparency when she attributes to the book the characteristics of "sencillez y una sola preocupación: referir lo ocurrido" and "la deficiencia [lingüística] de quien apenas conoce su idioma" (233) [simplicity and a single preoccupation: to tell what happened; the deficiency of one who barely knows her own language]. Edith Negrín's 1990 article "Benita Galeana o la escritura como liberación" [Benita Galeana, or writing as liberation] takes a thematic approach to the text and summarizes the many obstacles that poverty and patriarchy impose on the social destiny of a peasant girl in Mexico. All three critics refer to *Benita* rather loosely as *testimonio* and/or autobiography, but they do not situate the terms in the current critical debate. Completing the scant bibliography are my 1997 biographical essay "Benita Galeana; en la lucha," published in *Las desobedientes: Mujeres de nuestra América*; and "Speaking from the Soapbox: Benita Galeana's *Benita*" (2000).[6]

Benita is a unique example of women's life writing from a decade that produced a large number of male-authored autobiographies in Mexico, and it is made more exceptional by the fact of the author's marginal literacy. "De ella se podría decir que *sabe escribir*, pero *no sabe leer*" (1940, 7 my emphasis). [About her it could be said that she knows how to write, but not how to read.] This extraordinary statement appears in the prologue to the first edition of *Benita*, written by Galeana's husband and fellow Communist Party activist Mario Gill. Illiteracy is, to say the least, a formidable obstacle to sustained writing and in that light the surprising history of the composition of *Benita* merits consideration. Three sources provide an explanation of how Benita Galeana knew how to write without knowing how to read: references in the autobiography itself to the narrator-protagonist's struggle for literacy; Mario Gill's "Palabras preliminares" for the 1940 edition; and Galeana's words as recorded in an interview that I conducted with her in Mexico City in June 1994. Essentially the same story consistently emerges: that Galeana, unaided, wrote a first version of her autobiography using a typewriter and spelling the words phonetically according to her rudimentary knowledge of the alphabet. A facsimile of one page of the resulting manuscript, reprinted in the original 1940 edition, can be deciphered with some difficulty, but the text bears little resemblance to standard Spanish prose and it is best read aloud in order to "hear" the story without the visual interference of massive misspellings, irregular word boundaries, and an almost complete lack of punctuation. At

Galeana's request Mario Gill edited the manuscript to the extent of standardizing the orthography and providing consistent punctuation and chapter breaks. Galeana is insistent upon the point that Gill did not alter the language or the structure of the story beyond the minimum necessary corrections and that when she heard the book read back to her, she recognized the story and the language as her own. That said, it would be naive to deny that Gill's editorial intervention had some impact on the published text, but it is impossible for us to determine the extent and the nature of the impact.

Galeana published her book in 1940 with a Communist Party print shop, Imprenta Mels. The first edition numbered one thousand copies, which she reports were quickly sold out. The front cover and the title page identify the book as *Benita (Autobiografía)* by Benita Galeana. The volume includes Gill's "Palabras preliminares" and a series of engraved illustrations created by members of the Taller de Gráfica Popular, a breakaway group from the Liga de Escritores y Artistas Revolucionarios, which was closely associated with the PCM and produced illustrations for the Party newspaper, *El Machete*. *Benita* was out of print until 1974 when Editorial Extemporáneos, a socialist publishing house in Mexico City, reissued it. This second edition made three critical and unfortunate cuts to the manuscript by deleting Gill's "Preliminares," the engravings, and the final chapter of the autobiography titled "Bajo la Bandera de la Internacional" [Under the flag of international communism]. No subsequent edition has restored these elements, and therefore they are effectively lost to today's reader.[7]

The history of the writing and publishing process begins to make a case for reading *Benita* as a testimonial autobiography and a virtually unique creation in Latin American letters. First, Galeana's book fulfills the necessary condition for the autobiographical pact given by Philippe Lejeune: the identity of author ("I, the undersigned"), narrator, and protagonist established by the shared proper name. Benita Galeana's life story can also be seen to conform in general terms to Lejeune's well-known definition of autobiography as the account of an exceptional life and personality, although Galeana is a radically untypical and unlikely autobiographer vis-à-vis the male autobiographical tradition and that created by elite women writing in the West. Just as *Benita* can be identified as an autobiography within established conventions of reading, readers of *testimonio* will also find themselves on familiar ground owing to structural, linguistic, and thematic aspects of this unusual book. Most testimonies include a prologue or introduction, usually written by the editor of the text in the case of mediated testimonies. This framing piece attests to the documentary or nonfictional nature of the life story to follow, and it often describes the writing or editing process. In the case of *Benita*, Mario Gill's original foreword and the different prologues added to more recent editions (1974, 1990, and 1994) fulfill these functions and demonstrate the ever-changing context for the book's production and reception.[8] Galeana is usually described as both an exceptional individual and a representative woman of the people, further strengthening the book's status as an unrecognized precursor to the *testimonios* that would be written years later in Latin America. To the degree that the "truth effect" of *testimonio* is enhanced by the marginal literacy of its speaking and acting subject, *Benita* can claim this privilege too.[9]

For reasons of gender, class, ethnicity, and political affiliation, Benita Galeana lived and wrote from the margins of power and its discourses in early twentieth-century Mexico. Nevertheless, she did not remain silent, and her autobiography gives us the opportunity to examine the languages that constitute her narrative voice and to see that the relationship of discourse to subjectivity is neither monolithic nor deterministic, but fluid and reciprocal. Benita Galeana did not model her life story on the basis of literary precedents. She neither imitates nor subverts traditional autobiographical writing in any direct, deliberate way for the simple reason that she had no access to it. Nonetheless, cultures have many ways other than literature to communicate life scripts and stories that women or men may enact or, exceptionally, modify or reject. The life narrated in *Benita* responds to the shaping pressure of patriarchal ideology on a poor woman's choices, and it also pushes back against it. Within the overarching reality of male dominance and female subordination, three specific discursive practices are fundamental to Galeana's narrative voice. They are the popular oral storytelling tradition of her childhood; the language of Soviet-style communism of the 1930s conveyed by Party speeches and *El Machete*; and to a lesser extent, I believe, the Catholic confessional. Using the linguistic and discursive tools available to her, Galeana writes her story both in obedience to and against patriarchy, and she inscribes a respectful and a resistant perspective on the Mexican Communist Party, its Stalinist ideology, and its hierarchical organization.

The thirty short chapters of *Benita* are divided into two long sections, "La infancia" [Childhood] and "En la lucha" [In the struggle]. "La infancia," about one-third of the book, covers approximately the years 1907–24, and "En la lucha" picks up in 1924 and carries the story through to 1938 or early 1939. Although the narrative is chronological, moving from childhood through adolescence and into adulthood with very few narrative anachronisms, time is only weakly accounted for. The story develops for long periods without measuring the passing of time or marking it with milestones such as dates or the protagonist's age. Within the annual cycle, significant days such as Independence Day, Christmas, and May 1st are sometimes recalled, but the year is rarely noted. This is particularly true in the chapters of "La infancia," and it is a logical consequence of very limited contact with the world beyond the village. "En la lucha" is almost equally vague, but references to Mexico's presidents and to historical events help the reader reconstruct a rough time line of Benita's activities from 1924 to 1938.

"La infancia" narrates Benita's impoverished childhood under the abusive tutelage of her older sister Camila. After the death of their mother when Benita was two, Camila took charge of her younger siblings. Their father was also present in the household, and Benita portrays him with warm affection. He died when she was six years old, leaving her entirely at her sister's bidding. Hard work, frequent beatings, material want, and lack of schooling define a scenario of victimization and hopelessness for the young protagonist. Within that scenario, the child Benita does two things. First, and contrary to the script of female passivity, she actively explores the limited options for self-improvement in an isolated rural village. Once she raises a suckling pig in order to buy a gold necklace with the profit from its sale, but before she can do so, Camila secretly butchers the pig and feeds it to the family. Unable to attend school, she pores over an alphabet book at home. Later Benita tries to run away from San Gerónimo with a few other discontented girls, but their families chase them down and punish them severely for their daring. Second, parallel to these scenes of thwarted rebelliousness, Benita also entertains more conventional dreams of escape: escape from familial oppression through marriage, and escape from the desperate, confining geography of her birthplace via migration to Mexico City. A constant theme of "La infancia" is the hope of meeting a stranger who will marry her and take her to the capital, but her first real opportunity for change comes when a sister who lives in Acapulco returns home for a visit and takes Benita back to the coast with her. Benita has her first boyfriends in Acapulco, and a decisive turning point occurs when she accepts an offer of engagement from a young office worker, and later has a child with him out of wedlock before the relationship breaks off.

It is not hard to recognize the patriarchal mythology of brave male heroes and beautiful (virgin) damsels in distress in Benita's daydreams of escape. Overall, she conceives of her individual liberation in highly conventional terms according to the limited scripts available to a poor, young woman. In "La infancia" the patriarchal myth predominates with the cruel stepmother and the kind but ineffectual father playing their usual roles. At the same time, the protagonist occasionally poses a bold challenge to the status quo by acting on her own behalf in order to survive. In addition to the obvious instances of rebellion already mentioned, other more subtle aspects of "La infancia" reveal the imperfect fit between Benita's individual needs and experiences and the conventional, gendered roles available for her. The portrayal of her father is a case in point. As the earliest eligible "knight in shining armor" in her life, Benita characterizes her father as generous, loving, and protective in contrast to her cruel older sister/stepmother, and she identifies closely with him. He is further romanticized as the inconsolable widower who ceaselessly grieves his wife's death. However, equal attention is given to his frequent absences from home, his bouts of heavy drinking, and his careless management of the family's once extensive properties. Weak and irresponsible, he is incapable of being the hero who might rescue his younger daughter from harsh treatment at the hands of her surrogate stepmother. However, in writing her life story, Galeana tries, consciously or not, to rescue her father from failure and censure. Her expressions of love are direct and profuse in contrast to the indirect and rationalizing depiction of his neglect, and she casts the male as hero even as she must save him from himself in an exemplary, if unknowing reflection on the predicament of women under patriarchy.

Late in the first section Benita travels throughout Guerrero in the company of a *mezcalero* or mezcal salesman, while her infant daughter remains in the care of relatives in Acapulco. In one deserted location the couple is attacked by a band of soldiers loyal to the minor rebel leader Rosalío Radilla, and the *mezcalero* is taken hostage. This episode again shows Benita in the position of rescuing her male protector, when she uses her wit and courage to free him from the rebels. Soon afterward, Benita abandons the *mezcalero* and makes her way to Mexico City (with money stolen from him) sometime in 1924. In Mexico City, Benita is anxious to save enough money to retrieve her little girl, and she works for a time as a servant and then as a barmaid. She also enters into several short-term alliances with men, including a common-law marriage with Manuel Rodríguez, a taxi driver who becomes a member of the PCM. When he is arrested at a May 1st demonstration, other Party members contact Benita for help in winning his release from jail. It is significant that Benita's introduction to communism and political activism comes through an appeal to her roles as wife and mother. Her economic dependency and her loyalty to Manuel, who has promised to send for her child, are factors that make her receptive to the communist cause. The outstanding episodes of the rest of the book, covering the period from 1927 or 1928 to 1938, have to do with Benita's militant activism in the communist movement. That is, there is a striking shift from the depiction of futile suffering in "La infancia" to purposeful, although often dangerous struggle in "En la lucha."

In *Benita* the narrator describes her political awakening in a moment of crisis: her first arrest while advocating for her husband's freedom at a rally. The loss of her own freedom and the injustice of her arrest shock her into an awareness of the need to fight against injustice and oppression in the larger society. Her new political and social consciousness leads her to work on behalf of the Party by distributing pamphlets in factories, attending marches and demonstrations, meeting with her cell, hawking *El Machete* on the streets, and giving speeches at impromptu rallies and at planned events. Galeana joined the PCM just at the time that it was declared illegal and subjected to severe repression under the governments of Emilio Portes Gil (1928–30) and Pascual Ortiz Rubio (1930–32). During these years PCM leaders were routinely sent to the infamous prison of Islas Marías in Sinaloa, and the Party offices were sacked and its press destroyed. *El Machete* went underground in the fall of 1929 and it continued to appear about every two weeks during the period of prohibition (until 1935), at great risk to those who, like Benita Galeana, distributed it. Galeana reports having been arrested and imprisoned fifty-eight times in the period between 1929 and 1934. In her confrontations with the police, Benita invents numerous ways of defying their authority and subverting the prison regimen. Once, in order to delay being transferred to a more isolated and secure prison, she strips off her clothes and waits naked in her cell, much to the astonishment of the prison matrons. By playing on social taboos, Galeana engaged in a strategic exposure of her body in order to protect herself from a greater threat to her safety.

In the chapter on "The Engenderings of Self-Representation" in *A Poetics of Women's Autobiography*, Sidonie Smith describes three ways in which the autobiographer may resolve the dilemma of self-representation from the marginal position of woman. *Benita* seems to inscribe the first of Smith's three narrative models, in which the woman autobiographer assumes the postures traditionally associated with male selfhood under patriarchy. In adopting the male script, she will represent herself as an autonomous, adventurous, and unique individual and identify with the father while repressing the mother and daughter in herself. Her narrative will tacitly accept and endorse the culturally constructed fiction of man as the positively valued ideal and the equally constructed fiction of woman's inferiority. Smith notes, however, that a woman will never be wholly successful in rewriting herself as a representative man, and her life story will betray her dilemma. Galeana's narrative exemplifies Smith's thesis in many respects.

In *Benita* the narrator-protagonist displays some signs of an "unfeminine" vocation for self-defense and rebellion in childhood. Her determination to escape family and village life and her aggressive refusal of her much older brother-in-law's sexual advances, for example, are acts of self-affirmation that go beyond mere survival. Her rebellion against patriarchal social structures takes typically masculine forms: running away from home and fighting off her brother-in-law with a machete. At the same time, as I noted, she clings to the hope of being rescued by a man who will be her lover and her protector. Once she joins the PCM she enthusiastically assimilates the male script of political militancy. In recounting the many adventures and misadventures of clandestine political activity, the narrative voice is inflected with language absorbed from *El Machete*, PCM pamphlets, and political speeches, and Benita wholeheartedly adopts the ideology of workers' rights and world revolution as expressed therein.[10] The predominant message of *Benita* is one of gratitude and unconditional support for communism as represented by the PCM, and she structures her life story to trace an ascending, triumphalist movement that is well in line with the communist promise of collective liberation through popular struggle. The two-part division of the autobiography into "La infancia" and "En la lucha" sets up a sharp contrast between the protagonist's suffering prior to joining the Party, and the new consciousness that "saves" her and propels her into a bold and unceasing activism. She summarizes the trajectory from victimization to victory through purposeful struggle in the last chapter of the 1940 edition, the book's "lost" chapter: "Tampoco me importa lo que he sufrido si es el precio que pagué por encontrar al fin el camino de la felicidad, de la felicidad basada en el trabajo, en la independencia y en la lucha por la liberación de la Humanidad del yugo capitalista" (239). [It doesn't matter how much I suffered if it is the price I paid to find the road to happiness, happiness based on work, independence, and the struggle for the liberation of Humanity from the yoke of capitalism.] This chapter is a call to arms to Mexican women to join the workers' struggle and to reject their confinement to the domestic sphere by embracing a masculine model of political militancy.

Nevertheless, in spite of the benefits of her association with the PCM, Benita cannot ignore or silence the fact of her ambiguous position within a Party that perpetuates class and gender subordination while leading a struggle for liberation. Numerous passages reveal the tensions inherent in that position. Throughout "En la lucha" Galeana portrays herself in a dual role vis-à-vis the PCM. On the one hand, she has finally realized her youthful rescue scenario with the heroic male Party taking the place of the husband that she formerly sought. As a rescued, redeemed woman she voices her grateful obedience to the Party line. On the other hand, she is a militant hero in her own right and an engaging public speaker who has experienced the excitement of drawing a crowd and holding them with her voice. These experiences empower the narrator-protagonist to perceive and to criticize the Party's mistakes and to speak out in defiance of its determined silencing of dissent. A recurring theme is the regret and resentment triggered by the PCM's neglect of her education and its refusal to help her find employment when she needs it. In a discussion of capitalism and communism, Galeana recognizes that the institution of marriage privileges men and takes rights away from women under either system. She also criticizes the in-fighting, the frequent purges of Party members, and the double standard of sexual conduct perpetuated even by "camaradas muy capaces e inteligentes" (115) [capable and intelligent comrades]. Although the instances of direct criticism are relatively infrequent compared to her professions of loyalty and support, a careful reading of the text detects these and other expressions of resistance.

In another contradictory move, the final, militant chapter makes explicit the confessional dimension of the text, linking it back to traditional autobiography. In the Catholic practice of confession, a priest reinterprets and regulates the experiences confessed according to the normative codes of the Church. Communism has also used confession for purposes of disempowerment and control. Galeana had experienced the frequent investigations and purges of Party members in the 1930s, and in the final chapter she seems to have assimilated their lesson of obedience by interpreting her life as a journey from ignorance, submission, and error toward understanding, confidence, and militancy. She confesses, as if speaking before her Party cell, that her relationship with her former husband Humberto Padilla was a personal defeat because he tried to contain her and alienate her from the Party and from her working-class roots. She resolves never to fall into the same error. "Bajo la bandera de la Internacional" threatens to become a monolithic and propagandistic call for social change through one exclusive channel, international communism, and to close off the debate over issues raised in other parts of the autobiography. Nevertheless, Galeana's consciousness, already demonstrated, of being a woman in a society that oppresses all women even more severely than it oppresses working-class men, permeates her writing in both subtle and obvious ways and at least partially dis-cernes the inheritance of patriarchal values and norms.

Finally, the text's silences are as powerful as its words in showing how the autobiographical-I is not only constrained by imposed scripts, but is also shaped and limited by what a culture's discourses *exclude* from speech. When Benita first comes to Mexico City, she leaves her young daughter behind in Acapulco, and during their separation the hope of regaining custody is a constant theme and a principal reason for seeking work and/or accepting support from a man. After they are reunited, her daughter apparently lives with Benita in Mexico City throughout the late 1920s and 30s, but curiously, the reader learns virtually nothing about her. The narrator gives other, more transient characters a visible presence in the book, but she is almost silent about her daughter, whom she names only once—Lilia—in one hundred pages. One could speculate about psychological reasons—perhaps the topic is too personal or too painful or the sense of guilt too great to tell. The obvious trauma caused by raising a child in uncertain and dangerous circumstances that include being hauled off to jail on a regular basis supports such a reading. However, another answer emerges more directly from my analysis of *Benita*. As Adrienne Rich poignantly and powerfully showed in *Of Woman Born*, the discourses of patriarchy in the West have precious little to say about mothers and daughters. Nor would the rhetoric of Stalinism in its most clichéd forms have provided Galeana with the words to speak of her daughter. It is one thing to recognize, remember, and protest against a problem that has a name. It is a far more difficult intellectual and linguistic task to recognize and recreate what lies outside of our habits of speech, and a daughter simply has no identifiable place and no identifiable name in the life story that takes shape in *Benita*. In all likelihood, the historical Benita Galeana nurtured her daughter, knew her well, spoke with her often. Nonetheless, in writing her autobiography the linguistic and cultural codes at her disposal did not give access to a language that could inscribe the mother-daughter relationship, and both mother and daughter are effectively, even if not deliberately, silenced.

Benita Galeana's writing of her life story was necessarily shaped—empowered and constrained—by the socially constructed discourses of her culture and the power relations that they describe and enforce. This situation is common to all human subjects, although our different and unequal relations to power are factors to be considered. Galeana, for reasons of gender, class, and political affiliation, lived and wrote from a marginalized position within Mexican society. She was additionally marginalized to some degree within the Mexican Communist Party at the same time that her membership empowered her to take action in defiance of conventional gender and class roles. Whatever its limitations, the practical struggle for tangible gains for workers and for a broad notion of human liberation within a socialist framework provided Galeana with a model for activism that transformed her from silent victim into speaking subject and agent of change. *Benita* is a record, however "impure," of the problems and the potential of that transformation.

Juan Pérez Jolote: Biografía de un tzotzil by anthropologist Ricardo Pozas Arciniega offers another distinctive variation on modes of life writing in Mexico in the twentieth century. The "biography" narrated in the first person by its eponymous protagonist was first published in 1948 in the student journal *Acta Anthropológica* (Escuela Nacional de Antropología e Historia), and reissued as a book four years later by the Fondo de Cultura Económica. Since 1952 it has been reprinted about two dozen times and translated into several languages including English, French, Polish, German, Japanese and, most recently, Tzotzil (1994). Variously labeled a biography, an autobiography, an ethno-testimony, and a novel, Pozas conceived the book as an ethnographic document recording the life story of one of his Tzotzil informants in Chamula, Chiapas. Unlike his scholarly study *Chamula. Un pueblo indio de los Altos de Chiapas* published in 1959, Pozas wrote *Juan Pérez Jolote* with the general reading public in mind and not strictly for specialists in his field.

The research for the project was based on a series of interviews that he conducted in the early to mid-1940s, with a final encounter between anthropologist and informant taking place in San Cristóbal de las Casas in 1948. Pérez Jolote, whose first language was Tzotzil, learned Spanish as an adolescent, and he was therefore able to communicate directly with Pozas, who did not himself speak the language of the Chamula community that he studied.

In 1927 at the age of fifteen, Pozas spent a year working as a rural teacher and a community activist in his home state of Querétaro under the Vasconcelos model of public education as a project of civic service and nation building. He went to Mexico City in 1928 to continue his education and to teach urban workers attending night school, and in 1938 he entered the Escuela Nacional de Antropología e Historia. While he was a student he participated in ethnographic field research in Michoacán, Oaxaca and, primarily, Chiapas, and his work in the Chiapan highlands resulted in the writing of not only *Juan Pérez Jolote*, but also his 1957 graduate thesis, the aforementioned study of Chamula, and numerous scholarly articles. During the 1930s and 40s, Mexican anthropology was characterized by two dominant tendencies: an effort to distinguish itself from traditional Mexican archaeology, with its overwhelming interest in the indigenous cultures and achievements of the past; and a strong connection to national politics and post-revolutionary nationalism.[11] Under the influence of Manuel Gamio, Gonzalo Aguirre Beltrán, the German scholar Paul Kirchhoff, and University of Chicago anthropologists Sol Tax and Robert Redfield, Ricardo Pozas and his peers sought to understand and to represent in their publications the social organization, economic structures, and religious practices of present-day indigenous communities. In their field research, Mexican ethnologists and social anthropologists of the era pursued a fundamental objective to integrate the indigenous population of Mexico into the national life under the premise expressed in the 1917 Constitution that Mexico is a unicultural, mestizo nation. Anthropologists participated in policies of assimilation and homogenization that were implemented to turn the Indian into a mestizo citizen, according to Scott Cook in his review essay of six books treating Mexican sociocultural anthropology, "Struggling to Understand Complexity" (204).

In a practical sense, this meant that anthropologists felt a responsibility to apply their research to the development of government programs designed to improve the material conditions of life in rural areas and to promote the mestizoization of Mexican Indians. Andrés Medina summarizes the approach to the field that was proposed and defended by Aguirre Beltrán in the following terms: "En pocas palabras, de lo que se trata es de elaborar una compleja y afinada construcción teórica que otorgue a la política indigenista del gobierno mexicano el rango de ciencia" (23). [In brief, it is about elaborating a complex and finely-tuned theoretical apparatus that grants the status of science to the indigenist policy of the Mexican government. My translation.] Ricardo Pozas was an important exponent of the idea of social science in the service of public policy, and he was strongly aligned with the revolutionary nationalism of his time. As much an activist as a scientist, he took seriously the obligation to contribute to the solution of the perceived ills of rural Mexico: poverty, class divisions, lack of access to education for the majority, and overall "backwardness," at the same time that he respected and sought to promote the understanding of many aspects of "traditional" rural, indigenous life.

Juan Pérez Jolote is frequently identified as a groundbreaking work for a number of reasons. In the 1930s and early 1940s there was little existing research on the Tzotzil-speaking peoples of Chiapas, and Pozas was in the vanguard of a growing interest in Mexico's Maya-speaking population. Further, there was no tradition of producing biographies of Mexican Indians comparable, for example, to those written by ethnographers in the United States about members of the Navajo, Hopi, and Crow communities (Castro 15). The Pozas book is based on extensive, direct observation of the town of Chamula, and it seeks to recuperate the voice of a Tzotzil Indian, albeit a voice "once removed" from its community by virtue of speaking to the anthropologist in Spanish. This is in contrast to most indigenist literature of the first half of the twentieth century, which was conceived and written from an almost exclusively elite perspective. The character Juan Pérez Jolote is, within the framework of a text edited by another, the narrator and protagonist of his own story, and not wholly the object of an elite writer's gaze and imagination.

Although Ricardo Pozas regarded *Juan Pérez Jolote* as an ethnographic piece, the book quickly moved from the category of scientific writing into that of literature, where it remains today. In 1952 when the Fondo de Cultura Económica issued the first widely available version in book form after its limited dissemination via *Acta Anthropológica* in 1948, the publishing house catalogue listed the title in its literature section. Carlo Antonio Castro quotes the FCE *Catálogo general, 1934–1954* as announcing that the book has been an enormous critical success due to its literary qualities. The catalogue also refers to *Juan Pérez Jolote* as a novel, in spite of its having been written as an anthropological document (Castro 17). Rosario Castellanos, in her article "La novela mexicana contemporánea y su valor testimonial" published in *Hispania* in 1964, attests to the book's reception as a literary work, and most of the subsequent scholarly attention paid to it similarly treats it as indigenist literature. In an interview in 2007 with the Mexican cultural anthropologist Rossana Reguillo, she expressed the view that *Juan Pérez Jolote* survives and is studied today not in social science classes, but in the context of the humanities and literature.[12] In the reading that follows, I will approach this example of life writing from three angles: the book's claim to factual status, its relationship to the subsequent phenomenon of Spanish-American *testimonio*, and the inscription in the text of cultural hybridity.

As is often the case in nonfiction literature, *Juan Pérez Jolote* is a framed narrative, and the framing devices are primarily responsible for establishing its claim to factual status. The book opens with an introduction signed by Ricardo Pozas A., and it concludes with a section of ninety-two explanatory endnotes. Between the introduction and the notes, the main body of the text presents the auto/biography of Juan Pérez Jolote. In the brief (six-page) introduction, Pozas takes a number of steps to invite a reading of the story as fact-based. First, he calls the book a biography and further states that it should be regarded as a monograph of Chamula culture, that is, as an ethnographic piece. Without giving any details about the individual identity of the biographical subject, Pozas moves to the main purpose of his introduction, which is to provide background information on the dual economic structure within which the Chamula Indians live. Recognizing that a life story is not likely to give a systematic account of economic relationships, Pozas devotes three pages, or half of the introduction, to describing the interplay between the remains of pre-Hispanic forms of economic life and the dominant national system based on Western capitalism. The remaining two pages offer a concise list of other aspects of the target culture including social organization, political and religious life, the centrality of the family, and fundamental traits of the "personalidad básica" (12) [basic personality] of the Chamula man or woman.[13]

Strikingly absent from the introduction is any accounting of the methodology used to produce the text. Pozas does not identify Pérez

Jolote as an interview subject or tell where and when he met him; he does not address the question of the original language, Tzotztil or Spanish, in which the research was conducted; and he says nothing about the process of selecting and ordering the material that comprises the life story. The reader must locate a reference to Juan Pérez Jolote as "the informant" in note 6 at the back of the book, and any further clarification that the book is based on extensive conversations in Spanish between Pozas and his informant can only be found outside of the text in articles and interviews. The endnotes lend the weight of fact to the narrative by offering considerable explanatory information about geographical references, local customs, Tzotzil terminology, religious beliefs, and economic and political practices that appear in the story. Overall, the components of the narrative frame make a clear claim to factual status for *Juan Pérez Jolote*, while leaving considerable gaps in the reader's knowledge of the methodology used and the identity of the subject.

Like Benita Galeana's autobiography, *Juan Pérez Jolote* predates the phenomenon of Spanish-American testimonial literature and the accompanying theoretical debates of the 1970s, 80s, and 90s. However, in contrast to *Benita*, Pozas's work has a direct link to *testimonio* because it can be shown to be a predecessor to Miguel Barnet's foundational *Biografía de un cimarrón* (1966). Amy Nauss Millay, in her study of orality in Spanish-American narrative, reveals that Pozas taught a course on ethnographic fieldwork methodology at the Cuban Academy of Science in the early 1960s when Barnet had begun his interviews with Esteban Montejo. Barnet took the course, and Pozas attended some of his interviews with the 103-year-old former slave who is Barnet's "cimarrón." Millay cites a 1996 interview in which the Cuban writer explains that Pozas's mentoring and his own reading of *Juan Pérez Jolote* exercised a strong influence on the way that Barnet shaped the Montejo material into his groundbreaking work (Millay 128).

Parallels between *Juan Pérez Jolote* and the most canonical examples of *testimonio* are easy to identify. It is the life story of a subaltern member of society that was produced through collaboration between an elite researcher/writer and the testimonial subject. The protagonist is at once characterized as a representative member of his community and an exceptional individual. The life story portrays a previously hidden or silenced dimension of the national reality with the objective of educating and perhaps politicizing the reader, who is assumed to be of the privileged sectors of society. It is generally not read by members of the community to which the subject belongs. For example, forty-six years would pass before *Juan Pérez Jolote* was published in Tzotzil. The oral quality of the written text recalls its origin in interviews and the low level of literacy of the protagonist. An introduction and notes are virtually always present to frame the *testimonio*. However, in a notable contrast to later testimonies, *Juan Pérez Jolote* is not directly conceived as a response to crisis, and especially not as a response to political crisis and repression, gross human rights abuses, or the impending destruction of a community. The protagonist's voice is not a call to action, and although his story records many ways in which the Chamulas are exploited by the larger society, the ethnographic project prevails, as it does in *Biografía de un cimarrón*.

While factual status must be claimed by the writer of a book and encoded into its structure and language as shown, it falls to the reader to determine factual adequacy. In general, *Juan Pérez Jolote* has met the expectations that readers hold for nonfiction writing, and its reception has supported Ricardo Pozas's stated aim of educating an audience of ordinary, albeit culturally elite readers about the Tzotzil. The anthropologists Ricardo Frank Cancian and Julian Pitt-Rivers in reviews dated 1963 and 1964, respectively, identify the book as a biography or an ethnographical document, and Cancian specifically confirms the authenticity and reliability of its information based on his own fieldwork in the region (Cancian 1372). Literary scholar Mario Valdés cites *Juan Pérez Jolote* as one of two outstanding mid-century narratives treating the Tzotzil (the other is Rosario Castellanos's *Oficio de tinieblas*), and he mentions the presence of extensive information about the economic, social, and religious structure of Chamula society that is documented by carefully observed and recorded data ("Literary Social Symbol" 393–94). Nevertheless, a closer look at the text with an eye toward the question of what a non-Indian reader might learn about Tzotzil life and culture reveals certain gaps in information and obstacles to comprehension.

Juan Pérez Jolote presents, without a doubt, a rich density of verifiable facts and ethnological data that serve as traces of the real and anchor the life story to a knowable external world. As I have already summarized, the content of the narrative, clarifed at times in the endnotes, treats many aspects of daily life and long-established customs, thus strengthening our acceptance of its referential nature and its responsibility to an extratextual reality. In the very first paragraph the narrator further impresses upon the reader that this reality is a durable, even a virtually permanent one, by identifying his land as that of his ancestors, and by predicting that when he dies, his soul will know how to return to his house. In contrast to his firm sense of spatial grounding, however, the narrator's temporal moorings are remarkably loose. Also on the first page, he declares that "No sé cuándo nací" (15) [I don't know when I was born], and throughout the book there are only infrequent and tenuous references to time as it is experienced and measured in the intended reader's world of clocks and calendars. The absence of a consistent accounting of the passage of time may push the reader into the role of a detective, searching the narrative for clues to locate key moments in the protagonist's life. The first reference to a known year occurs when Pérez Jolote, a youthful runaway, lands in jail after witnessing a murder. He speaks of the assassination of the president and the civil war that ensues between the forces of Huerta and those of other Revolutionary chieftains. Clearly the year is 1913 and the unnamed president is Francisco I. Madero. The reader does not know how old Pérez Jolote is in 1913, but we can deduce that he is an adolescent based on the time that he has already spent living apart from his family and on the way that others treat him. He seems to be still a youth, but not a child, as he is recruited for Huerta's army (his ticket to get out of jail), but at the same time the adults whom he meets tend to be quite protective of him. The protagonist also has his first sexual experience during his several years as a soldier, first serving Huerta, then Carranza, and finally Villa. His on-and-off soldiering could conceivably have lasted until about 1917, and after that he speaks of seeking agricultural work in Veracruz, Tuxtla, and Ixtapa as he slowly makes his way home to Chiapas. The second date mentioned in the book is 1930 when Pérez Jolote says that he returned to Chamula and began to live in his community once again. This means that he was absent from home for roughly seventeen or eighteen years, and it explains both his loss of fluency in his native language and the degree to which others perceive him to be highly ladinoized upon his return. The period from 1917 to 1930 is extremely condensed in the narrative, occupying a scant two pages of text, and the stated return date therefore comes as a surprise.

Having done all of this detective work, it remains to be said that the determination of dates and the measuring of time in a linear fashion are the reader's preoccupation and not particularly a concern of the Tzotzil protagonist. Juan Pérez Jolote does take time very seriously in following the yearly cycle of the seasons and, especially, in tracking the month and day of the festivals celebrated in honor of the community's saints. In this regard, Pérez Jolote achieves a relatively high standing in the community within a few years of returning to Chiapas, because his ability to read permits him to understand the annual calendar and ensure that feast days are commemorated in a timely fashion in order to avoid giving offense to the saints. While the imprecise accounting of the years might frustrate some readers, it is one reminder that the subject of the life story speaks from within a cultural logic that is significantly different from that of the dominant society in which his story has been published, sold, and consumed. It is both an obstacle and an opening to the reader's understanding of the individual protagonist and his community, and Pozas's refusal to impose a more exact scheme of dates can be seen as a positive act of recognition and respect for cultural difference.

A second challenge to the reader's acceptance of the factual adequacy of the text stems from the nature of the facts given by the narrator and the manner of their presentation. It is useful here to recall Hayden White's definition of a fact as a verbal description of an event, and therefore as a mediated and ideologically charged representation of reality. Cultural values, inscribed in language, produce the "already enfigured form" that even an apparently objective set of facts takes ("The Real, the True" 15). Equally pertinent to a consideration of the facts of Juan Pérez Jolote's life is James Wilkinson's recognition that eye-witness accounts tend to leave out what is understood to be common knowledge or what is taken for granted by the community to which the witness belongs. Evidence is, as a result, often presented in a kind of verbal shorthand that assumes a shared, unspoken store of contextual information ("Choice of Fictions" 83). To an outsider who lacks specific cultural competence, some narrative facts may appear to be obscure, irrelevant, illogical, or "imaginary" and not "real." These nuances of factual representations are highly visible in *Juan Pérez Jolote* due to the cultural differences that exist between the narrator and the implied reader.

A passage that exemplifies the cultural shaping of facts and the existence of gaps in individual testimony is one that narrates an illness suffered by Juan Pérez Jolote and the cure that he undergoes at the hands of an *ilol* or healer. The protagonist reports that he fell sick at the time of his father's death, but the declaration "estuve enfermo" (94), [I was sick] is given without any description of physical or psychological symptoms. The healer, after taking his patient's pulse, diagnoses *komel*, the Tztotzil word for fright or dread, suggesting a psychological malady. Later the *ilol* explains his illness as rooted in *rencor* or a grudge, although Pérez Jolote doesn't recall having quarreled with anyone. In spite of this contradiction, the cure proceeds, and it is based on the fact that each person has a *chulel* or a wild animal that shares and in some ways determines the person's health and welfare. For example, if one's *chulel* goes hungry or is injured or killed by a more powerful animal (perhaps one belonging to an *ilol* or to a witch), then the human being will suffer illness, misfortune, or death. The cure consists of freeing the *chulel* by appeasing its captor through an appeal to God, who is evoked in the text through language that blends Christian and Mayan concepts of divinity, and with gifts of incense, liquor, flowers, and a sacrificial rooster. No explanation is tendered as to the value of these particular offerings, although alcohol consistently plays a central role in any ceremony or official act throughout the book. The non-Maya reader is left to wonder at their significance and efficacy, symbolic or otherwise. The illness of *rencor*, the existence of a *chulel* hierarchy, and the curative powers of a healing ritual based on sacrificial offerings may well challenge most readers' sense of factual adequacy, which is determined by the reader using the standards of his or her own cultural horizons; in this case, a knowledge of Western medicine. Pozas's decision to leave Tzotzil terms such as *ilol*, *chulel*, and *komel* in the text and to relegate their Spanish translation or definition to the section of endnotes also pays tribute to the difficulty of rendering facts convincingly across cultural and linguistic boundaries, and so the life story presented here both satisfies and resists a Western reader's sense of factual adequacy.

The analysis carried out thus far points toward a number of manifestations of textual and cultural hybridity in *Juan Pérez Jolote*. In its most basic sense a hybrid, derived from the Latin word for mongrel, is simply the product of a mixture of dissimilar origins or of disparate components. In linguistics, the etymology of a hybrid word reveals its origins in two languages, such as many terms in English that combine Latin and Greek roots. In biology, a hybrid is the offspring of two animals or two plants that are of different breeds or species. Colonialist discourse frequently cast hybridity into a highly negative light by claiming the putative physical, intellectual, and moral inferiority of mixed-race individuals and defending the superiority of an illusionary racial purity. Twentieth-century literary and cultural theory, however, has overturned the negative connotations of hybridity and has substituted a variety of positive uses for the term as part of a wider challenge to received notions of racial and cultural purity and hierarchy. In *The Dialogic Imagination* Mikhail Bakhtin attributes some of the creative power and the disruptive originality of novelistic discourse to its propensity for hybridization, or the deliberate mixing of two social languages in the text. He characterizes the artistic mixture of linguistic forms as a "collision between two different points of view on the world that are embedded in those forms," giving rise to an open-ended dialogue of distinct voices (*Dialogic* 360–61). The concept of hybridity has been pushed in another direction by postcolonial theorists. Homi K. Bhabha, one of the key proponents of a contestatory view of hybridity as an antidote to the essentialism and racism of colonialist thought, starts from the premise that all cultures are inherently and inescapably hybrid and there is no purity or true originality in human social formations. Colonization brings *already* hybrid cultures into contact with each other, and the process of their encounter, while asymmetrical with regard to relations of power and influence, results in a further mutual (not to say equal) exchange of cultural forms and symbols and the creation of new ones. In the introduction to his collection of essays *The Location of Culture*, Bhabha speaks of the need "to think beyond the narratives of originary and initial subjectivities" (1), and to avoid reading cultural difference "as the reflection of pregiven ethnic or cultural traits in the fixed tablet of tradition" (2). All cultures undergo continuous processes of transculturation, or borrowing and lending of the practices and values that constitute their defining religious, artistic, economic, political, and social activities. The attention to a textual dialogue of voices and the rejection of a unitary, stable image of culture are useful for a reading of *Juan Pérez Jolote* as a work that crosses the conventional boundaries between biography and autobiography, and science and literature, and that represents the life story of a migrant, ladinoized Mexican Indian in a way that privileges the story of his return to and reintegration with his "original," "native" Chamula community over the story of his departure and his travels.

Juan Pérez Jolote is the product of a dialogue between two social actors who speak from within two different cultures and who occupy different and complementary positions in the ethnological interview that structures their conversation. Ricardo Pozas, whose signature establishes his claim to authority and credit for the writing of the book, occupies the roles of the scientific expert, interviewer and, ultimately, editor of the text. Juan Pérez Jolote, the informant or interviewee, is the object of study, the "Other" to Pozas's I, and yet also a speaking subject in his own right and the agent of the actions recorded in the life story. The relationship between the two, one an elite-class scientist and the other a subaltern informant, is therefore asymmetrical but not unilateral. Pozas's determining agency largely defines the ethnographic project, which he deliberately initiates, carries out, and concludes according, at least in part, to his own research interests and scientific assumptions and objectives. However, the work of an ethnographer-interviewer is two-sided and open to pressure from the interviewee, in that the researcher sets a direction by formulating questions, but the project's success hinges on his willingness to listen and adapt to new directions motivated by unexpected answers. Two voices, in this case two voices belonging to two very differently located subjects, come into play in an exchange that is unequal but also dynamic. I will argue that the written record of this exchange manifests the hybridity of Chamula culture while also defending a desire for essentialism on the part of Pozas.

Juan Pérez Jolote is divided into three distinct pieces, as I have already described. It could be said that the framing introduction and endnotes "belong" to Ricardo Pozas, and the central life story pertains to the narrator-protagonist, but that would ignore the complex interrelationship and interdependence of the parts within the whole. Jacques Derrida's essay on the use of frames in visual art titled "The Parergon" (1979) deconstructs the conventional opposition of frame to work, or exterior to interior by demonstrating the intimate, essential connection between any framing device and the work that it helps to structure (24). In the text under study, the tension between a recognition of cultural hybridity and a demand for cultural essentialism is present in Pozas's introduction and influences our reading of the life story. The first sentence of the introduction begins to formulate this tension. "*Juan Pérez Jolote* es el relato de la vida social de un hombre en quien se refleja la cultura de un grupo indígena, cultura en proceso de cambio debido al contacto con nuestra civilización" (7). [*Juan Pérez Jolote* is the story of the social life of a man in whom the culture of an indigenous group is reflected; a culture in the process of change due to its contact with our civilization.] Here the auto/biographical subject is offered as a representative member of another culture, an indigenous group, viewed from the side of "our civilization." The contact between "their" culture and "ours" has already produced changes in the former, implying an emerging hybrid form and perhaps assuming that behind or before the changes there existed an original, untouched society. Notably, there is no consideration paid to the idea that the contact taking place between the Indians and the Hispanic-dominant, mestizo-aspiring nation might have a reciprocal impact on the mainstream of Mexican society as well, or on the individual anthropologist. Both cultural change and the act of viewing, assessing, and representing it seem to be one-way processes in which the dominant society and its representative play the determining role.

Juan Pérez Jolote's identity as an authentic Chamula is critical to Pozas's project of using him as a model of Indian life, and he insistently characterizes him as typical, ordinary, perfectly normal, and just like all other Chamula men. This means, among other things, that Pérez Jolote speaks Tzotzil, wears the traditional dress of his town (traditional, that is, since the imposition of Catholicism), and fully participates in the economic, religious, and social life of his community. The reality that daily life and ritual in Chamula are thoroughly hybrid, (a hybridity that dates from well before the period of Spanish colonization, but is usually conceived as a product of the Spanish conquest), is seen in the description of farming practices and implements that combine indigenous and European elements, interactions with ladinos in towns outside of Chamula, the economic necessity of migrating to the lowlands to work on coffee plantations, and forms of religious worship that mix "ritos paganos" [pagan rituals] with the cult of Catholic saints (11). This background information, given to create a context for reading the individual life story, emphasizes a kind of benign blending of pre-Hispanic and Western cultural and economic features in Chamula, although the use of the word "pagan" betrays an assumed hierarchy of religious values that favors Christianity over Mayan beliefs.

Two unresolved contradictions illuminate the tension between a dynamic hybridity and a stable essentialism that are attributed to the Chamulas in the introduction. The first contradiction is merely hinted at and will be further developed in the life story that is the centerpiece of the book. It is that Pérez Jolote, our representative, ordinary Chamula, has had certain exceptional experiences that would seem to set him significantly apart from other, more "typical" men of his village. Pozas alludes only briefly to two of these formative experiences by mentioning within parentheses his subject's exceptional participation in the Mexican Revolution, and by referring in a mysterious, veiled way to unnamed reasons for his leaving Chamula. Pozas's choice of an other than "normal" Chamula, no doubt driven by his informant's command of Spanish, apparently needs to be defended by both protestations and omissions, but the reader will carry over some uncertainty and skepticism into the reading of the narrative. That is, no amount of declaring that Pérez Jolote is perfectly ordinary will make him so against the evidence of his exceptionality. In addition, aligning the protagonist with a set of so-called normal behaviors in order to prove his authenticity, begs an important question: Was Juan Pérez Jolote a Chamula during the more than seventeen years that he spent outside of his village traveling as far as Mexico City and Veracruz, wearing ladino dress, speaking Spanish, forgetting Tzotzil, and failing to worship his patron saint? Did he become a ladino during that time? Although Pozas, working within the historical, political, and disciplinary parameters for Mexican anthropology in the 1940s, does not use the example of Pérez Jolote to open up a larger debate over the meaning of ethnic identity, the gaps and inconsistencies in the text that he wrote in order to educate his readers about a specific Indian group within the national borders challenge the usefulness of such classifications based on a culture's presumed profile and an individual's presumed typicality.

The second major contradiction exists between the exposition of the hybrid aspects of Chamula society summarized above and the attempt on the final two pages of the introduction to fix a list of uniform and presumably stable traits for Chamula identity. Among the attributes that constitute the fundamental character of the Chamula are physical athleticism, aptitude for simple mechanical tasks, respect for human life, violent temper when inebriated, firm religious beliefs, fear of revenge, and distrust of outsiders. Rather than solidifying a convincing portrait of the Chamula personality, the dubious universality and the disparate nature of this conglomeration of physical, intellectual, and cultural traits undermine the validity of the very project of attaching essential identity signs to a human group. By reading the introduction against the grain, it can be shown that the frame, far from "containing" the picture of Juan Pérez Jolote's life and orienting the reader toward an interpretation of his story as a reliable and comprehensible representation of the Chamula "other" within Mexican society, raises questions about the constitution of group and individual identities and suggests the primacy of the hybrid over the essential. This subversive function of the frame may have been unintentional on the writer's part, but it is no less effective for that reason.

On the first page of the auto/biography per se a discussion of the protagonist's name immediately calls further attention to cultural hybridity, the signs of which permeate the entire life story. The name Juan commemorates his birth on the feast day of St. John, and he is called Pérez Jolote simply because that was his father's name. An endnote translates "jolote" as the word for turkey and states that it is common among the Chamulas to use the name of an animal as a surname. Pérez is one of a limited number of Hispanic surnames that are used by Tzotzil-speaking peoples, as Pozas elaborates in his monograph *Chamula: Un pueblo indio* (36).

The roughly one hundred pages of the life story (the "work itself" in contrast to the "frame") comprise a retrospective narrative structured in a continuous form without divisions into chapters. The overarching story line traces a movement of separation, prolonged absence and eventual reintegration into the community that spans from childhood to, perhaps, early middle age. Of his early years and family life, Pérez Jolote recalls the hard work of cultivating the land and collecting firewood, and frequent beatings by his father. In fact, the memory of physical abuse surfaces immediately and is reiterated numerous times. This abuse is the very cause for his leaving home as a mere child, which Pozas did not specify in the introduction. Perhaps somewhat defensively, Pozas adds a note to the third mention of beatings in three consecutive paragraphs in order to clarify that this is not typical of child-rearing in Chamula. On the contrary, the anthropologist maintains that children are treated with great patience and consideration and rarely run away. Apropos of the endnotes, there are eight referencing the first two pages alone, and the appearance of a superscript number in the text alerts the reader to interrupt the reading of the narrative and seek out the supplement of Pozas's explanatory interventions. The endnotes exemplify Derrida's theory of the frame as connected to a lack or a perceived lack in the interior of the work ("Parergon" 24). The writer compensates for a lack in the informant's ability to give an adequately clear and complete account of his own life and culture, and he supplements the "shorthand" of the first-person testimony with his own interpretative observations.

Pérez Jolote does not say at what age he left home for the first time. He might have been eight or nine years old judging from his ease in finding substitute families and the rather simple chores that he performs for them. By his own reckoning he is absent for seven months before he is returned to his family by civil authorities representing the national government. He leaves again an indeterminate amount of time later to work on a plantation in Soconusco, and he finds himself in jail in 1912–13. He does not return to Chamula until 1930. His experience as a soldier occupies the next phase of his life, and overall he paints a relatively undramatic and untraumatic picture of the Mexican Revolution of 1910. His military training, his movements from town to town, his passage from one army to another, occasional hospital stays, and his duties as part of an occupying force in various Mexican towns are recounted with very little specific detail or emotion, and there are only a few references to participation in actual combat. The protagonist's ignorance of the reasons for which a civil war was being waged is similar to the portrayal of peasant soldiers in other accounts of the Mexican Revolution. He is equally content to serve government forces under Huerta or rebel forces under Carranza and Villa. The period of about thirteen years between leaving the army and returning to Chamula is passed over extraordinarily quickly, and suddenly it is 1930, the protagonist is a grown man, and he is back with his family. Seeing that he has forgotten how to speak Tzotzil and has adopted ladino dress, the villagers perceive him as an outsider, and Pérez Jolote undergoes a long period of adjustment and reacculturation during which he gradually ventures out of the family circle and takes his place as an adult member of Chamula society. The second half of the life story is devoted to his reintegration and his full participation in the life of the community over a period of about four or five years. This includes his return to linguistic fluency and traditional dress, his economic contribution through working the family land and traveling to coffee plantations, his eventual marriage, the death and burial of his father, and his assumption of various *cargos* or positions of responsibility and authority in the civic and religious structure of Chamula. The story ends rather abruptly with the narrator-protagonist's admission of alcohol addiction and his hope to avoid succumbing, like his father, to an early death due to complications from alcohol abuse. External sources cited earlier explain that the closing lines were recorded by Pozas in his final conversation with Pérez Jolote in 1948, a number of years after the initial interviews took place.

The first-person narrative voice represents the bilingual-I of Juan Pérez Jolote speaking Spanish mixed with some Tzotzil vocabulary. More accurately, it represents a version of a once-living voice in contact with the speech of another, and later mediated and modified through the necessary work of transcription and editing. It is not possible to discern the narrator's "real" voice speaking on the page, nor is it possible to ascertain what his priorities were, what things he said that were later omitted, what he emphasized or downplayed, or what he might have said had the unknown interview questions been phrased differently than they were. Was Ricardo Pozas "faithful" to his informant or did he manipulate the testimony to his own purposes?[14] These are purely speculative and ultimately fruitless concerns, although the framing of the book as an ethnographic document based on interview material might logically encourage a mimetic reading in search of the voice of a "genuine Indian." However, by letting go of the preoccupation with an elusive authenticity, the reader can ask other, more pertinent questions of the text at hand. To conclude this analysis I will return to aspects of the representation of cultural hybridity in the life story.

Juan Pérez Jolote's narration of his daily activities and his explanations of Chamula economic and religious practices illustrate the inherent hybridity of culture and the degree to which that hybridity is invisible to the members of a human group. While the anthropologist is concerned to differentiate activities, material goods, and beliefs that have Mayan origin from those with Hispanic roots, the informant experiences his diversely constituted culture as a coherent whole. In *Juan Pérez Jolote* the introduction and the endnotes are the obvious signs of the scientist's preoccupation with unraveling the weave of Chamula life and tracing its threads to their sources. I am not suggesting that there is nothing to be learned from such an endeavor, only that the life story demonstrates the degree to which a given community internalizes disparate influences and accommodates a certain level of internal contradiction. Also, in the study of cultural change over time there is no starting point from which to measure the distance traveled or the loss or gain of original and new attributes. The Maya and Hispanic cultures were themselves "mongrels," to recall the root meaning of hybrid. It's mongrels all the way back.

The human awareness of the passing of time is a universal condition that takes a variety of specific forms and is endowed with a variety of meanings. The temporal structure of the life story of Juan Pérez Jolote displays the intersection or overlapping of distinct time values as the narrator-protagonist lives time according to more than one system. The experience of time as a linear progression from the past toward the future, an attribute of Judeo-Christian ideology, shapes the presentation of events from childhood to adulthood in a chronological sequence with few anachronisms. This is a shape that may very well have been imposed by Ricardo Pozas, although during the years spent away from the Chamula township, Pérez Jolote would have himself experienced the forward thrust of Mexican history, marked by Revolution and the changing names of those in power: Madero, Huerta, Carranza. The few identifiable dates given in the story are primarily linked to events occurring at the level of the national life insofar as they touch the protagonist (the Revolution) or the Chamula community (the annual arrival of new civil authorities). The measurement of time in weeks and months generally pertains to the life activities of the protagonist experienced outside of his town, including the careful counting of the days spent working for wages on the lowland plantations, where each day holds a small monetary value against the debt contracted prior to the season of planting or harvesting.

Pérez Jolote equally experiences the cyclical nature of time that governs life in an agricultural society. The seasons circle around, tracing a predictable pattern of rainy and dry periods and an accompanying rhythm of clearing the land, planting, tending, and harvesting the crops. The steady repetition of the natural cycle might contribute to the sense of permanence and continuity across generations, which is evoked in the opening paragraph of the life story. Pérez Jolote is sure of his unchanging attachment to an identifiable piece of land and is also sure of the continuity of existence across the fluid boundaries of life and death: "Cuando yo muera y venga mi ánima, encontrará los mismos senderos por donde anduve en vida, y reconocerá mi casa" (15). [When I die and my soul returns, it will find the same paths that I walked in life and it will recognize my house.] The scant attention paid to dates of birth and the resulting imprecision with regard to a person's age means that a life is not measured in years, but in the larger expanses of time that comprise childhood and adulthood. The matter of the tracking of religious festivals is an interesting case, because it combines an adherence to the ends-oriented calendar of Western Christianity and the timeless repetition of significant events in an annual cycle that denies the linear progress of history. The constant and effortless shifting among different temporal schemes finds its literary expression in the seamless form of the narrative, with its sporadic and inconsistent references to dates, its long gaps in coverage, and its detailed accounts of ritual activities such as festivals and the conferring of *cargos* that give meaning to membership in Chamula society.

A second, striking example of cultural hybridity can be found in the version of the story of the life of Jesus that Pérez Jolote learns from his *yajuatiquil* or elder mentor at the time of assuming the position of *fiscal*. The *fiscal* keeps track of the saints' days and advises the other municipal functionaries who are in charge of their celebration. He has to know the important attributes of each revered saint and what aspect of the life of Chamula that each one protects. St. Sebastian, for instance, is the patron saint of sheep, and Santiago protects beasts of burden such as mules and donkeys. As part of his orientation to his new job, Pérez Jolote quotes his mentor giving a highly condensed account of Jesus's life—birth, miracles, and crucifixion—that clearly blends elements of the biblical story with pre-Hispanic motifs.[15] In summary, before the birth of Jesus, also called St. Emmanuel, the Lord Saviour, and St. Matthew, the sun was as cold as the moon and the earth was plagued by *pukujes*—devils, also identifed in this context as Jews—who ate human beings. Jesus was born in a stable in Bethlehem to the Virgin Mary and St. Joseph, and at that moment the sun began to give off light and heat to protect all people from destruction at the hands of the *pukujes*. Within three days of his birth the baby Jesus was performing the work of an adult by fashioning a door out of a tree trunk, and later he cultivated his own *milpa*. He was persecuted and had to flee to safety, and he prepared a feast for his people immediately before his death. The crucifixion is represented somewhat ambiguously as an act of murder and as an act of self-sacrifice through which Jesus saved the world from the *pukujes*. Most Western readers would be able to sort out the primary elements from the Christian tradition from those rooted in Mayan culture, although some elements such as the identification of a deity with the sun and light, a metaphor for truth and the literal source of life, are common to both. Pozas provides interpretative commentary to trace and explain the hybrid origins of the Jesus story in his book *Chamula: Un pueblo de indios*. Written as a life story and not as a scientific treatise, *Juan Pérez Jolote* nevertheless successfully captures the way in which hybridity informs the religion of the Chamulas, their distinctive dress, their economic life, and their material culture, such that it serves as an illustration of the dynamic tension and balance between disparate cultural influences and between tradition and change in any human community.

Benita and *Juan Pérez Jolote* are two early examples of life writing in Mexico that portray the experiences of subaltern subjects "in their own words." In the analyses carried out in this chapter I have examined a number of ways in which both texts problematize the narrative voices of their protagonists and challenge a facile assignment of qualities of "authenticity" and "originality" to them. As with the autobiographies of elite social actors, a careful reading discovers the presence of shaping, empowering, and constraining forces on the narrator-protagonist of a life story produced from a popular perspective. Gender, class, race, ethnicity, religion, and political ideology are some of the defining categories of the complex subject positions occupied by each of the autobiographical protagonists studied, and their individual lives and voices attest to their dynamic relationship to these determining forces and to the hybrid constitution of all cultures and all writing.

5

Chronicling Crisis

Late Twentieth-Century Manifestations of the Literature of Encounter

> The chronicle repositions itself today against the all-encompassing discourse of the supposed *logos* of modernity, by confronting it with another form of reason that takes into account the instability of disciplines, genres, borders that delimit discourse. The chronicle, by its characteristic presence, is able to recuperate diverse spoken languages, play with the appetite for experience. . . .
>
> If, as I believe, every crisis is also an opportunity, the chronicle ought to be viewed as more than a limited, defined and definable genre. It ought to be regarded as a language of encounter, a place from which communication, that primary vehicle of our sociability, can extend a bridge between worlds.
>
> —Rossana Reguillo, "Border(line) Texts"

I open this chapter on the chronicle in late twentieth-century Mexico with a quote that efficiently synthesizes the core characteristics and concerns of this abundantly produced and widely read mode of nonfiction literature. The qualification of the chronicle as a hybrid genre that is flexible in form, the prominent orality of its language and its blending of diverse voices, its inscription of the real and in particular the reality of crisis, and its textual reenactment of encounters with the other are attributes that are found in the work of most of the chroniclers who have been active in Mexican print journalism and mass communications in the past fifty years. In this chapter and the next I study selected chronicles that treat three moments of crisis and opportunity for Mexico in the period

1984 to 2000: first, the gas explosions of November 1984 in San Juan Ixhuatepec and the gas explosions of April 1992 in Guadalajara; and in Chapter 6 the January 1, 1994 Zapatista uprising in Chiapas. All three events, two human and environmental disasters, and a political movement devoted to reforming a history of human disaster, occupied the attention of the Mexican nation in a spectacular way, and they demanded a complex confluence of responses and remedies ranging from material aid for victims to legal investigation and prosecution of responsible parties, new roles for civil society, sustained and profound critiques of the ruling political structures, and an examination of the meaning of citizenship and nationhood with regard to the identity markers of social class and ethnicity. They also revealed the extent of institutional resistance to change, the insidious effects of corruption on Mexican society, and the amnesiac power of the passing of time. The initial steps of the process through which these events are being written into history have taken place within the parameters of the flexible form, the encounter of languages, and the "appetite for experience" that characterize the chronicle. The primary texts to be studied here are Carlos Monsiváis's chronicle of the gas explosions in San Juan Ixhuatepec (popularly known as San Juanico) and Rossana Reguillo's mix of chronicle and anthropological study of the similar explosions in Guadalajara. In the following chapter, writings by Elena Poniatowska, Carlos Monsiváis, Juan Villoro, and Alma Guillermoprieto portray the Zapatista rebellion and its leader Subcomandante Marcos at three specific historical junctures.

In 1999 and 2000 when Ignacio Corona and I were assembling an anthology of essays about the contemporary Mexican chronicle, it was still appropriate to lead off our introduction to the book with Carlos Monsiváis's now much-quoted lament about the marginalized position of the genre in literary history and criticism. His important 1987 essay "De la Santa Doctrina al Espíritu Público" [From holy doctrine to public spirit] gives an overview of the history of the genre, and it opens with Monsiváis's protest that the chronicle, which has been an abundantly produced, widely read, and highly influential genre since the time of the Spanish conquest of Mexico, has been largely neglected within the realm of literary history and criticism. In the twentieth century alone, writers as diverse and as prominent as Salvador Novo, Vicente Leñero, Elena Poniatowska, Carlos Monsiváis, Guadalupe Loaeza, Cristina Pacheco, José Joaquín Blanco, and Juan Villoro have contributed to this persistent and ever-changing literary form. However, more than ten years after the publication of "De la Santa Doctrina," we found that there was still no comprehensive treatment of the contemporary chronicle, and the existing criticism consisted of relatively few articles dispersed among many different journals and volumes of essays. Aníbal González's groundbreaking 1983 book on the *modernista* chronicle in Spanish America had not been matched by a similar study of subsequent manifestations of the genre in Spanish America as a whole or in Mexico.

This gap has begun to be addressed in the last decade starting with the publication in 2001 of Linda Egan's monograph *Carlos Monsiváis: Culture and Chronicle in Contemporary Mexico*, which includes extensive background material on the genre as well as a detailed analysis of Monsiváis's writing. *The Contemporary Mexican Chronicle: Theoretical Perspectives on the Liminal Genre* by Corona and Jörgensen and Anadeli Bencomo's *Voces y voceros de la megalópolis: La crónica periodístico-literaria en México* appeared in 2002, offering studies of the work of numerous *cronistas* and enhancing our understanding of the chronicle's place in Mexican culture. The preparation of these three books occurred virtually simultaneously in distinct academic sites in the United States at a time when scholars interested in the chronicle were just beginning to disseminate their work and identify each other's contributions to the field. A more recent addition to the growing scholarship is Esperança Bielsa's very interesting comparative study of the urban chronicle in Guayaquil and Mexico City titled *The Latin American Urban Chronicle: Between Literature and Mass Media* (2006). *The Mexico City Reader*, Rubén Gallo's anthology of translations of thirty-seven chronicles by twenty writers published in 2004, now makes the Mexican chronicle more accessible to an English-speaking audience. Therefore, as I write these pages and undertake an analysis of selected examples of chronicles published since 1985, Monsiváis's complaint is somewhat less pertinent than it was twenty-odd years ago, and the studies that have appeared in the past decade are a rich resource within which to situate my own readings.

There is a general consensus among chroniclers and critical readers alike regarding the common characteristics of the Mexican chronicle as it has been produced since the 1960s. I believe that this is in part due to the considerable visibility and influence of the work of Elena Poniatowska and Carlos Monsiváis as preeminent practitioners of the genre, and to the latter's efforts to place it into a historical and literary context. Monsiváis's introduction to his 1980 anthology *A ustedes les consta: Antología de la crónica en México* and the 1987 essay that I have already cited are fundamental to our understanding, in that they provide a history of the chronicle's presence since colonial times, and a point of departure for formulating a poetics of the genre. At the time that they were written, they stood virtually alone in the critical landscape. A good portion of "De la Santa Doctrina" was reworked for his essay "On the Chronicle in Mexico" that appears in Corona and Jörgensen's edited volume, and this has also increased the circulation of his ideas. Linda Egan's study, which is unmatched as a theoretically sophisticated and highly readable treatment of Monsiváis's work and of the poetics of the chronicle in general, further contributes to the consolidation of the prevailing view.[1] By this I do not mean to suggest that the chronicle is a homogeneous body of texts that look and sound alike, or that there is a dominant model to follow. On the contrary, chroniclers adopt, adapt, and innovate a wide variety of literary and nonliterary devices and languages in order to communicate about a diverse and ever-expanding set of social and cultural phenomena. However, within a diversity of forms and a plurality of voices, certain textual and extratextual markers identify the writings that most authors and readers would agree to place under the rubric of chronicle, and several key terms consistently appear in any attempt at a definition.

The phrase "literary journalism" may be offered as a snapshot answer to the question: What is a chronicle? It reflects the tension between the genre's close kinship with journalism, and in particular with the newspaper, and those aspects of its form and language that distance it from conventional reporting. Since the nineteenth century, chronicles have primarily been published in newspapers and their cultural supplements, and they are identified in the mind of readers with print journalism. Like all news reporting, the point of departure for a chronicle is a real event unfolding in time or a known human being whose existence can be verified by sources outside of the text. As such, the chronicle claims factual status. It is a form of literary nonfiction and it promises to communicate a measure of reliable, empirical information. The reader seeks traces of the real and expects that the referential function of language will be predominant. Chronicles appeal to our desire and our need to know about our own immediate reality and about worlds outside of our experience.

At the same time, like the North American New Journalism, to which the contemporary Mexican chronicle owes a certain debt, it is a hybrid genre that moves among a variety of discourses and seamlessly blends fact with fiction, and the urgency of on-location reporting with a more literary attention to style and aesthetics. At home in the throwaway medium of the newspaper, chronicles are also collected into books and given the more durable form granted to works of literature. The genre openly defies traditional notions of journalistic objectivity and it freely borrows characteristics of the short story, the essay and the ethnographic narrative in offering a perspective that frequently runs counter to official or authorized versions of events. Documentation and invention are at play in the representation of both real and fictional characters and in the inclusion of recorded or recreated dialogues. Editorial commentary and analysis may interrupt the narrative. Written and oral discourse coincide to create a textuality that is highly literate, often ironic and/or densely intertextual, and that also incorporates testimony, excerpts from interviews, and other traces of colloquial speech patterns. Finally, there is no narrative without a narrator, and the chronicler him- or herself is usually assumed to be the unifying voice who speaks through a variety of guises: casual or involved observer, protagonist, passerby, one of the crowd, partisan, reporter, voyeur, informed expert, or ingenuous witness of the events or the phenomena portrayed. Whatever the stance, the chronicler-narrator is an active observer and listener who works out in the open—on the streets or in the stadium, the plaza or the subway—and who engages in a dynamic encounter with the other.

The chronicle is primarily an urban literature, dedicated to representing, interpreting, and inventing the modern metropolis (or megalopolis) for a readership of city dwellers. The writings of Salvador Novo were the most compelling and influential manifestation of this trend in Mexico in the first half of the twentieth century, and all of the later chroniclers whom I have mentioned focus primarily on urban life and culture.[2] A variety of approaches to encountering and inscribing the heterogeneous and ever-changing realities of urban spaces and urban populations have coexisted over the past fifty years. Daily life and customs are frequent objects of the chronicler's observation and recreation, and they may be viewed with an eye toward resisting the processes of change, when change is experienced and interpreted as loss. Elena Poniatowska's collections *Todo empezó el domingo* [1963, It all began on Sunday] and *El último guajolote* [1982, The last turkey] contain nostalgia-tinged evocations of the typical activities, locales, and human actors of the popular classes in Mexico City. An afternoon in Xochimilco, La Lagunilla market, a wedding, Sundays in Chapultepec, street vendors, dance salons, pulquerías, and knife sharpeners are the objects of Poniatowska's sympathetic eye. In contrast, Carlos Monsiváis brings a decidedly ironic perspective to his chronicles about the urban "rituals" that draw together masses of people: a rock concert, a ride on the metro, or the December eleventh mass at the Basilica de Guadalupe are examples from his "book of hours" *Los rituales del caos* [1995, Rituals of chaos]. José Joaquín Blanco also contributes to this trend, and his work opens a space for the representation of homosexuality in the chronicle.[3]

Since 1968, the chronicle has played a crucial role in the Mexican public discourse by responding to situations of political urgency, social crisis, and human and natural disaster, as in the well-known body of work that treats the 1968 student movement, the 1985 Mexico City earthquakes, and the 1994 rebellion in Chiapas. In carrying out a critical investigation of events such as these, the chronicle has earned a reputation as a contestatory discourse, a committed literature, a counterversion to official history and rhetoric, and a voice of the poor, the marginalized, the oppressed, and the discriminated in Mexico. Central to many of the best-known writings of Poniatowska, Monsiváis, and also Hermann Bellinghausen and Julio Scherer, is a sustained and thorough critique of the structures and exercise of power and Mexico's prevailing authoritarianism. Through this critique and by highlighting the presence of alternative, often grassroots social movements, the chronicle not only exposes social and political ills, but it also encourages and promotes the democratization of Mexico, the strengthening of civil society, and the recognition of difference that many believe are necessary conditions for a better future for the nation. The texts that I have chosen for analysis belong to this rich vein of chronicle writing.

Catastrophic Chronicles

Narratives of disaster have a long history, and nonfiction plays a particular role in documenting and making sense out of the violence, destruction, and suffering that accompany floods, earthquakes, hurricanes, bridge or building failures, major fires, and similar "natural" or human-made catastrophes. There is no doubt that the modern news industry thrives on disaster, knowing that it can hold huge audiences with day and night coverage of spectacular events and their aftermath. In reporting on disaster, the staging of suffering in sensationalist terms is an irresistible opportunity or a constant risk, depending on one's commercial or ethical point of view. The sensationalism that is inherent in portraying scenes of injury, violence, and death sells newspapers and airtime, as crime stories, accident reports, and the journalism of disaster prove time and again. Part of their appeal for the reader or spectator is the combination of horror and relief that is felt when "witnessing," albeit from a safe distance, terrible events. Alternatively, reporting on disaster can manifest a sense of responsibility for challenging the public's understanding of events rather than feeding its emotions with a sensationalist account, and it can also take on an advocacy role by reporting on the news in such a way as to support a struggle for change over merely passive reception. This kind of reporting entails investigation into the contributing causes of disastrous events (poor building code enforcement, environmental degradation, individual or institutional irresponsibility, corruption, poverty) and into the underlying reasons for the often inadequate response that aggravates the effects. It does not take for granted that disasters are accidents after which the best one can do is clean up and move on. On the contrary, it exposes the many political and economic interests involved in the rhetoric of "moving on" and making promises of better precautions in an ever-elusive "next time." Elena Poniatowska's series of chronicles on the September 1985 earthquakes in Mexico City that were published as the book *Nada, nadie: Voces del temblor* [1988, *Nothing, Nobody: The Voices of the Mexico City Earthquake*, 1995] and Carlos Monsiváis's "Los días del terremoto" [Days of the earthquake] from his collection *Entrada libre* are two examples of disaster narratives that go far beyond the recording of personal "tragedy" (a much over-used term in today's media) in order to delve into both the existing structural factors that cause or exacerbate catastrophic events and the potential for a constructive challenge to the status quo. Both are works of nonfiction and derive a measure of their rhetorical and analytical power from their respect for the exigencies imposed by claiming factual status for a written text.[4]

In 1984 and 1992, poor and working-class neighborhoods of Mexico City and Guadalajara were blasted apart by explosions originating in nearby Pemex installations. The chronicles of these two separate and yet related gas explosions by Carlos Monsiváis and Rossana Reguillo, like the histories of the 1985 earthquakes, demonstrate the genre's capacity to combine the power of storytelling with the power of critical commentary and analysis within the authorizing frame of nonfiction discourse. In her study of Carlos Monsiváis's five collections of chronicles published between 1970 and 1995, Linda Egan reads an overarching narrative about Mexico's problematical entry into modernity and its dual struggle against authoritarianism and toward democracy in the second half of the twentieth century. Monsiváis represents this ambitiously conceived story by chronicling such diverse topics as political events, social movements, popular culture, well-known personalities, and experiences of daily life in Mexico City. According to Egan, a persistent but realistic optimism runs through even the most ironic, parodic, or critical of Monsiváis's writings, and his belief in the nascent power of an emerging civil society that is pursuing the means of self-governance in the face of institutionalized abuse of power is most clearly on display in the seven pieces of *Entrada libre: Crónicas de la sociedad que se organiza* [1987, Free admission: chronicles of the society that is getting organized] (Egan 196). The longest chronicle in the book, exceptionally long at over one hundred pages, treats the September 19, 1985 earthquakes, and it documents an unprecedented degree of solidarity, civilian organization, volunteerism, civil disobedience, and personal heroism on the part of massive numbers of citizens of all social classes in the capital city.

Monsiváis's earlier text on the 1984 gas explosions in Mexico City, "San Juanico: Los hechos, las interpretaciones y las mitologías," can be seen as a kind of prelude to "Los días del terremoto" in its representation of a disaster that shook one neighborhood and that moved a previously unorganized and nonactivist population to start a struggle for economic and social justice. The grassroots efforts of neighborhood groups were ultimately frustrated by the power of the government bureaucracy and private economic interests, but "San Juanico" is an exemplary chronicle that records, analyzes, and continues the work of revindication that was begun on the ground in 1984. The chronicle is divided into two main sections: "Panorama del desastre" and "De las consecuencias sociales." These are in turn comprised of twelve very brief parts with their own subtitles. The breakdown facilitates our reading and the subtitles offer an opportunity for the chronicler to insert his own editorializing interventions in a very condensed but visible form. The title of the entire piece lays bare a three-part structure to its content: first, "los hechos," the empirical information that tells what happened and when; then multiple and conflicting interpretations of those events as articulated by official sources and by residents of the neighborhood; and finally a deconstruction of the self-serving mythology by means of which the authorities politicized the disaster to their own advantage, and the racist and classist mythology manifested in an "epidemic" of San Juanico jokes ("San Juanico" 144). By taking each section in order and focusing on the narrative voice, we can trace the movement from an uninvolved and yet clearly sympathetic reportage, to an increasingly caustic criticism of the specifics of the official (governmental and business sector) response to the disaster, and a more generalized critique of Mexican capitalism, racism, and indifference to human life.

Readers of chronicles have in common with readers of essays the expectation that the narrator of the text is to be identified with the *cronista* or the essayist him- or herself. This is at odds with the assumption made for a novel or a short story that its narrator is a fictional entity constructed by the author for the purpose of telling the tale in a particular way. The identity between writer and narrator is characteristic as well of other forms of nonfiction, as we have seen in the study of autobiography. A chronicle's claim to factual status is supported by the authority of the one who signs the text, and the signature of Carlos Monsiváis is highly credible in all matters pertaining to contemporary Mexican society and culture, given his many years working as a journalist in the more respected and less controlled Mexican newspapers and magazines.[5] The voice or voices that he creates for himself in each individual piece are an important component in the message that he wishes to convey. The opening pieces of "San Juanico" are narrated by an apparently distant, impersonal voice who functions primarily to compile and deliver information that has already been composed by others. "La catástrofe," "El heroísmo" and "El éxodo y la solidaridad" [The catastrophe; Heroism; Exodus and solidarity] establish the measurable dimensions of the disaster. Here a relatively neutral narrative voice who is neither a participant nor a direct witness of the events communicates a wealth of information, cites sources, and maintains a sober but urgent tone in recounting scenes of horror and devastation. His primary concern is to set up the chronology of the events and to record the documentable and verifiable facts concerning the number of explosions, the estimated height of the flames, the size and weight of the gas tanks that shattered under the pressure of the blast, the number of houses destroyed, and the number of people killed, injured, and displaced. These sections move along at a rapid pace, and the compilation of long lists of noun phrases and simple sentences creates a telegraphic effect that communicates urgency and an unrelenting assault on reason and on the senses. The lists create an ever more intense accumulation of details, each endowed with equal value and none privileged over the other. The first explicit signs of the narrator's critical perspective and his role in creating meaning out of the data can be detected toward the end of these introductory sections when he comes to the defense of the genuine, spontaneous solidarity that was manifested in the flood of donations of food, clothing, money, and blood immediately after the disaster occurred. Rejecting accusations of media manipulation of public sentiment, the narrator sees in these acts of generosity "un esfuerzo democratizador desde abajo" [128, an effort at democratization from below], which mirrors the theme of the other chronicles in *Entrada libre*.

Starting in the fourth section, "La nueva fundación de Aztlán," the investigative, analytical, and critical function of the narrator comes to the fore. The history of the settlement of the land now known as San Juanico, one of the "lost cities" on the margins of the capital, is revealed to be one of unplanned and unregulated growth from which a few businessmen made their fortunes in the 1960s and 70s. An increasingly sarcastic tone is used to describe the machinations of property owners and government officials who benefitted from the arrival of massive numbers of immigrants from the countryside in need of a place to set up their cardboard shelters and have access to the marginal employment opportunities available in the growing metropolis. The use of capital letters to parody the self-importance of officials and official rhetoric, a frequent monsivaisian ploy, appears in this section as well. In this case, the narrator points to the "Administradores Públicos" who profit from "administering" their posts while maintaining their distance from the "public." Throughout the rest of the chronicle, the narrator moves the story of the explosions and their aftermath across a timeline of about two months, and simultaneously organizes and analyzes the facts that he has assembled through careful research to create the necessary evidence for his principal accusation: that the explosions were not an accident, but the consequence of the institutional negligence and corruption that are endemic in Mexican politics and Mexican business. Monsiváis specifically condemns Mexican capitalism in its rush always to increase production without regard for safety and quality. In other words, the explosions were the logical outcome of the prevailing politics, and the word "accident" was misused in order to deflect blame and derail the search for objective causes. In its critique, the chronicle exposes fatal flaws in two reigning mythologies of twentieth-century Mexico: the myth of "Progress" as the highest good for the nation, and the myth of a paternalistic, all-protecting government. The narrator undoes the official post-disaster rhetoric of sympathy and concern, promises of material aid, and the tragedy of suffering by showing it to be a ploy to distract the public from insisting on a full investigation that would lead to the determination of responsibility. This pattern will be repeated on a much larger scale less than a year later after the September 1985 earthquakes.

Against the dismal picture of official cover up and impunity, "San Juanico" also offers two potential antidotes to the cycle of corruption and public apathy and resignation toward entrenched power. First, it credits television, specifically the Televisa network, with the power to mobilize people into action when it steps outside of its usual broadcast habits and uses the camera and the microphone to make urgent situations immediately visible and to subject the authorities to scrutiny during on-air interviews. In contrast, the two government-run channels downplayed the effects of the explosions and quickly scapegoated a private gas company in order to take attention away from Pemex. Another vehicle for change is illustrated by the rapid organization of grassroots efforts to demand both a careful accounting of the dead and a just settlement for those who were injured and who lost family members, homes, and livelihoods. However, it is shown that ultimately none of the demands were met, and the brevity of the section devoted to portraying these positive actions is emblematic of a short-lived, thwarted struggle against powerful vested interests.

The final sections of the chronicle, grouped under the title "De las consecuencias sociales," also deconstruct a negative mythology of urban Mexico by presenting an anthology of the San Juanico jokes that circulated in Mexico City within a couple of weeks of the catastrophe and by undertaking a critical examination of their cultural significance. The narrator rejects any move to interpret the jokes as in some way cathartic or as an example of legitimate black humor. Rather, he analyzes and condemns them as a sign of the Mexican middle- and upper-classes' arrogance and sense of superiority over their poor, generally darker-skinned compatriots. He classifies them as a subcategory of "naco" jokes, and he takes a very hard line against the underlying racism and classism of this brand of humor. Ultimately, the interweaving of narrative and analysis in "San Juanico" demonstrates the depth of knowledge that the *cronista* brings to his writing, and the complex and wide-ranging connections that can—and must—be drawn among social, economic, and political phenomena in order to challenge both the official story and the public's tendency to accept it. "San Juanico" exemplifies the chronicle's ability to present a forceful and persuasive alternative version of events, and it reveals the need for an increasingly critical and thoroughgoing investigative journalism in Mexico in order to counteract the more controlled media outlets. The next work to be considered demonstrates how the discipline of anthropology can usefully and effectively integrate textual practices associated with the chronicle into a social science-based critique of contemporary events. In the writings of Rossana Reguillo, the embedded chronicle is part of the process of analysis and it enhances the appeal of academic publications to readers outside of the field.

On April 22, 1992, a working-class neighborhood of Guadalajara suffered a series of early morning gas explosions that were sadly reminiscent of the San Juan Ixhuatepec disaster of 1984. Parallels between the two catastrophes are easy to identify: the residents' reports of a strong odor of gas in the days preceding the explosions, the involvement of a Pemex facility in the disaster, the extent of the loss of lives and the destruction of homes and businesses, accusations of government negligence, corruption and cover up, unfulfilled promises of aid, an initial but temporary activism on the part of the media, the emergence of neighborhood organizations, and even the appearance of humor targeted at the disaster, all recall the earlier events. Rossana Reguillo has published books and articles that document these similarities and also reveal important differences between the explosions in the two cities, and her writing incorporates elements of the chronicle into what are essentially research studies in intriguing ways that demonstrate the flexibility of the genre and its centrality in creating an oppositional record of Mexican society.

Rossana Reguillo Cruz, a native of Guadalajara, is a social and cultural anthropologist who specializes in the study of the mass media and contemporary urban society. She is a research professor at the Instituto Tecnológico de Estudios Superiores de Occidente in Guadalajara, and she was appointed as a UNESCO scholar in Barcelona for the year 2004. Reguillo is a prominent member of a new generation of Mexican anthropologists who have broken with the traditional study of Mexico's indigenous past in order to bring contemporary social science theory to bear on present-day social and cultural phenomena. Her early research yielded the 1991 book *En la calle otra vez: Las bandas: Identidad urbana y los usos de la comunicación* [Back on the street: gangs: urban identity and the uses of communication], which examines the criminalization and the scapegoating of urban youth by the Mexican government and press and seeks to understand the contradictory blend of violence, vulnerability, and inventiveness manifested by socially excluded youth as they struggle for survival. Her work has expanded throughout the 1990s and into the new century, as she has undertaken a comparative study of the social construction of fear and the uses of fear as a mechanism of social and political control in four Latin American nations: Colombia, Mexico, Puerto Rico, and Argentina. One constant dimension of her work is her attention to the influence of the mass media on the citizens' perception of their society, and the media's dual potential to act either as a counterforce to challenge official rhetoric or as a support to the political uses of fear and otherness. The need to rethink violence from within a given society rather than seeing it as an ill that enters society from the outside, and the imperative to analyze the structural violence of poverty, unemployment, lack of access to education, and official complicity in criminal organizations are other pressing concerns that Reguillo has confronted in her research.[6]

Although Rossana Reguillo is a social scientist and not a journalist or a literary author, she participates in the production of chronicles in several ways. Ignacio Corona addresses the relevant link between chronicle and anthropology in his essay "At the Intersection: Chronicle and Ethnography" (Corona and Jörgensen 2002). Corona approaches this intersection along various routes by bringing together insights and questions posed by social science and literary theory and practice, and his analysis of the contemporary Mexican chronicle convincingly illuminates its common ground with ethnography in terms of textuality, thematics, self-reflexivity, narrativity, the interpenetration of the personal and the putatively objective, and a persistent privileging of the visual.[7] He notes that Rosario Castellanos, Elena Poniatowska, and Carlos Monsiváis have had links to the discipline of anthropology, and that the kinds of knowledge produced by ethnography inform their work as chroniclers. In the case of Rossana Reguillo, we have a social science researcher who openly acknowledges the place of the chronicle in her work, who has written an essay that explores some of the features and the functions of the genre, and whose research studies frequently embed narrative segments that could be considered chronicles in their own right. In "Border(line) Texts," from which I quoted at the beginning of the chapter, Reguillo expresses agreement with the widely accepted view that the chronicle straddles journalism, social analysis, and literature. It is a form of storytelling that responds to the "endless cycle of emergencies" that characterizes late twentieth-century social life ("Border(line)" 52). Reguillo attests to the chronicle's "appetite for experience" and for the real, which it tries to narrate in open-ended, heteroglossic forms (54–55). The chronicler is a nomad who moves through the world always listening as well as observing. Finally, she affirms that "in the social science realm of cultural studies, [the chronicle] is gaining space and visibility as a discourse that seeks to analyze social reality at the same time that it wants to become an effective and aesthetic device for self-reflexivity" (55).

Two of Rossana Reguillo's publications particularly foreground her engagement with the urban chronicle. *Ciudadano N: Crónicas de la diversidad* (1999, Citizen X: chronicles of diversity) "narrates the many cities that exist within one city" ("Border(line)" 57) by mapping the complex identities of a large number of urban characters encountered in Guadalajara. A journalistic and ethnographic impulse motivated the researcher to undertake a sustained project of interviews of the many socially constructed "others" who inhabited the city in the mid 1990s. The book's seven chapters organize dozens of vignettes of individual lives and identities under loose categories of experience such as economic survival, intimacy, political opposition, and coming of age. The sketches are based on face-to-face conversations between Reguillo and her subjects, and she calls it a bilingual book because it combines the language of anthropology and the language of the street. The diversity of age, socioeconomic class, gender, sexual orientation, ethnicity, employment, political views, civil status, educational level, and other identity markers documented in *Ciudadano N* and the brevity of each vignette prevent the reader from extracting a generalized image of the city "as a whole" and force a recognition of the internal human complexity of a single urban space. At the same time, poverty, participation in the informal economy, and a sense of insecurity and marginalization are common denominators for many of the subjects, who nevertheless assign different interpretations and meanings to them. There is little uniformity in the narrated experiences even in response to shared conditions. *Ciudadano N* represents a unique attempt to record the voices of a large number of city residents. It is a self-conscious and conscientious effort to condense and juxtapose their stories in such a way that it preserves the autonomy of each one. This design challenges the search for coherence that the act of reading most often implies, and it discourages an easy identification with or sentimentalization of the characters who comprise these "chronicles of diversity." It also counters the facile stereotyping that Reguillo has studied and critiqued in Mexican press accounts of urban youth, in particular.[8]

In a 2002 interview, Reguillo said that the two major components of her research projects are statistical analysis and narrative, both informed by a rigorous engagement with theory. "Our challenge is to move at two levels at once. One level is the analysis of structure, which is to say the analysis of the big picture, the statistical analysis. In this day and age, statistics are a fundamental and necessary element of understanding world configurations. But this alone is not enough . . . It's also important to look at the ethnography of daily life, the smaller story. My epistemological and methodological position is this: neither the story without the structure, nor the structure without the story" (Jaramillo Hoyos 3). *La construcción simbólica de la ciudad: Sociedad, desastre y comunicación* [The symbolic construction of the city: society, disaster and communication], Reguillo's study of the 1992 gas explosions in Guadalajara, manifests this determination to "move at two levels at once" in order to achieve a comprehensive perspective on events which bridges the global structures and the language of local barrios. The book was published within four years of the disaster, which means that its research and writing were carried out with the urgency and intensity of many chronicles of crisis, notwithstanding the meticulous theoretical work that frames its analysis of how civil society, government, and the media respond to catastrophe. In fact, Reguillo had already collaborated in an even more immediate project treating the explosions, a co-edited volume of essays and chronicles titled *Quien nos hubiera dicho* [1993, Who could have told us]. Both titles respond to a single imperative: "Asumir de frente el compromiso y el reto de registrar la sociedad, para no sólo contar lo que pasó, sino entender lo que pasó" (*Construcción* 19). [To meet head on the commitment and the challenge to register society, not only to tell what happened, but to understand it.] In-depth investigation rigorously informed by a profound knowledge and application of social theory distinguishes Reguillo's writings on disaster from other, more journalistic forms of the chronicle of crisis.

La construcción simbólica de la ciudad has seen two reprintings, and the 2005 edition carries a new introduction that resituates the 1996 study in a post-September 11 world. In introducing the first edition of her book, Reguillo emphasized that the magnitude and the impact of the

Guadalajara explosions demanded both immediate action and thoughtful, longer-term analysis, and that disasters often lay bare the internal contradictions of the society that produces them. These are her points of departure for undertaking a study of the sociopolitical dimensions of disaster and especially the solidarity that arose among the affected populations in Guadalajara. In 2005, the researcher acknowledges that intervening events and the changing conditions of urban life have served to erode the outrage that inspired collective action and grassroots organizing against the political status quo in spring 1992. The increased sense of fear and defenselessness experienced by many sectors of society and in many countries since September 11, 2001, the public's short memory, and the government's power to assert its version of the past against alternative versions combine to pose a threat to the community-building and the sense of solidarity across social boundaries that tend to arise in the aftermath of catastrophe. These developments create a pressing need for writing that registers the chronicler's early immersion in the immediacy of events, as well as the researcher's extended reflection on their meanings. In the new introduction, Reguillo also states explicitly her interest in social change and her perception that disruptive events such as wars or disasters can potentially engender a new order. When the continuity of experience is profoundly disturbed, individuals and communities undergo a sense of loss of the past and uncertainty about the future. Familiar ways of thought and established relationships are shaken, and the immediate aftermath is a time of tension and of negotiation and activism toward constructing the future. Reguillo calls this period an "intermediate space" and she estimated it to have lasted for about six months after the gas explosions. Her study focuses on this time period during which new forms of civil society emerged and old practices of defending the status quo and the institutions of authority persisted and defended themselves (*Construcción* 2005, 18).[9]

The presence of the chronicle form as a component of an anthropological study is most clearly seen in chapters three and four of *La construcción simbólica de la ciudad*. These two chapters narrate, document, and analyze the sequence of events and the efforts toward community organization that began on April 22, 1992, and the particular ways in which belonging to a given urban space or neighborhood shapes a person's daily life and social relations. Reguillo identifies the source materials that she employs throughout the book in chapter two, and these include her own direct observation, in-depth interviews, video-recorded material, her personal field journal, and press accounts of the disaster (98–99). In the narrative reconstruction of the events and in the accompanying analysis in chapters three and four, there is a complex intersection of the voices of the affected population, the perspective of other people who became involved in the matter, and the vision of the researcher herself (128). On the first page of chapter three, "Conciencia sacudida. Cronología de un desastre" [Shaken consciousness. Chronology of a disaster], Reguillo reiterates the crucial acknowledgment that the account of events given by its eyewitnesses and its protagonists is already an interpretation, and this interpretation is built upon the subject's position with regard to the event as well as his or her direct or indirect experience of it (127). Paul Ricoeur's thesis that all human subjects create meaning through storytelling and that our experience is shaped by the narratives that are available to us, is highly relevant here. In examining portions of these two chapters of Reguillo's book as a form of the chronicle, I will identify traces of the process of meaning-making undertaken by the social actors interviewed, and the narrative devices employed by the writer to structure the overall meaning that she draws from her encounter with diverse languages and perspectives in the months following the explosions.

Roughly the first twenty-five pages of chapter three comprise a combination of chronicle and analysis under the heading "La emergencia" [The emergency], while in the final ten to twelve pages, "La batalla por la historia" [The battle for history], the discourse of social science analysis predominates. In contrast to other contemporary chronicles, Reguillo's "chronology of a disaster" does not present a visible I-narrator whose subjectivity is clearly on display. The chronicler, assuming the role of a scientist, positions herself as an observer, an interlocutor, and a reader who gathers, deconstructs, and reassembles information produced by others. The predominance of an impersonal register can be seen in the high frequency of use of the "se"-passive verb forms, while the occasional use of the first-person plural merely emphasizes the absence of an individualized first-person narrative voice. Nevertheless, the chapter is structured in accordance with an interpretative design that emerges from the researcher's active engagement with her source materials and with social and cultural theory. The main thrust of chapter three is to show how the explosions served as a catalyst for articulating a series of grievances against the government, how the affected population briefly came together to make a series of demands and then split into several groups in conflict with each other, and how the authorities initially failed to grasp and manage the situation, but eventually regrouped and reassumed control of the process of investigation, reconstruction, and interpretation. The official government report on the disaster, issued well after the initial activism had lost its momentum, assigned no blame and freed all of those who had been accused of responsibility. Reguillo's analysis of civil society's largely unsuccessful attempt to organize for change in Guadalajara in 1992 concludes that a number of factors combined to diminish the effectiveness of grassroots efforts toward social change. The lengthy process itself discouraged individuals from continuing to press their demands, the government successfully divided the groups against each other, and the January 1, 1994 rebellion in Chiapas and the upcoming national elections diverted public and media attention toward new concerns. Ultimately, as Carlos Monsiváis found in San Juan de Ixhuatepec, time is a strong ally of those who hold power. Their control of material resources, media access, and the legal and bureaucratic structures necessary to defend their position permits them to make the official version of history prevail.

In spite of the careful erasure of the most obvious signs of the chronicler's presence and the blending of diverse sources into a coherent narrative, a clear pattern of meaning is established in favor of the affected population in their conflict with the authorities. Two narrative devices in particular contribute to this effect. First, Reguillo inserts into her chronology a variety of directly quoted materials that she has selected but presumably has not rewritten. A limited number of testimonial passages transcribed from interviews convey the urgency of the lived experience and create sympathy for the victims of the disaster. Examples of official reports, on the other hand, betray a bureaucratic culture that reduces a complex reality to a set of quantifiable and strangely equivalent categories: numbers of the dead and wounded are listed on a par with the number of houses destroyed and vehicles lost. The reproduction of political cartoons and the text of leaflets distributed at demonstrations in the aftermath of the explosions illustrate that the initial media and public response to key incidents was highly critical of the political leadership and their actions. By thus laying bare the heterogeneity of her sources, Reguillo participates in a tradition of chronicle-writing whose best-known practitioners include Elena Poniatowska and Carlos Monsiváis.

A second and highly effective editorializing device is the insertion of subtitles throughout the chapter. The tenor of the subtitles is more explicitly emotional and judgmental than the language of most of the sections of the narrative, and, like the inclusion of eye-witness testimony, they shape our reading in the direction of sympathy for the affected population and skepticism toward the government. Highly charged phrases such as the examples that follow appear across a few pages of text, and their cumulative effect supports the conclusions that have been derived from the process of research and analysis: "En las entrañas de la tierra, la tragedia se agita" [128, In the bowels of the earth, the tragedy stirs]; "¿Por qué nadie nos dijo nada?" [129, Why didn't anyone warn us?]; "La pesadilla estalla" [130, The nightmare erupts]; and "Culpabilización itinerante" [131, Wandering process of blame]. These subtitles invite the reader to consider the dreadful nature of the events that are to be represented (tragedy, nightmare); and they also point toward the irresponsibility of the authorities and their ultimate impunity. As subtitles, they frame the narrative in an active, informing sense of the verb "to frame," and they are a clear sign of the chronicler's shaping subjectivity.

Chapter four, "Bautizarse en abril. Territorio, percepción y nacimiento de la organización" [April baptism (or baptism by fire). Territory, perception and the birth of organizing] departs from the premise that "los actores sociales ordenan su relación con el mundo a partir de su pertenencia a un territorio" [165, Social actors order their relationship with the world on the basis of their territorial affiliation]. Given that the physical space that one inhabits helps to determine a particular form of daily life and contributes to an individual's understanding of the larger social world, Reguillo analyzes the early efforts at organizing as a function of the affected population's relationship to their neighborhoods. Analco, the oldest neighborhood, is the primary object of study, while the newer subdivisions of Quinta Velarde, Atlas, and Olímpica are brought in for purposes of comparison and contrast. All of these neighborhoods are socially and economically different one from the other, and each one also encompasses an internally heterogeneous population. Reguillo strives to account for difference as well as commonality of perception and response to the disaster by focusing on the most heavily damaged area, Analco.

Roughly the first ten pages of the thirty-page chapter map the most important community spaces and collective experiences of the residents of Analco before and after the explosions. The markets, the churches, the main streets. and people's homes were the central locales that defined the neighborhood in the years before April 22, 1992. These were the stages for special events such as Christmas season *posadas*, weddings, and funerals, and here the relative tranquility and stability of the daily routine of work, domestic life, worship, and sociality were experienced. After the explosions, both the heavily damaged or destroyed spaces, and whatever buildings remained standing, acquired new uses and new meanings. Churches became shelters, homes became centers for organizing, the streets became places to eat and sleep. The memory of how things were "before" creates a powerful tie to a radically disrupted geography of "home," and the experience of dramatic and sudden loss drives the transformation of Analco from a typically complacent urban neighborhood to a site of organizing and protest for material, political, and legal reparations.

Much of chapter four has the textual quality of a chronicle due to three elements: the chronological component of "before and after" that structures the narrativizing of space, the inclusion of fragments of testimonies, and the skillful employment of free indirect style in the telling of the story. I will focus on this third element that strongly informs the description of the Analco of the recent past and that of the stunned narrative present. To a greater degree than what is apparent in other chapters of the book, the narrative voice in "Bautizarse en abril" subtly adopts the speech patterns of the residents whom Reguillo interviewed, and their voices are woven into a powerfully conversational account. In the introduction to the chapter, an impersonal "we" presents the working hypothesis and the organization of the study to follow. However, under the rubric of a "dense description" of Analco, there is an almost immediate change in the narrative voice. This section starts by orienting the readers to the main streets of Analco and the extent of their destruction. Emotionally charged phrases such "lo demás es silencio" and "Todo es desolación" [167, the rest is silence; everything is desolation] signal the shift to a highly subjective point of view. In the following pages, the use of free indirect style creates the illusion that the residents are speaking to the readers without the mediation of a narrator: "La vida en el barrio era tranquila, bonita, sabrosa. Claro que con el traslado de la Central Camionera, pues mucha de la actividad económica se acabó" [167–68, Life in the neighborhood was peaceful, pleasant, very nice. Of course, with the bus station's moving out, well, a lot of the economic activity disappeared]. Throughout this section markers of informal speech such as "claro" and "pues" [sure, well]; the emphatic "sí;" the deictics "aquí," "allá," "antes," "ahora" [here, there, before, now]; and the use of diminutives pepper the narrative even when witnesses are not being directly quoted. The use of free indirect style transforms what would otherwise be an impersonal inventory or map of Analco into the record of a lived geography whose destruction is deeply felt. Reguillo's subsequent analysis of the residents' unwillingness simply to move away and her account of the organizing activities that they undertook to demand reparations and to influence the reconstruction of Analco are persuasively framed by this chronicle of loss.

Taken as a whole, *La construcción simbólica de la ciudad* is a detailed and theoretically sophisticated record and analysis of the disaster that occurred in Guadalajara on April 22, 1992 and the processes of social change and institutional resistance and inertia that followed. I have been primarily interested in the sections of two chapters that intersect with the practice of the chronicle in contemporary Mexico. Nevertheless, the largest portion of the book is a socio-anthropological analysis and not a chronicle. It illuminates the ways in which social institutions and actors who exist in unequal relations of power negotiate order out of disorder in the aftermath of crisis. A fundamental tension can be documented between those forces that struggle to reinterpret and thereby challenge the prior order and those that strive to restore the status quo during a period of transition that Reguillo calls the intermediate space. Chapter two of the book gives an overview of the work of the social science theorists whom Reguillo finds to be most helpful and provocative in carrying out this kind of study. Her working hypothesis, regarding the confrontation between the civilians residing in Analco and the institutionalized power of the government and industry, is based on a complex synthesis and critique of an extensive body of theory. Foremost among the names cited in chapter two and throughout the book are Victor Turner, Anthony Giddens, Francesco Alberoni, Pierre Bourdieu, Georges Balandier, and Jüren Habermas, but this list is far from being comprehensive. I point this out not to engage in a discussion of Reguillo's theoretical grounding, but simply to acknowledge again the difference between her limited employment of the chronicle as part of a larger research project, and the more typical journalistic chronicle as a text that is presumed to be complete in and of itself. In *La construcción simbólica de la ciudad*, the chronicle proves to be a flexible and effective textual practice for recording the perceptions of the social actors whose organizing efforts are the object of the study, as well as the researcher's interactions with them. In addition to chronicling disaster, however, Reguillo subjects the discourses of crisis, disorder, and return to order to a careful, systematic scrutiny under the light of social theory. This highly elaborated dimension of her work responds to the imperative that she succinctly expresses at the end of chapter three: "El desastre entonces no se agota en su propia naturaleza, ni en un dictamen, ni en el aparente triunfo de la impunidad. Los procesos desatados por el 22 de abril exigen rescatar lo que subyace a lo aparente" [161–62, Disaster, then, does not exhaust itself in its own nature, nor in one report, nor in the apparent triumph of impunity. The processes unleashed by April 22 demand that we rescue what lies beneath the surface].

Reguillo's investigation draws other meanings from April 22, 1992 that are not limited to impunity, governmental reassertion of control, a return to the status quo and the failure of grassroots activism. Her work shows that in the intermediate space of April to October 1992, diverse sectors of civil society in Guadalajara engaged in a reinterpretation of familiar structures of urban life and politics and posed a significant challenge to entrenched authorities and what is usually taken for granted about their hegemony. They did this in ways that could not have been foreseen absent the occurrence of a disruptive, traumatic event. Their activities can be seen as part of a long, at times imperceptible process of transformation of society, including transformation of the relationship between the governed and the government, and between individuals and their communities. All of the social theorists quoted by Reguillo view society as a living, dynamic web of relationships in which a variety of forces exert pressure toward stability or toward change. Reguillo's study, in spite of the conclusion that time was the ally of the powerful and that the grassroots movements largely failed to achieve their ambitious objectives, also reveals a great deal about how change takes place and what factors block change. The activism of 1992 may have set the stage for future social movements by modeling new forms of civil society's participation in more democratic structures and by transforming individual and collective consciousness in subtle ways. *La construcción simbólica de la ciudad* contributes to the realization of that potential by making a unique contribution to our understanding of the complex cultural meanings and repercussions of disaster.

Carlos Monsiváis and Rossana Reguillo have produced chronicles of catastrophe that are striking both for the similarities between the events and the themes portrayed and for the methodological differences that define each work's unique textuality. Monsiváis provides the canonical model of literary journalism in Mexico, while Reguillo, belonging to a younger generation much influenced by the monsivaisian chronicle, relocates the form into a social science discourse that is quite distinct from the genre's customary home on the pages of the newspaper. The versatility and adaptability of the chronicle make it an ideal writing practice to respond to a variety of events and historical figures and to convey diverse voices and perspectives in their engagement with the real. In the next chapter, I expand on this understanding of the chronicle by reading four prominent writers' representations of a contemporary subject of history and an object of media fascination, the Zapatista leader Subcomandante Marcos.

6

Making History

Subcomandante Marcos in the Mexican Chronicle

> La máscara y la apertura de su discurso [de Marcos] permiten que cada quien le asigne su destino favorito.
>
> —Juan Villoro, "Los convidados de agosto"[1]

Disaster and politics are intimately related, as we have seen in the previous chapter's discussion of two chronicles about (un)natural catastrophe and its human consequences. In this chapter I will continue the study of the contemporary chronicle and politics by examining a manifestation of one of the genre's principal contributions to public discourse in Mexico: the representation of new social movements and political crises from a nongovernmental perspective. The student movement of 1968 initiated a significant disruption in middle-class complacency with the social and political status quo of 1940 to 1968 as defined by the ruling party (PRI, Partido Revolucionario Institucional) and the myth of the "Mexican Miracle." In the face of an authoritarian and monologic one-party regime, the students demanded a dialogue with the government and a more open democracy. In the realm of literature, *La noche de Tlatelolco*, Elena Poniatowska's 1971 oral history of the movement, is widely acknowledged to have reinvigorated chronicle-writing and inspired a generation of journalists in the 1970s and 80s. By preserving a detailed, well-documented account of the goals of the student movement, the government's rejection of dialogue and the violent repression that led to the October 2, 1968 massacre of demonstrators in the Plaza de las Tres Culturas, Poniatowska's book effectively resisted and unmasked governmental censorship and the silencing of the voices of the movement after October 2. *La noche de Tlatelolco* has few peers as a monument to the contestatory power of nonfiction writing, but in the 1970s, 80s, and 90s other important books of chronicles also aimed to realize this potential by narrating critical moments in a changing society. Poniatowska's *Fuerte es el silencio* documents social movements such as land invasions and urban guerrilla groups, and both Poniatowska and Carlos Monsiváis published widely-read chronicles about the 1985 Mexico City earthquakes in *Nada, nadie: Las voces del temblor* and *Entrada libre*, respectively. Like the treatment of the gas explosions studied in the previous chapter, the earthquake chronicles combine a narrative of disaster with an analysis of the civil response to crisis and a critique of the government's handling of the emergency. The hybrid nature of the chronicle is fully exploited in all of these texts in order to balance the narrative and analytical elements.

When the history of Mexico's transition from the twentieth to the twenty-first century is written, the Mayan uprising in Chiapas will be a key episode of the national narrative. The surprising incursion into four Chiapan cities by the Zapatista Army (Ejército Zapatista de Liberación Nacional or EZLN) early on New Year's Day 1994, the government's military response to the rebellion, and the mobilization of civil society in support of the rebels and their spokesperson Subcomandante Marcos opened what many observers saw as a new chapter in the long, fraught story of the Mexican nation's relationship to its own indigenous population. Although the armed phase of the rebellion lasted only twelve days and ended with a cease-fire called by the government of then-President Carlos Salinas, the often interrupted process of negotiations over indigenous rights to land and local self-rule, the intensive militarization of Chiapas, and the response by Mexicans from all over the country to the Zapatista call for a truly democratic and multiethnic society are still unfolding.

Future historians will rely on verbal and visual documents of many kinds to create their interpretative versions of a past that Mexico is still living. At a decade's or a century's remove from current events, the researcher investigating the Zapatista movement in search of its inner dynamics and its lasting significance will necessarily refer to contemporary representations of its events and its cast of characters—representations that are already a mediated, interpretative retelling of "the real thing." Among these documents, the prolific output of letters, communiqués, speeches, manifestos, interviews, and short stories signed by Subcomandante Marcos in his starring media role are certain to figure prominently. Marcos's writings, brilliantly disseminated through selected print media outlets and through the Internet since the earliest days of the rebellion, combine the art of representing the collective experience and aspirations of the indigenous communities of Chiapas with the art of self-representation.[2] The skillfully deployed combination of self-effacing subordination to the community that he serves and his individual charisma has made the rebel leader into a source of fascination, speculation and admiration in Mexico and around the world. Who is Marcos, the masked, pipe-smoking, Borges-quoting guerrilla on horseback, who uses presence and absence, speech and silence equally effectively as instruments of publicity and persuasion? Politicians, pundits, and ordinary citizens alike have been asking themselves that question for more than a decade now, and the answers they have formulated are many and contradictory.

Journalists, in particular, have written and rewritten Marcos at a feverish pace since January 1, 1994, and their published articles and interviews comprise both a resource for contemporary readers, and an ever-growing archive of so-called primary texts for future students of Mexican history. This chapter focuses on a very small selection of writings about Marcos and the EZLN by four widely-published Mexican chroniclers, Carlos Monsiváis, Elena Poniatowska, Juan Villoro, and Alma Guillermoprieto.[3] I have chosen to address chronicles that document three key moments: the Convención Nacional Democrática [National Pro-Democracy Convention] of August 1994; the "unmasking" of Marcos by the Mexican government at a press conference on February 9, 1995; and reassessments of the EZLN and Marcos in 1999 and 2000. The articles catch Marcos engaged in his own acts of self-representation, and they offer a variety of interpretations of their meanings. In the process of inscribing these events and the figure of Marcos into the broader cultural narrative, the four writers make an important contribution to the tradition of the political chronicle in Latin America. To a significant extent, the motifs of masks, theatricality, and spectacle recur in all of the texts, which offer both a representation of a specific movement and its leadership, and another way of addressing the perennial quest for an authentic national identity in Mexico that resonates, as I will show, with Octavio Paz's seminal essay *The Labyrinth of Solitude*.

The chronicle may be an ideal vehicle for writing Marcos and the Zapatistas into Mexican history. Its flexible, hybrid form and the frequent code shifting that mixes oral and written language, popular and elite culture, and essayistic, narrative and dramatic structures, define a heterogeneous textuality that is well-suited to Marcos's protean and elusive persona, and equally appropriate for the movement's ambitious demands for an inclusive, multiethnic, and multilingual society. Chronicles, or texts reclassified as chronicles years after their writing, have served as primary source material for Mexican historiographers since the colonial period.[4] The chronicles under study in this chapter speak directly to readers seeking to learn something true or factual about Marcos and the EZLN. That is, like history writing, chronicles invite their readers to receive their messages with an eye toward information as well as artistry. However, to recall Hayden White's groundbreaking work on the "tropics" of all narrative discourses, theorists of history writing must constantly grapple with the tension between a recognition of the provisional, constructed, and value-laden nature of written histories, and a fundamental reluctance to concede history entirely to the realm of unknowability. That is, most writers and theorists of history, while acknowledging the selective process and the figurative elements of its many manifestations, yet preserve a belief in the referential quality and the truth-seeking ideal that historiography aims to inscribe. With this in mind, the analysis of the contemporary chronicle may rightfully focus on the ways in which the chronicler has emplotted the facts and configured the events into a coherent, meaningful story that is never simply a transparent record.[5] Such an approach honors the analytical and critical impulse that informs chronicle writing itself.

The chronicles of the EZLN inevitably and logically refer to phenomena of theatricality and masking in their portrayal of a movement that has relied in part on the spectacle of mass mobilizations and street demonstrations and whose members wear black ski masks in all public appearances. Theatricality is a key concept in the pieces by Carlos Monsiváis, Juan Villoro, and Alma Guillermoprieto, (but less so in Elena Poniatowska's text), although the meanings that the writers attach to spectacle and to the mask are variable.[6] In a worldwide context, anthropologists who study the role of masks in human societies find certain common functions across many cultures, especially polytheistic cultures. A. David Napier's 1986 book *Masks, Transformations, and Paradox* establishes that masks are connected with phenomena of categorical change, and therefore they predominate during experiences of transition such as rites of passage, curative ceremonies, and funerary rites.

"Masks . . . testify to an awareness of the ambiguities of appearance and to a tendency toward paradox characteristic of transitional states," because masks are a medium for exploring boundaries and challenging fixed identities (Napier xxiii). Donning a mask is not a simple act of covering one's face, but a substitution of a new face and a new identity for the wearer. Modern Western culture, with its basis in monotheism, is suspicious of masks, seeing them as an expression of what is false and disingenuous in contrast to the authenticity of the human face and the stability of the single omniscient deity (Napier 2–4). Human identity is conceived as sameness to oneself, and the face is the primary identity marker in our culture, a culture that privileges the truth value of what can be seen. In contrast, a culture based in polytheism, with its division of powers, lack of a single figure of absolute authority, and potential for conflicts among the deities, often uses masks to assert control over an uncertain and unpredictable reality (Napier 5). Donald Cordry in *Mexican Masks* points out that pre-Hispanic Mesoamerican cultures held that the wearing of a mask removed the face and thus the identity and soul of the wearer and temporarily substituted a new face. This new identity, usually fashioned in the image of the deities, was believed to allow the wearer to exert control over the forces of nature in order to benefit human welfare, and it was therefore associated with power (Cordry 3–4). The tension between the idea of a mask as something false and untrustworthy, and yet also as something powerful and transformative, is at play in the four chroniclers' reactions to the masks worn by the Zapatistas and in particular by Subcomandante Marcos. The anonymity conferred by the ski mask when worn as a means of self-protection from the threatening, identifying gaze of the state is another factor to be considered.

Theatricality in the Latin American political sphere has taken on a highly negative connotation in many countries due to the recognition of the ways in which authoritarian regimes have successfully used the spectacle and theatricality of disappearance, mass meetings, and military display to maintain control over their populations. Diana Taylor's book *Disappearing Acts* on Argentina in the 1970s and 80s is one example of an analysis of how theatricality was used as an instrument of repression by the military junta. However, theater and spectacle may also be used to challenge structures of authority. In Mexico, the street theater that developed during the student movement of 1968, the figure of Superbarrio (also a masked man), and the cabaret-style shows of Jesusa

Rodríguez are a few examples of oppositional political theater. Likewise, the activities organized by the Zapatistas use theater to speak *to* power from a position of marginality, rather than as a practice of speaking *from* a position of power in order to maintain established forms of control. The manipulation of the scene and the wearing of masks become subversive strategies, which are either liberating and empowering, or threatening and dangerous depending on the perspective of the observer. Those seeking change may welcome this nonviolent form of challenging authority, while those like the Mexican government whose authority is at stake, will likely respond with scorn or even with violence.

A major event of the first year of the Zapatista uprising was the August 6–9, 1994 National Pro-Democracy Convention (CND) organized by the EZLN and held in the Lacandon rainforest. The purpose of the CND was to engage various sectors of civil society in a wide-ranging dialogue on democracy, justice, the rights of indigenous peoples, and civil rights in general in Mexico. To that end, roughly six thousand grassroots activists, academics, university students, members of NGOs, feminists, labor leaders, veteran members of the political left, and journalists were invited to an unprecedented encounter with an outlawed guerrilla group in open rebellion against the government. The first full day of the Convention was spent in San Cristóbal de las Casas, where there was a series of workshops and debates on the current crisis in Chiapas and in Mexican national politics. Then after a nearly twenty-four-hour bus trip into Zapatista-controlled territory in the mountains, the participants spent two days of speeches, discussions, and rudimentary eco-tourism at a hastily built "convention center" carved out of the rainforest and significantly named Aguascalientes, after the city where Mexico's 1914 constitutional convention was held. The convention chronicles written by Carlos Monsiváis, Elena Poniatowska, and Juan Villoro narrate the trajectory of the CND according to each writer's individual perspective. All of them refer to some extent to the journey itself, the makeup and motives of the participants, the encounter with the EZLN soldiers and their civilian supporters, the program of speeches and discussions, and the now legendary deluge of rain that put an early end to the proceedings shortly after Subcomandante Marcos's long-awaited speech on the night of August 8. Their versions of the convention engage to varying degrees the themes of masks and theatricality in Mexican society, and they suggest much about the three writers' own hopes and doubts about the Zapatista movement and their nation's future through the meanings that they attach to the figure of Marcos and to the popular response to him.

Carlos Monsiváis published "Crónica de una convención (que no lo fue tanto) y de un acontecimiento muy significativo" [Chronicle of a convention (that really wasn't) and of a very significant happening] in the weekly news magazine *Proceso* on August 15, 1994, and it was reprinted in the anthology of Zapatista documents, *EZLN: Documentos y comunicados I* in the same year. The title, with its parenthetical negative qualification of the convention "que no lo fue tanto" and the following affirmation that something significant did nevertheless happen there, prepares the reader for Monsiváis's highly skeptical and yet also hopeful take on the CND. The tone of the text thus recalls the chronicles collected in *Entrada libre*. Both Linda Egan and Anadeli Bencomo have read the earlier volume, with its emphasis on politics and grassroots organizing, as a cautiously optimistic take on the emergence of civil society after the 1985 Mexico City earthquakes (Egan 197–200; Bencomo 142–45). In *Escenas de pudor y liviandad* (1988) and *Los rituales del caos* (1995), in contrast, Monsiváis turns his attention to official culture, popular culture, and consumer society in what Bencomo sees as a renunciation of the civic and political commitment that is conveyed in *Entrada libre* and, I would add, is apparent again in his EZLN/Marcos writings.

To open "Crónica de una convención" the narrator composes a verbal wide-angle photo of the diverse groups who gathered in the new Aguascalientes. In the center of that image is the EZLN—two hundred soldiers, leaders, and civilian members of Zapatista communities—flanked by six thousand invited participants. Monsiváis offers the word picture as a way of fixing in the collective memory the hopes for peace, tolerance, and the continuing mobilization of civil society that the experience of the CND seemed to synthesize, just as the photo synthesizes the diverse "paisaje humano" [human landscape] that Mexico is and is not (313). After the opening shot, Monsiváis emplots the events of August 6–9 in the form of a chronological narrative. In contrast to the static "family photo" at the beginning, the narrative is dynamic, tracing continuous movement from the chaos and confusion of the day of gathering in San Cristóbal, to the exhausting tedium of the bus caravan into the jungle, the long wait on August 8 for the proceedings to begin, the climactic excitement and solidarity created by Marcos's speech, a sudden, torrential storm, the wet, interminable night spent under inadequate shelter, and the premature denouement of the convention on the morning of

August 9 under the threat of returning rains. Two constants define the reigning tension between exasperation and hope throughout Monsiváis's text: his unrelenting ridicule of the far left ("los ultras") and its shouted dogma and divisive politics; and his praise for the solidarity of the convention participants and the EZLN's offer of dialogue. The inclusion of the phrase "militantes de la izquierda de la izquierda de la izquierda" (313) [militants to the left of the left of the left] in the list of convention attendees introduces a concise and effective bit of sarcasm aimed at the traditional left very early in the chronicle. Later, Monsiváis continues his long time disparagement of the "canibalismo de las izquierdas" (315) [cannibalism of the left] and of those whose unremitting anger, self-righteous posturing, constant interruptions, and monopolization of the microphone are an enduring obstacle to substantive political dialogue. The narrator summarizes his rejection of their manichean world view thus: "Mientras ellos griten y no dejen hablar, el mundo, dividido desde el génesis entre revolucionarios y traidores, seguirá en su sitio" (315). [While they shout and don't let anyone else speak, the world, divided from the beginning into revolutionaries and traitors, will remain unchanged.] However, the narrator recognizes that the CND was not ultimately dominated by the "ultras," and other voices were heard—those of women, gays, lesbians, and, most importantly, those of the Zapatistas' indigenous members and supporters. A large portion of the second half of the chronicle borrows language from Marcos's communiqués and his August 8 speech, seamlessly incorporating his words into the text while easing off of the sarcastic tone directed at "the left of the left of the left."

The chronicle's narrative voice remains true to the persona that Monsiváis created for himself throughout many years of observing and recording the political and cultural life of Mexico. Part expert witness, part critic, part ironist, and part professional skeptic, the narrator portrays what the other participants do and say from a distance, always minimizing the degree of his own active engagement. When he does appear directly on the page as a participant and not solely a witness of the events, he is quick to point out his own failings and record his irritation in a self-deprecating manner. For example, we learn that Monsiváis is inexplicably denied entry to a debate during the day spent in San Cristóbal; then he gets lost looking for his bus, he sleeps very badly on the long ride, he trips over a rock and sprains his ankle upon arriving in Aguascalientes, grows impatient with the lack of organization, complains about the "hospitality" afforded by the convention's hosts, and mumbles sarcastic asides during the speeches to register and reinforce his skepticism. Neither prepared nor predisposed to be an eco-tourist, the Mexico City intellectual spares no one, not even himself, from his critical wit. At the level of the language of the text, a reliance on numerous distancing ploys also bolsters the narrative stance. A signature monsivaisian verbal tic is the use of parenthetical statements to self-correct or fine-tune key ideas, so that everything observed is qualified and judged, portrayed with reservations and ambivalence. His texts make very few claims without also stating an alternative, even an opposite interpretation.

The description of Marcos and his speech before the assembly offers a good illustration of how the narrator positions himself vis-à-vis the events and the people around him and his tendency to qualify and self-correct: "El turno en el podio es de Marcos. El instante es eléctrico, o así lo proclaman los rostros iluminados al ver que, por lo menos en esta magna alegoría, se cumple lo esperado desde 1914, o alguna otra fecha legendaria . . . El anfiteatro por así decirlo se vuelve una sola persona. A estas alturas ya no sé el significado de 'carismático' " (320). [It is Marcos's turn at the podium. The moment is electric, *or so* the shining faces proclaim it to be upon seeing that, *at least* in this supreme allegory what they have been waiting for since 1914, *or some other* legendary date, has come to pass . . . The *so-called* ampitheater turns into one single person. At this point *I no longer know* the meaning of "charismatic." My emphasis.] In this brief excerpt, one can see the characteristic use of the conjunction "or," and hedging phrases such as "at least" and "so-called" to qualify and complicate even the most basic details, including the narrator's understanding of the clichéd term "charismatic." The passage further shows how the event of Marcos's speech and by association the Mexican Revolution through the reference to 1914 are cast in theatrical terms (podium, allegory, ampitheater). This same tendency is pervasive in the novel of the Mexican Revolution, which often emphasizes the theatricality of the revolutionary struggle and its charismatic leaders (Pancho Villa, Emiliano Zapata), as can be seen in Mariano Azuela's *Los de abajo* and Martín Luis Guzmán's *El águila y la serpiente*. In other parts of the chronicle Monsiváis describes the parade of EZLN members and the passing of the national flag from Marcos to Rosario Ibarra as elements of an impressive spectacle. During the press conference held on the final day, Marcos offers to remove his mask, but the crowd shouts an emphatic, unanimous "No!" "Marcos sin pasamontañas no es admisible, no es fotografiable, no es la leyenda visible" (323). [Marcos unmasked is inadmissible, unphotogenic, no longer the visible legend.] Here Monsiváis, like Guzmán, implies that Mexicans prefer their reality to be dramatic and their heroes to be legendary, photogenic, disguised, and unknowable. He takes a critical stance toward this tendency to mythologize and thus obscure the nature of charismatic leaders through the uses of language that I have identified.

The narrator predictably stands apart from the electricity generated by Marcos's appearance and from the crowd's coming together into one rapt listener. In Monsiváis's analysis of Marcos's use of symbols (the black ski mask, the pipe, the Mexican flag) and the content of his speech, the chronicler remains aloof and critical, even while dropping hints that he too has somehow been affected by the experience. Monsiváis's chronicle, like the Zapatistas themselves, seems to wear a mask that resists our efforts to discern its message, that is, to see its hidden face/identity. One interpretation of the narrative strategies of distancing and qualification is as a response to the ambiguous nature of leadership within the Zapatista movement. Marcos's masked visibility as spokesperson and the mass embrace of him as the EZLN's leader, his subordinate position as a "subcomandante," and the existence of a governing council from which he claims to receive his directives send a mixed message that may accurately represent a fluid, inclusive structure of power within the popular movement or that may elevate the self-defined servant of the people to a dangerous position of public adulation. The final paragraph makes it clear, however, that it is not Marcos alone who inspires a degree of guarded optimism in Carlos Monsiváis, but rather he places his hope in the mobilization of a much larger community. "El regreso es, necesariamente, agobiante. Pero en los camiones y al paso por los pueblos la esperanza de paz se afirma y disemina. Si esto es así el viaje valió la pena" (323). [The return trip is necessarily exhausting. But on the buses and passing through the towns, the hope for peace is affirmed and disseminated. If so, the trip was worth the trouble.] Outside of the convention itself, in the necessary frame of the surrounding countryside and the small towns where the Zapatistas' supporters live, something important may have indeed happened for the Mexican people and for the chronicler.

Linda Egan describes Monsiváis's cautious, qualified optimism as the sort of optimism that a reader has to dig for in his writing. For fifty years, Monsiváis told the story of moments when Mexican civil society has managed to organize and take control of politics through grassroots movements for democratic change. His writings on the 1968 student movement and the 1985 earthquake are chapters in that story that attest to a deep-rooted but often disappointed faith in democracy. His articles on Marcos, beginning with "Crónica de una convención," start out deeply skeptical, but through time they reveal an ever greater willingness to invest the masked figure with the writer's own best hopes for Mexico. I will return to Monsiváis at the end of the chapter to examine an article and an interview published in 1999 and 2001, in which the chronicler's fascination with the paradoxical nature and the transformative potential of the Zapatista movement are even more clearly expressed.

In contrast to Carlos Monsiváis's diffidence and distance, Elena Poniatowska tells her tale of the convention with her customary enthusiasm for embracing popular struggles for social change in opposition to the established authorities. The author is famous for championing and chronicling socially progressive movements and their leaders, most recently in *Amanecer en el Zócalo* [Dawn in the Zocalo], her diary-chronicle of the Mexico City encampment of July to September 2006 in protest of that year's presidential elections and in support of the defeated Partido Revolucionario Democrático (PRD) candidate Andrés Manuel López Obrador. Her very brief article "La CND: de naves mayores a menores," [The CND: from big ships to little ones] was originally published in *La Jornada* (August 16, 1994) and was also reprinted in *EZLN: Documentos y comunicados I*. It is a more tightly focused narrative than Monsiváis's account. Poniatowska begins with the dramatic finale on August 8 by framing her chronicle with the storm that flooded the convention site that evening and lasted well into the night and the early morning hours. The storm, romantically cast as nature's thunderous and wise reply to Marcos's speech in the ampitheater, puts an early and timely end to the convention, before it could degenerate into a predictable and anticlimactic performance of endless bickering by the left. Personified as a wise and powerful woman, nature "resolvió problemas que la izquierda no ha solucionado en años. Ante todo la paz. Sobre todo la paz" (328). [Nature resolved problems that the left hadn't solved in years. First of all, peace. Above all, peace.] The text ends with the sunshine of the final morning, the prediction of a second storm, and the reluctance of the participants to go on their separate ways. Within this frame Poniatowska places short excerpts from the speeches of August 8 and quick sketches of Subcomandante Marcos and of individual convention participants who tended to the needs of others during the long, dark, muddy hours of the deluge, emphasizing acts of solidarity across boundaries of age, ethnicity, social class, and gender.

The chronicle's overall message is optimistic and the tone is overwhemingly celebratory in its identification and praise of real-life heroes. Marcos is clearly the inspiration for the narrator's hopeful enthusiasm. He is evoked primarily through quotes from his speech, which the narrator characterizes as a model for a new political rhetoric that is young, energetic, even brilliant, and totally different from the old, shop-worn discourse of the Mexican left. Marcos doesn't mention Yankee imperialism or the bourgeoisie, nor does he seek to hold onto power for himself. His expressed desire to pass the baton to civil society and "disappear" from the scene strikes a favorable chord with this chronicler and with others, including the notoriously wary Carlos Monsiváis. Interestingly, Poniatowska's account takes little notice of the famous ski mask or Marcos's dramatic offer to take it off, perhaps because she wishes to trust the spoken word and its transformative power rather than puzzle out the ambiguous function of the mask. Marcos is primarily represented in Poniatowska's chronicle by his language, and not through descriptions of his appearance. The question of theatricality or spectacle is not prominent either, except for the inevitable description of the procession of EZLN members and the references to being in an ampitheater. Poniatowska privileges the perceived authority and authenticity of Marcos's words, and she also emphasizes her witness to the acts of solidarity that many individuals carried out during the storm that followed the speech. She places these actions within the undeniably "real" phenomenon of nature that befell the CND. In this respect, Poniatowska's chronicle contrasts with the work of the other three writers and expresses a significantly less skeptical, less ambivalent reaction to the person or persona of Marcos and the events produced by the Zapatista movement. The narrator also describes the enthusiastic response of the crowd to Marcos, with which she identifies. The unqualified, unreserved collective embrace attests to the same charisma that Monsiváis attributes to Marcos. However, while Monsiváis distances himself from the Zapatista's spell and questions the meaning of charisma in the passage cited earlier, Poniatowska unabashedly writes herself into the highly charged atmosphere in the improvised ampitheater by frequently using the first-person plural form and emphasizing collective actions. Referring to Rosario Ibarra, the human rights activist who was elected president of the convention, Poniatowska writes "Los seis mil la abrazamos con los ojos" (324). [All six thousand of us embraced her with our eyes.] And on the morning after the storm, in spite of the weather forecast, "Todos, absolutamente todos queríamos seguir" (328). [All of us, absolutely all of us wanted to stay.]

In place of the mask, Poniatowska takes up the ship metaphor that Marcos himself employed to describe the convention site in an August 3, 1994 communiqué to four Mexican newspapers and again in his speech on the night of August 8, when he welcomed the assembly to Aguascalientes, Chiapas, "el Arca de Noé, la Torre de Babel, el barco selvático de Fitzcarraldo, el delirio del neozapatismo, el navío pirata" (305). [Noah's Ark, the Tower of Babel, Fitzcarraldo's jungle steamship, the delirium of neozapatismo, the pirate ship.] Poniatowska extends his allusion to Noah's divinely inspired ark and Fitzcarraldo's mad adventure to the more contemporary metaphor of the planet Earth as a ship or a spaceship on which we are all traveling together. This choice of metaphor is another demonstration of how she shapes her version of the events into a meaningful story of solidarity and interdependence. It supports her emplotment of the CND condensed into a narrative of the collective experience of the storm and the flooding and the positive energy of being part of a community, however improvised and temporary. Just as Monsiváis writes Marcos and the convention as another episode in his decades-long narrative of Mexico's halting steps toward democracy, Poniatowska's chronicle can be seen to express one of the constants of her long career as a writer: her desire to belong fully to Mexico, the country that the French-born writer has made her own. For Elena Poniatowska, writing Marcos is one more piece in the puzzle of a national and an individual identity that strives to construct itself around ideals of justice, dignity, and inclusion within a social context of inequality and exclusion.

The third of the *cronistas* who attended the CND is the Mexico City novelist, short story writer and social critic Juan Villoro. A generation younger than Poniatowska and Monsiváis, he grew up reading their work, and his take on Mexican society demonstrates a similar degree of skepticism and irony to Monsiváis's characteristic pose. His book *Los once de la tribu* [Eleven man tribe] compiles a selection of chronicles written from 1987 to 1995 that cover border-crossing popular culture icons (Jane Fonda, JR of *Dallas* fame), sports, literature and, in two articles, the Zapatista movement. In the introduction to the volume Villoro addresses what the chronicle as a genre means to him, echoing many of the ideas already summarized. With a nod to Tom Wolfe, he emphasizes the defining combination of documented facts with the subjective point of view of the narrator and the blend of journalistic and literary devices, as most other chroniclers also do. Like Rossana Reguillo, for whom chronicle writing is an art practiced in the open air, Villoro celebrates the genre's capacity to pull him out of the study and into the street, out of the solitude of writing fiction and into creative collaboration. At the same time and also like Reguillo, who spoke of the chronicle as an "uncomfortable witness to what shouldn't be seen" ("Border(line) Texts" 53), Villoro considers himself to be a "testigo incómodo" [an uncomfortable witness] casting an oblique, personal glance at the world around him (*Los once* 12). His account of the convention and Marcos's role in it illustrates his uneasy witnessing of the newsworthy "real," of which he states that it always happens far away from his own familiar world, in the jungle or in a five-star hotel. I believe that this uneasiness at "covering" the far-away real on assignment from his editors manifests a healthy reluctance to exoticize distant experiences and unknown others. "Los convidados de agosto" reiterates motifs seen in Monsiváis's piece and it connects directly to Villoro's later chronicle on Marcos's putative "unmasking" by the government through the elaboration of the metaphors of masks and the theater.

Villoro's convention chronicle takes its title from from Rosario Castellanos's well-known short story "Los convidados de agosto" [The August guests], creating a link to Mexico's best-known writer about Chiapas and its indigenous peoples. Castellanos's story of an aging "señorita decente" who harbors fading dreams of finding a man to fulfill her repressed desires would seem to have little in common thematically with Villoro's text about the CND. Both pieces, however, reflect on the hopes invested in an encounter with a stranger, and the potential for disappointment and even disaster that might result when a relatively closed community seeks contact with the world outside. Villoro's choice of an epigraph borrowed from the movie *Batman Returns* introduces a note of humor and irony that will permeate the entire text by associating Marcos with the comic book and Hollywood film superhero and therefore putting into immediate doubt any attribution of authenticity to the Zapatista leader: "Me encanta la franqueza de un hombre enmascarado" (259). [The direct approach. I admire that in a man in a mask.][7] From the opening lines Villoro, the uncomfortable witness, distances himself from the emotion of the event through the use of humor and ironic intertextuality. "En mi caso, como en el de tantos otros, operaba el vago protagonismo del testigo. 'Yo estuve ahí. Llámenme Ismael'" (266). [In my case, as in many others, the vague protagonism of the witness was in order. 'I was there. Call me Ishmael.'] In repeating one of the most famous opening lines in Western literature, Villoro ties his narrator to Herman Melville's reluctant, even horrified witness/chronicler to Captain Ahab's mad pursuit of the great white whale, Moby Dick. Melville himself drew upon the ancient stories of the Biblical Ishmael, who was the rejected, exiled son of Abraham according to the Hebrew tradition, and an honored prophet and founder of the Arab peoples according to Islamic teachings. Melville's intertextual gesture places his character ambiguously both outside of and central to the story to be told, a positioning that Villoro adopts for his eyewitness narrator.

Antithesis, at times resulting in paradox, is a hallmark of Villoro's chronicle, and can be seen in the first of its eight subsections. "La comezón de un líder" [A leader's itch] fixes on a trivial detail: the observation of Marcos scratching his nose during his speech before the assembly on August 8. Villoro interprets the scratching and the itch that it betrays as a sign of one—or both—of two alternatives: it might be the only spontaneous, uncontrolled, authentic gesture in the Subcomandante's carefully staged self-presentation, and/or it might be a deliberate gesture of pride and self-sufficiency. Other contradictory and yet not mutually exclusive themes in the article are the extreme human poverty and the enormous natural wealth of Chiapas, Mexico's celebration of indigenous cultures of the past and its contempt for indigenous peoples of the present, the discussion of peace and democracy in a space flanked by two standing armies, and the ultimate paradox of a revolutionary movement that desires to disappear. This final paradox is particularly ironic in the context of a nation whose Revolution of 1910 has remained spectacularly visible in the national politics and culture for one hundred years. The writer's perception and display of the discrepancies that exist between these antithetical realities contribute to the ironic dimension of the chronicle. The theatrical nature of the events of August 6–9 and Marcos's remarkable stage presence also capture Villoro's attention, as was the case for Monsiváis. Villoro states his thesis in plain terms: "la principal función de la guerrilla ha sido representarse a sí misma, poner en escena gestos, disfraces, textos políticos" (262). [The principal function of the guerrilla has been to represent itself, act out gestures, disguises, political texts.] The chronicler proceeds to deconstruct the speeches, props, and masks of the rebel movement and of its most visible, albeit masked leader: poet, bohemian, prophet, San Marcos.

"Los convidados de agosto" is organized as a roughly chronological narrative of the CND that incorporates a critique of the traditional Mexican left, which Villoro, like Monsiváis, detests for being dogmatic and humorless, and that paints an ambivalent portrait of Marcos. Following the opening reference to the assembly on the final night in Aguascalientes, Villoro returns in time to the summer and fall of 1993, when the markets of San Cristóbal de las Casas registered purchases of unusually large quantities of ski masks, olive green pants, and brown shirts. The shopkeepers didn't know that they were outfitting a rebel army, and the representation of the Zapatistas' early mobilization as a stealth operation supports the characterization of Chiapas as a nocturnal animal, waking while the rest of Mexico sleeps ("Convidados" 261). While this metaphor evokes the danger and mystery associated with the jaguar, the EZLN soldiers are later shown to be woefully underarmed and distinctly unthreatening, and not latter-day Jaguar Warriors. The material poverty of the Zapatista army and the youth and the small stature of its soldiers (average height 1.55 meters, average age twenty years), awaken a kind of admiring sympathy in the *chilango* intellectual, who muses "Es dificil imaginar un ejército más precario" (271). [It is difficult to imagine a more precarious army.] Following the initial image of Marcos and the aside regarding the improvised uniforms, the narrator relates his journey to San Cristóbal, the first day of sessions in the provincial capital, the long bus ride and hike to Aguascalientes, and the events of the convention, both human-designed and nature-imposed. In this way, Villoro's chronicle follows a similar narrative trajectory to the texts by Monsiváis and Poniatowska. "Los convidados de agosto" is, however, both longer and more multilayered than the other accounts of the CND. In addition to a strong intertextual component, it alternates between narrative and essayistic passages, all touched by generous doses of irony.

The portrayal of Subcomandante Marcos brings together all of the devices utilized throughout the text. I have already shown the irony created by the trivial and perhaps trivializing detail of the itchy nose. Marcos as a charismatic yet unknown figure, and as a leader who assumes a position of subordination are other features that arouse a kind of suspicious curiosity on the part of the chronicler. This suspicion informs Villoro's troubled response to the "masked man's" undeniable appeal and his ability to hold a crowd in thrall. During Marcos's speech, the narrator observes the effect that his language, the theatricality of his delivery, and his physical appearance have on the six thousand delegates. Refusing to succumb, Villoro dismisses charisma as a "simplification," an inevitable narrowing of the contradictory personality lying behind an attractive facade (274). Recalling Mexico's many charismatic and ultimately unsuccessful political leaders of the past, the weary narrator-witness Juan "Call me Ishmael" Villoro, like Monsiváis, questions this kind of appeal to public trust. On the other hand, like Poniatowska, he glimpses the potential for a different, more positive outcome in the Subcomandante's own, equally impressive capacity for humor and irony, his mastery of political rhetoric, his synthesis of indigenous and Christian parables, and his surprising message of self-cancellation (the oft-stated desire to be rendered unnecessary by an emerging leadership coming from civil society). Resistance and attraction to Marcos and the EZLN are at work throughout Villoro's reflections on the CND.

A persistent subtext of the chronicle is Octavio Paz's essay on "Mexican Masks," chapter two of *The Labyrinth of Solitude*. Villoro initially seems to express the same anxiety over masks as a sign of inauthenticity and weakness that informs Paz's treatise on the Mexican national character. Unlike masks that represent animals or gods or human faces, the ski mask is primarily a way to conceal one's identity, and it does not superimpose a substitute, individual identity on the wearer. The anonymity or emptiness of the ski mask and the openness of Marcos's language invite multiple interpretations as is reflected in the quote from Villoro's work that appears as the epigraph to this chapter. What fate and what identity does Juan Villoro assign to Marcos? On one hand, he credits the Subcomandante and the EZLN with a surprising capacity to survive and resist annihilation, and he sees the rebel leader's talent for communication as the key to this success. On the other hand, in the closing line of "Los convidados de agosto," the chronicler reads Marcos through Rodolfo Usigli's famous "gesticulador" [imposter] César Rubio, the protagonist of his 1947 play *El gesticulador*. Rubio, a failed college professor imposturing as a long-dead Revolutionary general, dies with his "identity" (mask) as a revolutionary hero intact, and his truth (face) forever obliterated. The death of the professor leaves his son (the next generation of Mexicans) in despair over the silencing of truth and the irrecuperability of authenticity. Octavio Paz alludes to *El gesticulador* as an example of the literary expression of the pervasive dissimulation and masking in Mexican culture. Villoro ends his chronicle with the following line that recalls both Usigli and Paz: "Su disfraz se había transformado: la máscara es ya su identidad" (277). [His disguise had been transformed: the mask is now his identity.] This ending may suggest that Marcos is likely to meet the false general's tragic end, demonstrating once again that it is futile to pursue idealistic ends and effect change through a means rooted in theatricality and self-deception. However, Marcos's unusual set of skills, which Villoro also acknowledges, leaves open the possibility that this time a masked, charismatic Mexican revolutionary may be able to engage in a successful play of disguises (poet, bohemian, prophet) that challenges the political status quo in a meaningful way and gives a new and lasting visibility to Mexico's indigenous communities and the struggle for social justice.

Within a year after the start of the uprising in January 1994, negotiations between the government and the Zapatistas had reached a stalemate. Early in 1995 the newly installed government of President Ernesto Zedillo lost no time in moving aggressively against the EZLN which, by some accounts, was losing a measure of its popular appeal after a year of electronic insurgency conducted via the Internet. The most curious—and ultimately least successful—strategy in the new government's anti-Marcos campaign was the public unmasking of the Subcomandante on February 9, 1995 and the formal charge to the nation's security forces to track him down and arrest him. Juan Villoro was again among the throng of journalists at the press conference in Mexico City, covering the latest development for the newspaper *La Jornada*. In "El guerrillero inexistente" [The nonexistent guerrilla], also included in *Los once de la tribu*, Villoro reiterates a key theme of "Los convidados de agosto": the idea that Marcos's mask allows everyone to assign him an identity and a destiny according to their own needs and desires. He lists some of the identities that have been projected onto Marcos: sex symbol, defrocked Jesuit, PhD in sociology, and lyric poet. On the government's part there is a clear desire to discredit the appealing image of Marcos as a mythic hero and recast him as a common criminal complete with a name, passport number, alias, and mug shot. Villoro discerns with absolute clarity the pressing need by those in power to reject and eliminate the paradox of masking, with its potential to make the wearer both visible and invisible and to assume a powerful and transformative identity. In Napier's study of the nature of masks that I referred to earlier, he suggests that when we confront a paradox we must accept the force of ambiguity and the possibility that something is not what it appears to be. Because change always implies that a thing is no longer what it was, our acceptance of change must be accompanied by an embrace of ambiguity. Marcos's mask paradoxically hides and reveals his identity, making him no one and everyone. The Mexican government, unable to accept the dangerous ambiguity of this paradox or to tolerate change, had to attempt to fix and control Marcos, by attaching a personal biography and a face to the masked man. Villoro's article focuses on the government's case for identifying Marcos as Rafael Sebastián Guillén Vicente, the son of a middle-class family and a former university professor of communications in Mexico City, and he exploits the comic backfiring of the clumsily staged unmasking and the government's accusations against him.

Villoro sets the stage for interpreting the meaning of the Zapatista rebellion and the government's attempt at unmasking by describing Mexico's economy and its middle class in late 1993, on the verge of the rebellion. Escalating consumerism, the proliferation of shopping malls, the high cost of locally produced goods, and the plummeting peso expose an image of the "Mexican miracle" that Villoro calls the new Land of Oz. In mimicking and mocking the speech and the consumer habits of his "yupiteca" peers, Villoro pokes fun at his own Coyoacán neighbors, and he also makes himself into one more victim of his ironic stance. The EZLN rebellion is represented in this context as a shocking but necessary wake-up call for the most privileged sectors of Mexican society.

The second half of the chronicle treats the February 9, 1995 news conference by poking fun at the government's use of slides projected on a large screen and the phony buildup of suspense in its presentation of the evidence of Marcos's "real" identity. Villoro emplots the event in the form of a television quiz show, a game of "Guess Who?" in order to mock and trivialize the seriousness of the charges brought against Marcos. Within a day or two of the press conference it is obvious that the government's decision to fight against the mask by an act of unmasking has backfired for a number of reasons that the chronicle's narrator seems delighted to reveal. First, Marcos jumped on the chance to portray himself as a victim of the Mexican army and government repression, and he won back a large measure of public sympathy and support by immediately writing a new letter dispatched from the jungle on February 10. The public response showed that, just as on August 9, 1994, the people did not want to see the "real" face of Marcos, and they reacted negatively to the government's call for his arrest. His mask allows everyone to identify with him and with his call for change, and thousands of people shouted "Todos somos Marcos" [We are all Marcos], at a demonstration in the Zócalo on February 11, 1995 (284). In a further, humorous blow to the government's prosecution of Marcos, under scrutiny Rafael Guillén turned out to be a pretty decent fellow. In fact, the more the public learned about him, the more he seemed to be, in Villoro's words, "el hijo-cuñado-yerno-novio perfecto para la gran Familia Mexicana" (283), [The ideal son, brother-in-law, son-in-law, boyfriend for the great Mexican Family.] With his middle-class roots, his family connections, and his Catholic school diploma and university degrees, Guillén cut a highly attractive figure. In an irony not lost on Villoro, a few days after Marcos was unmasked and "criminalized," a high-ranking appointee in the Ministry of Education was accused of falsely claiming to hold a doctorate for which he had never studied. Fausto Alzati was forced to resign over his fraudulent credentials, and "comparada con la trayectoria de los gobernantes, la vida de Marcos parecía un camino de virtud" (284). [compared to the shennanigans of the government officials, Marcos's life seemed to be a path paved with virtue.]

Toward the end of this very brief, tightly written article, Villoro goes back to the mask motif to remind the reader that in Mexican history masks and legends are more enduring than the long-lost and irretrievable realities that inspired them. The Revolution belongs to Pancho Villa, after all, and not to Doroteo Arango, and also, then, to Marcos, not to the ex-professor of communications, Rafael Sebastián Guillén. The ambivalence of the chronicler's position is not ultimately resolved in the piece, and the negative meanings of masks persist in spite of his ridiculing of Zedillo's ill-advised maneuver. Marcos is declared to be "el guerrillero inexistente," a mask that hides nothing and whose unmasking therefore reveals nothing. Nevertheless, in evoking Pancho Villa, Emiliano Zapata, and Che Guevara—all trinkets with Marcos in an ideological souvenir stand that is humorously described in the opening line of the piece—Villoro attests to the power of masks and myths that makes aspirations to notions of authenticity and fixed identity seem naive and unproductive.[8]

Alma Guillermoprieto was also present at the February 9, 1995 news conference, and she offers her take on "La desenmascarada" in her article of that name, originally written in English and published as "The Unmasking" in *The New Yorker* in March of 1995. Guillermoprieto occupies a unique position among contemporary Mexican chroniclers and her work complements theirs, because she has made a career of interpreting her nation and other Latin American societies for a First-World readership. From 1978 to 1994 the journalist lived for extended periods of time in New York City, Nicaragua, Brazil, and Colombia, and she traveled on assignment to virtually all of the countries of Central and South America. Her lengthy and detailed chronicles of diverse phenomena such as the Brazilian samba, Peruvian politics, the Colombian drug trade, the U.S. invasion of Panama, and Mexican *ranchera* music appeared in *The Guardian*, *The Washington Post*, and, most frequently, *The New Yorker* during that time. Representative selections of her articles have been compiled into a number of books both in the English original and in Spanish translation.[9] In March of 1994 Guillermoprieto returned to Mexico with the idea of taking a sabbatical from journalism and reacquainting herself with daily life in her home country. The assassination of presidential candidate Luis Donaldo Colosio on March 23, coming so soon after the January first Zapatista uprising, pulled her back into writing in order to try to make sense of a seemingly chaotic reality. Her work throughout her career exemplifies the correlation marked in Chapter 1 between experiences of crisis and the documentary impulse. In articles written in Mexico from 1994 to 1997 for *The New Yorker* and the *New York Review of Books* and published in their Spanish version in *Los años en que no fuimos felices: Crónicas de la transición mexicana* and in the English volume *Looking for History*, Guillermoprieto attempts to create order and meaning or at least to ask pertinent questions about the three stunning assassinations of 1993 and 1994 (Cardinal Juan José Posadas, Colosio and PRI secretary general José Francisco Ruiz Massieu), the Chiapas rebellion and the figure of Subcomandante Marcos. She places the unsolved crimes and the unresolved conflict in the context of Mexico's economic crisis, the growing drug trade, and the increasingly apparent disintegration of the PRI's one-party control over Mexican politics. Three of the eight "chronicles of transition," all originally published in *The New Yorker*, portray the EZLN and Marcos: "Los herederos de Zapata" ["Zapata's Heirs," May 16, 1994], "La guerra de las sombras" ["The Shadow War," March 2, 1995] and "La desenmascarada." In her prologue to the book, Guillermoprieto defines the period from 1994 to 1997 as a "new era" for Mexico, one that was initiated by the Zapatista rebellion, but that had its roots in the collective frustration of too many years spent waiting for change that was promised and never delivered. She narrates violent events primarily, and concludes that neither the PRI nor the Zapatistas offers an adequate solution to that violence (10).

Alma Guillermoprieto's chronicles are characterized by in-depth research into different kinds of source materials and a tendency to present a variety of perspectives on the issues at hand. Her stated goal is to open up questions and doubts in the minds of her readers and not to provide answers. She rejects any division of the key actors in Mexican society into gangs of good guys and bad guys, and she criticizes much contestatory journalism for polarizing public opinion and simplifying the complexity of social and political problems (15). In her EZLN chronicles one observes a rather more elaborate presentation of evidence and a somewhat weaker narrative dimension than in the texts by Monsiváis, Poniatowska, and Villoro. Her coverage of the press conference, for example, becomes a pretext for a broad analysis of Marcos's identity, the early years of the EZLN in Chiapas, and the conflict of the past year. "The Unmasking" is a chronicle that depends equally on research into published sources of information, Guillermoprieto's own interview with Marcos, her witnessing of the February 9 event, a visit to Aguascalientes in late February of 1995, and, perhaps surprisingly, rumor. Rumor or what "people are saying" provides a way to take the measure of the public's unverified but perhaps accurate knowledge about events that are shrouded in secrecy. The familiar motifs of theatricality, masks, and role playing appear in the piece, and there is some use of hyperbole for a humorous effect, especially in the depiction of the government's overwrought announcement of the Zapatista leader's identity and their game of peekaboo. The sweaty eagerness of the journalists packed into the conference room is also the target of the narrator's ironic gaze. However, the overall tone of the chronicle is relatively more dispassionate than the other texts discussed, and the first-person narrator is significantly less visible and less involved in the story. Also by way of contrast, Alma Guillermoprieto ultimately arrives at a pessimistic conclusion about the future role of the EZLN in national affairs, seeing the Zapatistas as a movement that is already running out of energy and support in early 1995. The epilogue to the collection, written in 1999 for the book and not previously published, voices a strong criticism of Marcos for adopting an ever more dogmatic, fundamentalist position, in contradiction to the flexibility and originality that was earlier praised by the other chroniclers.

The opening paragraphs of "The Unmasking" recreate the press conference and the identification of Marcos as Rafael Sebastián Guillén Vicente. The retelling is dramatic and humorous in its reenactment of the awkward theatricality of the "hide-and-go-seek" game of using a slide of a ski mask to uncover and cover a ten-year-old image of Guillén. The idea is to show that Guillén masked, unmasks Marcos's identity. Guillermoprieto dismisses the photographic evidence provided by the government, claiming that an equally conclusive "resemblance" could have been achieved by placing Marcos's masked image over one of Richard Nixon. The reference to the disgraced president, so radically different in age, appearance, and ideology to the rebel leader, captures the amusing absurdity of the show-and-tell of February 9. The narrator also pokes fun at the public for its fascination with Marcos and at the Subcomandante himself by piling up to comic effect the many personae attributed to him: "the dashing leader," "the hero of a thousand fervent letters," "the postmodern revolutionary," and "this masked idol," the second coming of Clark Kent (*Looking for History* 207).[10]

Nevertheless, the chronicler soon engages in a serious inquiry into substantive evidence for identifying Marcos as Guillén, as well as addressing the situation in Chiapas in its historical and contemporary dimensions. Interestingly, the first real act of unmasking that she carries out is directed at the government and not at Marcos. Guillermoprieto categorically rejects the official explanation of the recent movement of additional troops into Chiapas as a simple support mission for the federal police who are charged with arresting Marcos. Calling President Zedillo's words a transparent pretext for intensifying the militarization of Chiapas, the narrator directly challenges the official version fed to journalists and the public at large and unmasks the duplicity of official rhetoric. This challenge is also a critique of the military occupation of Chiapas, which Guillermoprieto suggests is responsible for the increase in the drug trade in the region. The humorous side of official foolishness should not overshadow the grave consequences of policies that a powerful government can impose. "Even as we watched the slide show, Army troops were preparing to move into the mountainous and overwhelmingly rural southeastern part of Chiapas" (208). The juxtaposition of the ridiculous and the threatening is a warning to readers not to be distracted or blinded by the immediate spectacle, but to discern the very real actions that are taking place outside of their view.

A lengthy portion of the text reviews the evidence concerning Marcos's "real" identity. This is where the chronicle shifts from parody to a more traditional, journalistic marshalling of the facts into an argument supporting a claim or an interpretation.[11] Guillermoprieto's evidentiary procedures include the textual analysis of writings by both Guillén and Marcos, interviews with Guillén's family and his former colleagues at the Universidad Autónoma Metropolitana, her interview of Marcos in April 1994, government reports, rumors about the history of the EZLN in the 1980s, and even a mural painted by Guillén in the university that resembles decorative elements encountered in the ampitheater in Aguascalientes. For example, by carrying out a kind of textual detective work through a close reading of Guillén's graduate thesis and Marcos's letters, the narrator identifies a common influence of the French philosopher Louis Althusser, a similar narcissism, and shared references to ants and orgasms (not necessarily in the same breath). In this way, Guillermoprieto builds a case for defending the government's hypothesis, after having ridiculed their presentation of it using photographic evidence. Ultimately, in spite of the evidence that she constructs, Guillermoprieto concurs with Villoro's observation about the results of the February 9 event. In political terms, what matters more than the verifiable, "real" identity of Marcos prior to 1984, is the government's utter failure to discredit the Subcomandante as a political entity or to disillusion his admirers, while Marcos capitalized on the incident with a new communiqué sent out a few days later. There is a consensus among all observers that Marcos's talent for public relations and communication is the key to the Zapatistas' hopes, however slim, of winning a war of words against the Mexican government.

It seems to be virtually impossible to write about Marcos without recurring to the language of theater and spectacle, and Guillermoprieto's chronicle shares a familiar lexicon with Monsiváis and Villoro. She also shares with them an uneasy appreciation of the meaning and the function of masks and Marcos's clever manipulation of theatricality. In "Crónica de una convención (que no lo fue tanto)" Monsiváis criticizes the Mexican fascination with dramatic, unknowable, and charismatic leaders by making ironic comments on the crowd's demand that Marcos not remove his mask in Aguascalientes. Villoro also refuses the appeal of charisma and looks for signs of authenticity—the urge to scratch an itch—within the tightly controlled spectacle of the Subcomandante's appearance at the convention. Alma Guillermoprieto's efforts to verify Marcos's identity as Rafael Guillén can be seen as another kind of resistance to the transformative power of the mask, but her chronicle cannot resist engaging with this motif in a way that grants it a certain grudging value, at least initially. Marcos is "a mesmerizing personality—self-possessed, courteous, ironic and theatrical" (209), who "has staged a very real, threatening war on the Mexican state based on almost no firepower" (211). It is a public relations war whose commander stage-manages events attended by civilian spectators, and whose soldiers parade with carved-wood imitation guns (216). This highly theatrical war has, in spite of its make-believe qualities, kept the Mexican government off balance for several years, but Guillermoprieto sees that any real shooting war that might start up "can only end in tragedy" (216).

The prediction that Mexico is headed toward tragedy occupies center stage in the epilogue written in 1999 for the publication of the chronicles in Spanish in *Los años en que no fuimos felices*. By that date the 1997 massacre at Acteal, the rape and murder of hundreds of women in Ciudad Juárez, and the violent deaths associated with the burgeoning drug trade are signs that "nuestra verdadera vocación es la tragedia" (*Los años* 219). [Our true vocation is tragedy.] If Marcos was once "el semidios travieso o tramposo" (220) [the mischievous, trickster demi-god] who made the nation laugh, the hardening of his discourse over time has turned him into a fundamentalist who is no longer able to give the gift of subversive laughter. Guillermoprieto's EZLN chronicles written between 1994 and 1997 represent the movement and its masked—or faceless—leader as defeated players in a national tragedy in which masks once again triumph over truth. Her presentation of evidence and her other uses of the languages of nonfiction are less open-ended and playful than what we have seen in Monsiváis and Villoro, and Guillermoprieto's writing leads to a set of conclusions that partially undermine her desire to create doubt and pose questions of importance for her readers.

Five years after the press conference that tried unsuccessfully to discredit and to criminalize Subcomandante Marcos, the EZLN continued to exist and continued to struggle, adopting new strategies in response to the changing policies first of President Ernesto Zedillo and, after the elections of 2000 and the watershed defeat of the PRI in the presidential race, Vicente Fox's regime. Among the four writers studied, Carlos Monsiváis has maintained a lasting interest in writing about Marcos and the EZLN. In order to bring this analysis of history-making representations of Marcos closer to the present, I will briefly examine an editorial essay written by Monsiváis in January 1999, and an interview that he and Hermann Bellinghausen conducted with the rebel leader in December 2000. I will also compare them to a piece published by Alma Guillermoprieto in 2001 that is part book review and part retrospective evaluation of the meaning of Marcos.

Carlos Monsiváis's essay "¿A quién le tienen que pedir perdón?" [To whom do they have to ask for forgiveness?], published in *Letras Libres*, is a short, concise summary of significant events and interpretations of the EZLN in the first five years since the uprising began. The title of the article, immediately recognizable to many readers, comes from Marcos's January 18, 1994 response to then-President Carlos Salinas's offer of an amnesty to the EZLN. The amnesty was conditioned on the Zapatistas' first asking for pardon for their rebellion. Marcos famously replied "¿De qué nos van a perdonar?" [What are they going to forgive us for?]; and through a series of rhetorical questions he cited a litany of just complaints and demands motivating the indigenous communities to rebel. Monsiváis considers this communiqué to have been a highly positive and influential statement early in the uprising, in that it signaled a turn away from armed conflict and dogmatic rhetoric, toward the struggle for indigenous rights through dialogue, which soon became the hallmark of the movement.

"¿A quién le tienen que pedir perdón?" is an essay rather than a chronicle *per se*, and it attempts not only to summarize a complex situation, but to mount a criticism of the government and a defense of the positive contributions made by the Zapatistas to the national debate over democracy and human rights. Due to the limited length of the text, it does not elaborate a full picture of any one event or of any one character. Marcos, nevertheless, is the topic of the final two paragraphs, and there is a notable difference between this new portrayal and the sly, ironic representation of his role in the August 1994 Pro-Democracy Convention. Now the emphasis is on the efficacy of Marcos's multifaceted strategies of persuasion, including his romanticism, occasional dogmatism and use of kitsch and humor, his undeniable commitment to his cause, and his constant defense of the rights and dignity of indigenous communities and other marginalized groups such as women, homosexuals, and lesbians. The reader who compares Monsiváis's texts of 1994 and 1999 will easily perceive the greater stature that the writer grants to Marcos, a shift that documents the effect of five years of his masked visibility and his gift for words.

In late December 2000, Carlos Monsiváis traveled to Chiapas with Hermann Bellinghausen to carry out his fourth interview with Subcomandante Marcos. Published in January 2001 under the title "Marcos, 'gran interlocutor'" [Marcos, great interlocutor], the text has two prefatory sections by Monsiváis and Bellinghausen, followed by a transcription of the recorded interview. Assuming an accurate transcription and minimal editing, it could be said that an interview is largely an act of self-representation rather than a representation of the other. However, the interviewer in his or her phrasing and ordering of questions plays an active role in shaping the dialogue and consequently in shaping the interviewee's performance. The relative sympathy or hostility of the interviewer, for example, will necessarily influence the interviewee's construction of himself or herself in the immediate context, just as the interviewee's replies influence the ongoing dynamic of the dialogue. In considering the published text as a representation of Marcos, it is important therefore to keep in mind the mutual interaction of voices.[12]

Monsiváis's introductory notes, again offering a summary of key events, return to the theatrical nature of the convention of 1994 in the negative sense of an empty, illusory, or false spectacle. While praising Marcos's speech, he criticizes much about the CND, and poses a skeptical question. In a society that embraces symbolic figures of salvation, will Marcos be able to distinguish between messianism and democratic leadership? Rereading "Crónica de una convención (que no lo fue tanto)" in light of this question suggests that the representation of the CND as a skillfully performed spectacle may well have reflected the chronicler's dread of a messianic role for the Zapatista leader. Six and a half years later, however, on the eve of the March 2001 arrival of EZLN members in Mexico City to speak before Congress, Monsiváis gives a positive answer to his own question. Marcos's capacity for dialogue and his persistence in the search for a dignified peace and democratic processes have proven over time to be authentic and worthy of respect. He has worn the mask not as a disguise, but to reveal his genuine identification with the rebellious indigenous communities of Chiapas and their struggle.

The rather lengthy interview touches on a broad range of topics concerning the evolution of the EZLN and its relationship with civil society. In the exchange of questions and answers, a genuine dialogue between two engaged Mexican intellectuals takes place. The questions, many of which are framed by lead-in commentary, give Marcos ample opportunity to elaborate on the positive contributions of the EZLN to the Mexican nation. Monsiváis identifies these contributions to include the dialogue between a revolutionary group and civil society, the increased visibility of and interest in indigenous peoples, the participation of women in a movement for social change, a heightened consciousness about racism in Mexico, and, most important of all, the oft-repeated vision of an inclusive society that accepts what Marcos calls "the right to difference." The interview strategy, while not stripped of elements of skepticism and criticism, expresses a remarkable degree of respect for a movement that began as a violent confrontation with the government, a course of action that Monsiváis, with his Quaker upbringing would not condone, but that knew how to transform itself with great agility and intelligence. Marcos, in turn, responds to the questions directly and in some detail, conveying the image of someone who, although forced to live in hiding, has nothing to hide ideologically. Like the ski mask that effaces his individuality, one characteristic of Marcos's speech is the use of the first-person plural form. Marcos's "we" refers to the marginalized people that he represents, and also to the ideal of a truly pluralistic and democratic society of the future. Overall, as a document that constructs yet another version of Marcos, the interview with Monsiváis and Bellinghausen is clearly the most positive and optimistic of the texts studied. At one point, Marcos declares that a crucial lesson taught to him by his indigenous allies was how to listen, and that capacity is very much on display in the article "Marcos, 'gran interlocutor.' "

If Monsiváis's fears that Marcos might become another in a long line of charismatic, messianic, and ultimately despotic leaders in Latin America seem to have been allayed over the course of almost seven years, Alma Guillermoprieto expresses a continuing disquiet over the role of Marcos in the EZLN. Shortly after Monsiváis's interview appeared and as the Zapatistas approached Mexico City on their long march to meet with Congress, she published the article "Historia de un rostro" [Story of a face] in the journal *Letras Libres*. Not exactly a chronicle, although certainly hybrid in form, the piece curiously combines two book reviews with information that Guillermoprieto presents as unquestionably factual, plus a fanciful portrait of Rafael Guillén lying in his hammock and writing, and an analysis of some of the Subcomandante's recent writing and the Monsiváis interview. The thesis of the article is that with the perspective of seven years of Marcos's presence in Mexico, it can be seen how his tight control of the public image of the EZLN has drastically shaped and limited our knowledge of its history and its goals, and that the appeal of *caciquismo* remains a clear and present danger in national politics. The books reviewed are two independently researched accounts of the EZLN and Marcos. One is highly critical of the Subcomandante, and one is sympathetic to the indigenous community of Chiapas and their efforts for change, but both were denounced by the left and by

Marcos according to Guillermoprieto. The book reviews make up the lesser portion of the text, and they serve primarily as a vehicle to convey the information about the EZLN that Guillermoprieto considers crucial to her evaluation of the movement. It is frequently unclear when she is citing the books and when she is summarizing common knowledge or her own investigations about Chiapas and the EZLN, because she blurs the lines among her several sources.

The transition from the book review to the verbal portrait of Rafael Guillén occurs about halfway through the text. Guillermoprieto imagines him writing himself or inventing the character of Marcos to play the protagonist's role in a story that turns out to be not an act of self-revelation but a labyrinth of mirrors reflecting an essentially false, untrustworthy reality. Someone who is or isn't Rafael Guillén or Marcos is fighting a war that isn't a war in a jungle that has ceased to be one (44).[13] Here the article enters the realm of fiction writing in order to explore a poetic truth. The privileging of imagination and invention within an ostensibly nonfictional essay is intensified by including a quotation from one of the many stories written by Marcos, and this move away from the language of facts reinforces the message that Marcos should be considered a fictional creation of Guillén and of the Mexican desire for change. Guillermoprieto seems to be struggling throughout the article with the tension between self-representation and self-invention, and between history as fact and history as rhetoric. The return at the end to a nonfiction mode in the form of an essay (not a story) by Marcos about a student strike at the UNAM and the interview between Monsiváis and Marcos that I have already discussed, is perhaps meant to bolster the persuasive power of the piece in support of its thesis. However, the repeated switching among distinct writing practices (book review, story, essay, interview) expresses the difficulty of determining an adequate language for telling the story or history of a face and its masks. At the end, doubts regarding the meaning of key themes predominate. To what extent does Marcos really lead by obeying? Will he know how to negotiate with the government of Vicente Fox? And, most critically, will a historically marginalized population again hand over their hard-won access to power to another *cacique*? (48).

A little more than a half century ago, Octavio Paz's *Labyrinth of Solitude* created an influential and seemingly indelible image of the Mexican historical, social, cultural, and psychological identity. In the chapter on "Mexican Masks" Paz draws heavily on literature—including

Rodolfo Usigli's *El gesticulador*—and on patterns of popular speech to denounce the hermeticism and the formalism that were the symptoms, he concluded, of the fundamentally defensive and inauthentic nature of the Mexican self, or more accurately of the Mexican masculine self. "The Mexican, whether young or old, *criollo* or *mestizo*, general or laborer or lawyer, seems to me to be a person who shuts himself away to protect himself: his face is a mask and so is his smile" (29). After the turn of the millennium fifty years later, the Zapatistas' insistence on masks and the Mexican public's fascination with reading and writing those masks as signs of change, may play a different and more constructive role in the nation's political and cultural discourse than the one recorded by Paz. By posing a sustained challenge to the Mexican government for more than a decade and providing a public face that is both masked and visible, Marcos, his writings, and writings about Marcos such as the ones studied here have invited an ongoing process of representing and reinterpreting Mexican politics. At a time when the idea of achieving and defending a stable identity—whether individual or national—has been replaced in the human sciences by theories of fluid subjectivities, perhaps Mexican masks are no longer to be cursed as a national flaw. As an instrument of transformation and a sign of the ambiguity of change, the Zapatista mask may better be celebrated as an effective way to dispute an imposed, hierarchical, and fatally static concept of the nation and its future, as it has been enforced by a long history of autocratic rule. A scant three weeks after the beginning of the rebellion, on January 20, 1994, Marcos himself addressed the "scandal" of the ski mask, and he challenged Mexican society to take off its mask and face reality: ". . . al quitarse su propia máscara, la sociedad civil mexicana se dará cuenta . . . que la imagen que le habían *vendido* de sí misma es falsa y la realidad es bastante más aterradora de lo que suponía" (*EZLN: Documentos* 18). [. . . upon taking off its own mask, Mexican civil society will realize that the image that they had been sold of themselves is false, and reality is quite a lot more terrifying than they imagined.] Between the poles of the mask as empty signifier, "el guerrillero inexistente," and the mask as universal identity sign, "Todos somos Marcos," lies a whole range of meanings still to be created for Marcos and for Mexican society. The hope expressed, however cautiously in these chronicles, is that the pro-democracy, pro-equality message emerging from behind the ski mask will ultimately exert a more powerful influence than the reductive, but tempting charisma of messianism, and will successfully challenge civil society in Mexico to assume its own leadership role.

Conclusions

Thinking Back, Looking Ahead

Thinking Back

As this study of nonfiction literatures in twentieth-century Mexico reaches its logical end point, it offers the chance to look back and draw some conclusions about the work that has been done and to think ahead about new writing practices and new directions for research. Early in the process of designing the project that has resulted in this book, two key objectives determined the scope and the nature of the study. My primary objective was to take seriously the category of nonfiction narrative literature commensurate with its prominence in Mexican print media culture of the twentieth century. In part, this objective responded to a perceived, and then easily documented gap in Spanish-American literary studies regarding nonfiction modes of writing. In a broader sense, my interest in the production and the reading of nonfictional discourses reflects the lived tension between a desire and need to know about the world in order to live in it and act upon it, and a deep skepticism toward how knowledge is produced and organized in language and in visual images. The second objective and a necessary first step in carrying out the analyses that comprise the core of the study, was to establish a theoretical framework that would be responsive to the challenges of reading the rhetorical devices common to nonfiction in general, and that would take into account the languages of distinct genres such as autobiography, diary, chronicle, historical essay, and ethnography. The five chapters of textual analysis treat a wide variety of works that represent events occurring across nine decades of Mexican national life, but in looking back four primary themes are shared among them: the writing of nonfiction as a response to the threat and opportunity of crisis; the negotiation between the writer's claim of factual status for a text and the reader's determination of factual adequacy; the constructed, narrative nature of human actions and identities (our "storied selves"); and the changing views of historiography and what constitutes historically and culturally significant events and persons for Mexican intellectuals. In the comments that follow I will briefly pull together these common threads.

The twentieth century in Mexico began and ended with armed insurgencies, albeit ones conducted on vastly different scales. Among social movements for structural change, revolutionary war creates extreme situations of upheaval and crisis to which writers in all genres have responded since ancient times. The ten years of warfare of the Mexican Revolution of 1910 and the twelve days of armed combat staged by the EZLN in January 1994 have compelled prominent intellectuals to wrestle with the challenges posed by societal crisis in the form of written texts with a strong documentary dimension. The struggle over leadership and legitimacy among Revolutionary chieftains that Martín Luis Guzmán and José Vasconcelos witnessed after the assassination of Francisco I. Madero is explored in the former's portrayals of Pancho Villa and in the latter's autobiography. The Mexican Revolution confronted these intellectuals with a conundrum that narrative could only represent and not solve. The EZLN and the figure of Subcomandante Marcos also presented elite writers such as those studied in Chapter 6 with puzzling questions of authenticity and legitimate leadership in a popular movement that seeks to address the centuries-old crisis of cultural and material survival that is endured by the indigenous peoples of Chiapas. Mexico's long history of *caudillaje* and of charismatic but corrupt leaders has conditioned contemporary writers to take a somewhat detached and ironic stance in evaluating the crisis in Chiapas and the opportunity for creating the more inclusive society that the EZLN claims to promote.

Crises of a more personal nature also drive people to write their own individual stories in an effort to impose meaning and order on experiences of struggle and change. José Vasconcelos's *Ulises criollo*, María Luisa Puga's *Diario del dolor*, and Benita Galeana's *Benita* offer three highly distinct responses to personal crisis and the threat that crisis poses to identity. Vasconcelos, the exiled "Moses" who is powerless to save his people from the treachery of Mexico's postrevolutionary leaders, uses autobiography to rescue himself from political defeat and oblivion. Puga employs the intimate, putatively private form of the diary to engage in a creative conversation with an intractable adversary, physical pain. In it she acknowledges the brokenness and the loss of her former self, while achieving a precarious equilibrium that allows her to sideline her unwanted companion and contemplate moving her writing life into new territory. Her death soon after the publication of *Diario del dolor* left that new territory unexplored. Benita Galeana, at a critical moment in her Communist Party activism, recorded a life story that begins in poverty and deprivation and moves toward meaningful participation in popular struggle. In all three cases, the writing process itself plays a crucial role in defending and affirming a besieged sense of self.

Finally, large-scale disasters impose conditions of crisis on communities of people who attempt to resignify the losses and the suffering of catastrophe as an opportunity to organize for change. Carlos Monsiváis and Rosanna Reguillo use the chronicle form to engage in an analysis of social and political causes and consequences of the localized disasters of two catastrophic gas explosions. By exploiting the narrative structure of the chronicle and embedding their analysis within an overarching story of exceptional events, both writers succeed in reaching a fairly wide reading public with a complex take on the possibilities and the limitations of late twentieth-century grassroots movements in the discouraging context of Mexican politics and class and ethnic relations.

Factual status and factual adequacy proved to be functional concepts for examining the production and the reception of nonfiction literatures. Eric Heyne's distinction between the claim for factual status that authors can make for their work and the inquiry into factual adequacy that is the prerogative of the reader allowed us to see how nonfiction involves its readers in an active, creative role and not one of mere consumption. Factual status assumes that nonfictional works bear a particular kind of responsibility to extratextual reality (events and persons). Therefore, they are read with an eye toward discerning and judging the rhetorical use of facts, proper names, chronologies, and diverse other forms of evidence. Doubt motivates the reader to consider the requirements of factual adequacy and is the crux of the distinction of nonfiction, and many of the analyses undertaken in the book reveal the ways in which the critical reader can deploy her or his own knowledge and competence and can also journey outside of the text in order to verify or undermine its claims.

I have shown that works such as *El águila y la serpiente*, *Cartucho*, and *Memorias de Pancho Villa*, when read as nonfictional accounts of the Revolution of 1910, pose a serious challenge to expectations for factual adequacy, while *Apuntes sobre la vida militar de Francisco Villa* and *The Wind That Swept Mexico* conform rather closely to them. In the case of autobiography, explicit references to fictional literature in the self-portrait, as in the case of *Ulises criollo*, do not necessarily violate the pact between the author-narrator-protagonist and the reader. One can consider some episodes of an autobiography to be fanciful or even wholly invented, but life writing that is based on the identity of the proper name remains squarely within the realm of nonfiction. Personal narratives such as *Benita* that are allied with *testimonio* and relate the experiences of non-elite social actors, may appeal to the reader's trust with the apparent "simplicity" and "transparency" of their language and narrative structure, but a careful critical analysis will not relinquish the right to doubt and to consider factual adequacy.

The ethnographic life story *Juan Pérez Jolote* and the chronicles studied in this book base their claim to factual status on two principal supports: the name of the author and the marshalling of evidence that is conventional for the specific disciplines of anthropology and journalism, respectively. Ricardo Pozas was a recognized authority in the study of indigenous peoples of Chiapas in the 1940s to 1970s, and he held positions of prestige in Mexican academic institutions. The widely read journalists Carlos Monsiváis, Elena Poniatowska, Juan Villoro, and Alma Guillermoprieto are able to interject their own subjectivity as chroniclers and employ irony in their work without losing credibility as chroniclers of verifiable events due to their long association with respected newspapers and journals and their reputation for taking a critical stance vis-à-vis official, government-sponsored versions of events. In all of these cases, the authors effectively utilize the scholarly and/or documentary conventions of their discipline, while also engaging in creative and at times parodic transformations of those conventions.

Ultimately, however, all of these readings provide reminders that a fact is an event *under description* or a discursive entity, and therefore any text bears a debt only to the recorded, discursive reality of that which has been spoken (Hutcheon 145) and cannot claim a direct relationship to that which has been lived. Factual status and factual adequacy are literary and cultural concepts that change over time and that are always at a significant remove from the world that the text would signify.

The constructed, narrative dimension of human actions and identities has been one of the most consistent themes of my analyses of nonfiction in this book. The written record of the process of making meaning of experience through story-telling discloses the ways in which we live stories and tell lives. This is perhaps nowhere more apparent than in the writing of biography, memoir, and autobiography, and the consideration of both elite and popular manifestations of life writing shows the many and varied sources of the scripts that the human subject follows, resists, and transforms in the trajectory of a life and its narrative version. Perhaps less obvious, but equally significant, is the informing presence of established cultural narratives in historical essays such as *The Wind That Swept Mexico* and in the chronicle, where the portrayal of individual personalities may play a secondary role to the narration of events. Nations, like individuals, live the stories that they tell about themselves, and those who write the national histories shape their versions by honoring or subverting well-known plots and motifs. Martín Luis Guzmán and José Vasconcelos craft counter narratives to the official history of the Mexican Revolution of 1910 and its triumphalist version of institutionalized revolutionary power. Anita Brenner attempts to rewrite the script of the United States' traditional ignorance toward Mexico by appealing to her compatriots' sense of self-preservation and their regard for democracy in *The Wind That Swept Mexico*. Juan Villoro cites the dilemma of the Mexicans' historical retreat behind masks and dissimulation as written by Octavio Paz; Carlos Monsiváis shows how the deep-seated disdain for indigenous Mexicans is revived and reinforced through gas explosion "humor"; and Elena Poniatowska, following Marcos's lead, draws on myths and legends shared by many Western cultures to describe the 1994 Convention site at Aguascalientes as a reenactment of Noah's Ark and Fitzcarraldo's steamship. These cultural narratives shape each writer's understanding of events and personages, facilitate and also constrain their interpretations, and serve as a common horizon of meaning against which the reading public can locate and assimilate the lessons of history.

The many genres of literary nonfiction trace changing views of what constitutes the field of history and historiography broadly understood as narratives of the past. Guzmán and Vasconcelos clearly inscribe a "great men" theory of history by emphasizing the military and political deeds of the most important leaders of the Revolution of 1910 in their works. Nellie Campobello's *Apuntes sobre la vida militar de Francisco Villa* also respects the traditional basis of history writing, while her *Cartucho* and Anita Brenner's *The Wind That Swept Mexico* expand the range of Mexico's historical actors to include women and anonymous soldiers, peasants, and workers. Life writing in the twentieth century occasionally showed a limited capacity to expand the parameters of the traditional accounts of the exploits and personalities of exceptional men and open a space in the "most democratic province of the republic of letters" (Howells 795) for the lives of working-class women and members of indigenous communities. One marginalized member of society claimed a place in the national narrative through her own testimonial life writing in the case of *Benita*, while another subaltern subject had his storied life taken from him and re-presented as significant for the nation through ethnographic life writing as exemplified by *Juan Pérez Jolote*.

Stories of civil society that privilege the actions and the impact of popular and grassroots movements rose to prominence in Mexican chronicle writing starting in the 1960s. Mass protest movements such as the 1968 student movement and the student strikes of the 1970s, and civil society's response to disaster after the Mexico City gas explosions in 1984, the earthquake in 1985, and the gas explosions in Guadalajara in 1994 demanded a literary-journalistic narrative that could express popular suspicion of the figures of power and invest hope for a future, more responsible and democratic Mexico in the actions of ordinary citizens. And what about the writing of Subcomandante Marcos into Mexican history? Did the initial fascination with Marcos signify a return to the appeal of "great men" for the Mexican imagination, or could he be seen as a legitimate representative of a popular, democratic movement to which he genuinely subordinated himself? The chronicles of the August 1994 Convention and many other texts concerning Marcos that have been produced since January 1, 1994 commemorate at one and the same time these diverse trends: the lingering appeal of charisma in a nation with a tradition of strong, personalistic leaders; the government's fear of the emergence of such a figure from outside of their control; the caution felt by leading intellectuals regarding any return to a messianic dream for how change will be achieved in Mexico; the precarious nature of popular movements in a context of an authoritarian political tradition; and the effective use of masks and a unique kind of anonymity in creating an individual focus of attention that can claim to represent a large and diverse group.

The object of history has been said to be the referent of the proper name, and so the question of the significance of names and acts of naming arises here. Spanish-American revolutionary movements have generated a wealth of internationally recognized *noms de guerre*, most famously Pancho Villa, Che Guevara, and Subcomandante Marcos. Deliberately assumed, these names mask or even obliterate an old identity, grant a new face and new powers to the bearer, and attest to the fluid, performative qualities of human subjectivities over fixed identities. In these examples, "false" names and legend surpass history's presumed responsibility to factual accuracy in the construction of enduring meaning out of the remains of the past. Names have other collective and personal values as well. Juan Pérez Jolote is the proper name for the hybridity of Mexican national identities, a hybridity that the eponymous life story conveys at cross purposes to Ricardo Pozas's homogenizing intentions. María Luisa Puga gives a name, "Dolor," to her pain, and by doing so she initiates an active, creative process of resistance to its corrosive power and ensures her survival as a writer.

All of the works included in this study both rely on and challenge the conventions of nonfiction writing in constructing versions of the past that appeal to the reader's search for knowledge and incite a degree of questioning and doubt about the adequacy of that version. The value and the distinction of reading nonfiction literature can be located in the experience of doubt and in the intellectual work that doubt requires of us. In my readings of these significant contributions to Mexican nonfiction narrative I have tried to follow the leading edge of doubt and to keep in the foreground of my analyses the rich complexity and deep partiality of the literatures of fact.

Looking Ahead

As the tumultuous period of history known as the twentieth century ceded not only to a new century but to a new millenium, print media, which had already shared the stage and the attention of readers for more than fifty years with radio and television, began to experience the effects of the competition of the digital media of the Internet and the World Wide Web. The Internet makes possible new and rapid forms of publication and dissemination of texts, and therefore it is having an impact on nonfiction narrative that is connected to but goes beyond the scope of this book. In closing, I will briefly identify some dimensions of this impact.

Marcos and the EZLN were one of earliest movements in Mexico to utilize not only traditional media outlets (newspapers) but the Internet to construct and distribute their message. They are also a prime instance of how the Internet allows others to take materials produced by a third party and upload them into public space with ease and speed and often with little regard for "ownership" as codified in copyrights. The enormous proliferation of Web sites that (re)publish Marcos's speeches and communiqués is only one simple example of how digital media are reshaping our access to the discourses of fact and transforming the status of authorship and the reliability of information. The digitally generated malleability of texts and other "evidence" in the form of still photos, sound recordings, and audio-video materials, all of which can be rather easily and imperceptibly manipulated, must raise new questions about our practices of reading and viewing what appears "virtually" right in front of our eyes. The recent controversy in U.S. politics over the firing of Department of Agriculture employee Shirley Sherrod based on a video clip posted by a conservative blogger, underscores the dangers of reading "truth" into segments of documentary records taken completely out of context. Readers, and since the invention of photography, viewers have always needed a dose of skepticism and critical perspective in order to discern the interests that are at stake in all putatively factual versions of events, but the rapid-fire dissemination of text, sound, and visual images on the Web may encourage an equally rapid and largely unreflective response, to the detriment of critical thinking and deliberative action.

Economic inequalities that exist in all societies, but that are especially deep and acute in Latin America, also create potential inequities of access to the new media and exacerbate already existing social divisions and hierarchies. The unequal status and opportunity that holds between the disabled and the nondisabled members of a society may also be increased if digital media develop without attention to a variety of obstacles to access. Alternatively, the falling cost and the remarkable portability of cell phones and computer technologies offer opportunities for increasing access to information in remote communities that have been underserved by more traditional means of disseminating information through books, newspapers, television, and radio. It remains to be seen how a globalized economy will foster greater or lesser disparities in the flow of information to diverse communities, and how all communities will employ the new technologies as instruments of cultural, economic, and political change.

Interactivity is a much-touted attribute of the digital media, and blogs are one obvious example of a highly interactive form of communication that is transforming the sites of production and delivery of factual discourse such as news items, scientific research studies, and work in the humanities, including literary criticism. An individual, without needing the mediating intervention of a peer reviewer and/or a publisher, can make his or her work available to readers quickly and without the need for paid subscriptions. Just as significant is the impact of blogs on a reader's ability to respond to posted material in an open forum that is creating a new culture of dialogue and exchange. This interactive component makes blogs a far more immediate, open-ended, and inclusive mode of communication than any that could be achieved through traditional printed newspapers, journals, and books and the corresponding response mechanisms of published op-ed pieces, letters to the editor, or book reviews. In these and many other ways, the digital media offer new modes of communication and new fields of research that scholars are just beginning to explore. The writing and reading of nonfiction is bound to be affected by these innovations, but many of the principles of analysis that are central to my study will continue to be relevant to new projects that focus on the transformation of documents, facts, evidence, authorship, narrativity, and representations of human subjectivity in the literatures of fact.

Notes

Introduction

1. See Chapter 3 of *The Writing of Elena Poniatowska*, "Creative Confusions: Readings of *Hasta no verte, Jesús mío*," especially pages 50–66.

2. Studies of Latin American *testimonio* proliferated in the United States and in Latin America in the 1980s and 90s, when influential work by John Beverley, George Yúdice, Doris Sommer, Elzbieta Sklodowska, Georg Gugelberger, Hernán Vidal, and many others established the terms of the debate over questions of authorship, authenticity of narrative voice, referentiality, the politics of collaborative projects, and the transgressive potential of testimonial literature.

3. E. L. Doctorow quoted by Phyllis Frus McCord in her esssay "The Ideology of Form: The Nonfiction Novel" (59).

4. The quote by Oprah Winfrey is taken from the transcript to *CNN Larry King Live*, January 11, 2006. http://transcripts.cnn.com/TRANSCRIPTS11/lkl.01.html

5. In returning to the "buscabiografías" Web site (December 10, 2009), I do not locate any links to best-seller lists. The fluid nature of Web sites poses a challenge to those using them for research. http://www.buscabiografias.com

Chapter 1

1. The description of history writing as a record of "what actually happened" is attributable to the nineteenth-century German historian Leopold von Ranke. The famous dictum comes from Ranke's book on the history of the Latin and Germanic peoples, first published in 1824 and translated into English in 1887.

2. The title of Chapter 1 of Hollowell's 1977 book is "Novelists and the Novel in a Time of Crisis." John Hellmann (*Fables of Fact*, 1981) emphasizes not only the crises of the 1960s, but the idea that the new realities seemed

fictive to the public, who looked to a revitalized journalism for meaningful, albeit ambiguous, versions of events.

3. Walsh's *Operación masacre* (1957) and Barnet's *Biografía de un cimarrón* (1966) are two of the texts that initiated what quickly came to be called "testimonial literature" in Latin American studies.

4. To the extent that a reader has doubts about the accuracy of what is related in a work of fiction, he or he is reading it against the grain. There are many examples of this kind of reading in the history of Mexican literature, including the reception of Martín Luis Guzmán's *El águila y la serpiente* and Vicente Leñero's *Los periodistas.* I will discuss how Guzmán's historical novel has been read in Chapter 2.

5. The English translation of "The Death of the Author" is included in the collection of Barthes's essays *Image-Music-Text* published in 1977.

6. In his essay "The Real, the True and the Figurative in the Human Sciences," Hayden White cites Arthur Danto and Louis O. Mink in defining facts as "events under description" (15).

7. Among Hayden White's many publications, the following titles produced over the course of twenty-five years represent milestones in theory: *Metahistory: The Historical Imagination in Nineteenth-Century Europe* (1973); *Tropics of Discourse* (1978); *The Content of the Form* (1987), and *Figural Realism* (1999).

Chapter 2

1. A few of the standard reference volumes on the novel of the Mexican Revolution are the following: F. Rand Morton, *Los novelistas de la Revolución Mexicana* (1949); Antonio Castro Leal, *La novela de la Revolución Mexicana* (1960); Adalbert Dessau, *La novela de la Revolución Mexicana* (1972); and Antonio Magaña Esquivel, *La novela de la Revolución* (1974).

2. Rutherford does not define what he means by "aesthetic pretences or qualities," but he seems to assume that the readers of a literary history such as this one will agree that the "artlessness," "ponderous melodrama," and "crude characterization" of the popular novel do not pretend to the status of literature, while irony, subtlety, and "evocative brevity" are proper aesthetic qualities (215–220).

3. In his article "Martín Luis Guzmán's Necessary Overtures," Juan Bruce-Novoa focuses on the often overlooked introductory chapters of *El águila y la serpiente* and *La sombra del caudillo* to show that they are an integral part of the overall design and meaning of the novels. David W. Foster in "Escrutando el texto de la Revolución" criticizes the limitations imposed by strictly documentary readings of the book, and he studies the rhetorical devices that Guzmán uses to shape his narrative of the Revolution.

4. I treat Philippe Lejeune's theory of autobiography in more detail in Chapter 3. Briefly, Lejeune describes autobiography as a mode of reading in which the identity of the name of the author, the narrator, and the protagonist

establishes a pact with the reader to accept the work as an account of the life of a real person written by him- or herself.

5. J. Patrick Duffey discusses the presence of films and cinematic techniques in *El águila y la serpiente* in his article "Pancho Villa at the Movies" (2001).

6. All translations from the novel are my own.

7. See Fernando Curiel, "La querella de Martín Luis Guzmán," 180.

8. In her book *Transparent Minds*, Dorrit Cohn proposes a theoretical framework for understanding the presentation of consciousness in fictional works. What she says about first-person (or autodiegetic) texts has some relevance for nonfiction as well, in that we tend to read the presentation of an autobiographer's consciousness as if it were a clear window into the mind.

9. Lucille Kerr's article "Gestures of Authorship: Lying to Tell the Truth in Elena Poniatowksa's *Hasta no verte Jesús mío*" treats the testimonial novel as a necessarily duplicitous form that nonetheless successfully appeals to the reader to accept the testimonial subject as the "real thing" (372–373).

10. This category is treated in Chapter 9 of Lejeune's book *On Autobiography*.

11. The 1909 date also appears in the interview with Campobello that is included in Emmanuel Carballo's book, where it can be assumed many scholars have encountered it.

12. Articles by Gary D. Keller (1970), Gabriella de Beer (1979), Catherine Nickel (1990), and Doris Meyer (1996) promote an autobiographical reading of *Cartucho*, for example. Although Keller hedges by calling the book an "autobiografía novelada," he states that "En el sentido psicológico *Cartucho* es un documento auténtico . . . sin distorciones ni estilizaciones" (143). [In a psychological sense, *Cartucho* is an authentic document . . . without distortions or stylizations.] De Beer and Meyer classify the book as memoir, autobiography, and testimony, while Nickel, reading directly against the grain of its highly fragmented structure and poetic language, attests to the "documentary style" of *Cartucho.*

13. This quote is from the essay "Life: A Story in Search of a Narrator," collected in *A Ricoeur Reader: Reflection and Imagination* (437, emphasis in the original).

14. The background information on Anita Brenner's family comes from Chapter 1 of Glusker's book *Anita Brenner: A Mind of Her Own* (1998).

15. Barthes states that in contrast to the fictional nature of language, a photograph "is authentification itself" (*Camera Lucida* 87).

16. *Times Literary Supplement*, quoted on the back cover of *The Wind That Swept Mexico*, paperback edition, University of Texas Press.

Chapter 3

1. Gusdorf's foundational essay "Conditions et limites de l'autobiographie" was first published in 1956, but it became widely read and discussed when Lejeune reprinted it in French in 1970 and James Olney translated it into English in 1980.

2. Excellent overviews of the changing directions in theories of autobiography can be found in the books by Sidonie Smith (1987), Paul John Eakin (1999), and Linda Anderson (2001).

3. These titles refer to books and book chapters by Liz Stanley, Domna Stanton, Sidonie Smith, and Linda Anderson, respectively.

4. Estelle Jelinek's introduction to her 1980 edited volume *Women's Autobiography: Essays in Criticism* characterizes women's life writing in the ways summarized and questioned by Sidonie Smith.

5. In the first chapter of her book *A Poetics of Women's Autobiography*, Sidonie Smith argues against the claim made by French feminists of the 1970s and 80s that women's "true autobiography" has yet to be written because women have only reinscribed male writing (18). Smith's study considers formal autobiography in the Anglo-American tradition, and she describes the "rhetorical woman" as a product of both historical and psychosexual phenomena (19). She strives to show that there are other rhetorical choices open to women that are not limited to silence (and therefore absence from history) or to writing like men (18).

6. The four volumes and the periods of life treated are: *Ulises criollo*, infancy to the 1913 assassination of Francisco I. Madero; *La tormenta*, the Huerta and Carranza presidencies, ending in 1920; *El desastre*, 1920–1928, including Vasconcelos's appointment as Secretary of Public Education by President Obregón; and *El proconsulado*, 1929 through the early 1930s and his exile to Spain.

7. Noé Jitrik poses this question in the beginning of his article "Lectura de Vasconcelos" published in 1988 (261).

8. Received notions of racial and gender identity inform the reviews of *Ulises criollo*, with race being a major concern. For Ramón Puente, the rigidity of Vasconcelos's thought betrays his mestizo blood, implying that a lack of flexibility characterizes the indigenous "race" (811). On the contrary, Miguel Mazón Cervantes attributes Vasconcelos's conservative politics to his being a creole, that is, of the "race" of the conquerors (829). For her part, A. Izquierdo Albiñana takes for granted the sacred status of motherhood and the noble, sacrificial nature of the Mexican mother in her criticism of Vasconcelos's portrayal of women, and especially his praise of prostitutes (841–42). In referring to these reviews, I have deliberately represented the examples as judgments of José Vasconcelos as a real person living in the world and not as a figure of writing, because of the highly personal nature of the reviewers' language.

9. All translations from the Spanish original of *Ulises criollo* (Claude Fell's critical edition) are my own. The existing English version of the autobiography, published in 1963 as *A Mexican Ulysses*, was translated and abridged by William Rex Crawford, and therefore was not suitable as a source of textual quotes.

10. In a profile of María Luisa Puga written by George Szanto, the author explains her view of writing as a necessary activity in the construction of our humanness and as part of any attempt to create and preserve freedom. Her strong belief that many more people should write and read took concrete form in her long time involvement in leading writing workshops for youth and adults all over Mexico, but especially in Michoacán (Szanto 7).

11. For an example of the autobiographical analysis of Puga's fiction, see the article by Irma M. López, "Autobiografía interminable: La novelística de María Luisa Puga."

12. It is worth noting that the move to Zirahuén meant going directly against the current of many decades of Mexico's massive internal migration from all parts of the country to Mexico City. For an established writer it additionally meant abandoning the center of the nation's cultural life and literary production and positioning herself to write from the margins.

13. Robert Edwards's essay "Exile, Self, and Society" (1988) offers an extremely useful and interesting discussion of exile that traces the notion from Roman times in the work of Publilius Syrius through its meanings in the Middle Ages, using among other examples the *Poema de Mío Cid* and Dante's *Paradiso.*

14. Kristeva's essay "Un nouveau type d'intellectuel: le dissident" was first published in 1977 in the journal *Tel Quel.* My references are to the English translation done by Sean Hand for the book *The Kristeva Reader* (1986), edited by Toril Moi.

15. Kafka, Joyce, Mallarme, Celine, and Artaud are a few examples of the writers studied by Kristeva, who can be said to have produced a revolution in literary language.

16. Puga quoted in an article written for *La Jornada* on December 26, 2004, one day after her death from lymphoma.

17. I am referring to Emily Hind's interview with María Luisa Puga, which is included in her book *Entrevistas con quince autoras mexicanas.* The published version contains no references to Puga's illness, although her disability must have been visible by that time.

18. There is a large critical literature on Holocaust testimonies and diaries, and also on life writing in response to illness. I have drawn these characteristics, which are also seen in Puga's work, from the essays "Holocaust Diaries: Writing from the Abyss" by Victoria Stewart and "Cancer Diaries: Writing as Fighting for Wellness" by Henrietta Nickels Shirk.

19. Lucy Bending uses the work of Elaine Scarry as an example of the view that pain destroys language in order to counter her argument with expressive examples taken from literatures dealing with illness and disability. I believe that it is necessary to recall that Scarry's study specifically treats the pain experienced under torture, when abuse is being deliberately inflicted by one person on another. This quite a different set of conditions than the experience of pain due to illness or injury, and can account for Scarry's conclusions about the body reduced to pre-linguistic screams and cries.

Chapter 4

1. I am referring to the most widely read and exhaustively studied mediated testimonies such as *Biografía de un cimarrón* by Miguel Barnet, *Me llamo Rigoberta Menchú y así me nació la conciencia* by Elizabeth Burgos and

Rigobeta Menchú, and *Si me permiten hablar . . . Testimonio de Domitila* by Moema Viezzer and Domitila Barrios de Chungara.

2. Elena Poniatowska posed this rhetorical question in an essay treating the literature of "La Onda" published in her collection of essays *¡Ay vida, no me mereces!* (193).

3. The matter of Benita Galeana's year of birth is a source of some confusion and I have seen three dates published: 1903, 1904, and 1907. I do not know of archival research to support one date over the others. The lack of a birth certificate for a child born in a small village early in the century is not surprising. As an adult member of the workforce Galeana applied to the governor of Guerrero for documentation. She told me that this paperwork lists her birth year incorrectly as 1907 and that she was actually born in 1904. The 1904 date makes better sense in terms of dating her activities and calculating her age at certain critical turning points of her life. When I interviewed her in June 1994, she spoke of being 90 years old, going on 91.

4. Throughout the analysis I will refer to the historical woman as Benita Galeana or Galeana, and I will only call the narrator-protagonist of the text by her first name alone, Benita. It is still common in writing about testimonial literature to see women *testimonialistas* referred to by their first name (Rigoberta and Domitila, for example), a practice that I find to be condescending. This is notably not the case for male testimonial subjects. No one writes about Esteban (Montejo) or Omar (Cabezas). Men are consistently referred to by surname.

5. For reasons of economy I will sometimes use the abbreviation PCM to refer to the Mexican Communist Party.

6. Robert D. Woods includes *Benita* in his valuable bilingual reference book, *Mexican Autobiography/La Autobiografía Mexicana*, 1988.

7. A number of years ago when I first heard about *Benita*, I requested a copy through my university's interlibrary loan service. Although I didn't specify the first edition, to my good fortune a 1940 book was located and shipped, giving me what I later learned was a rare opportunity to compare it to the more recent editions. Galeana herself did not have a copy in her possession in 1994, and I left her photocopies that I had made of the "Palabras preliminares" and the engravings of 1940. Amy Diane Prince apparently did not know about the discrepancies among the different editions while working on the English translation, which she based on the 1990 Lince text.

8. In "Speaking from the Soapbox" I give a more detailed description of the differences among the various editions of *Benita* and the ways in which each new prologue shapes the reading of the text.

9. See John Beverley, "The Margin at the Center" (15).

10. In the book and in our interview Galeana attests to the fact that other PCM members read *El Machete* aloud to her.

11. This characterization of Mexican anthropology is outlined in several sources including Andrés Medina, "Ricardo Pozas en la trama de la antropología mexicana" (1994), and Claudio Lomnitz, *Deep Mexico, Silent Mexico* (2001).

12. This assessment is from an unpublished interview with Rossana Reguillo conducted by the author in May 2007.

13. All translations into English of passages quoted from *Juan Pérez Jolote* are my own.

14. It is not difficult to correlate the predominant themes of *Juan Pérez Jolote*, conceived as an image of Chamula society, with Ricardo Pozas's well-documented interests as an anthropologist: the economy, first and foremost; and also religious practices, structures of authority and power in the township, the healing arts and marriage customs. It is not my purpose to explore those links as "proof" of Pozas's intentions or biases, but to focus on the inscription of cultural hybridity in the text.

15. The account that Pérez Jolote gives of the lessons told by his mentor is repeated almost verbatim in Ricardo Pozas's later book, *Chamula: Un pueblo de indios*. Either Pérez Jolote was his primary informant on matters of religious beliefs and practices, or the anthropologist intercalated a composite version of his findings into the individual life story.

Chapter 5

1. Two chapters of Egan's book directly take on the challenge of articulating a poetics of the genre: Chapter 4, "Carlos Monsiváis, Cronista. The Art of Telling the Truth" and Chapter 5, "Voicing a Poetics of the Contemporary Chronicle in Mexico."

2. Mary K. Long's published articles (1996, 2001) on the chronicles of Salvador Novo discuss his contribution to the development of the urban chronicle in Mexico and the chronicle's role in defining national identity.

3. Other collections of chronicles that portray aspects of daily life and representative or idiosyncratic social types include José Joaquín Blanco's *Función de medianoche* and *Los mexicanos se pintan solos*; and Cristina Pacheco's *Cuarto de azotea* or *Sopita de fideo*. Each writer brings a unique perspective ranging from sympathy to skepticism, and contributes a unique language to the diverse category of the chronicle.

4. For a detailed analysis of the earthquake chronicles by Poniatowska, Monsiváis, and Cristina Pacheco, see my chapter "Matters of Fact: The Contemporary Mexican Chronicle and/as Nonfiction Narrative" in Corona and Jörgensen.

5. Petra María Secanella's classic study of political journalism in Mexico, although now significantly outdated, exposes the traditional relationship of dependency of the Mexican press on the institutions of power. Governmental subventions to newspapers, the buying of space for articles produced by the government, the heavy reliance by reporters on official sources, and other ways of limiting press freedom resulted over the years in a distrust of print journalism as a source of reliable information and stymied the development of investigative journalism (*Periodismo político* 7–15).

6. Some of Reguillo's recent publications that treat these issues include *Emergencia de culturas juveniles: Estrategias del desencanto* (2000), "The Social

Construction of Fear: Urban Narratives and Practices" (2002) and "Ciudades y violencias: Un mapa contra los diagnósticos fatales" (2003).

7. In his chapter "At the Intersection: Chronicle and Ethnography," Ignacio Corona refers to such well-known social and cultural theorists as Jean Baudrillard, Pierre Bourdieu, Néstor García Canclini, and Clifford Geertz to make his case for the "intersection" of chronicle and ethnography, using examples from works by Juan Villoro, Ricardo Garibay, and Dante Medina.

8. In the first chapter of her book *Emergencia de culturas juveniles*, Rossana Reguillo critiques the prevalent press stereotyping of urban youth and of the poor as dangerous and as responsible for urban decay and violence, and she rethinks the youth culture in Latin America.

9. Throughout the analysis of *Construcción simbólica de la ciudad* all quotes and references to the text will be taken from the 2005 edition and will correspond to its pagination.

Chapter 6

1. The mask and the openness of his language allow everyone to assign his or her favorite destiny to him. (Unless otherwise noted, all translations are my own.)

2. Marcos directed many of his early communiqués to a selected group of newspapers: *La Jornada* (Mexico City), *El Financiero* (Mexico City), *Tiempo* (San Cristóbal de las Casas); and weekly news magazine *Proceso.*

3. I do not address the groundbreaking work of Hermann Bellinghausen, who spent a significant period of time living in Chiapas and reporting on the Zapatistas from within their own territory. This omission has two motivations. First, Bellinghausen's writings merit a lengthy study of their own that is quite outside the scope of this article. Second, the well-known scholar Cynthia Steele is currently working on such a study for publication.

4. Christopher Columbus's diaries and Hernán Cortés's letters were not written as chronicles in our present-day acceptance of the genre. However, readers over time have reconstructed the diaries and the letters as chronicles in that they recorded with an element of immediacy and urgency, real-world experiences to which the authors were witnesses and even protagonists.

5. Hayden White in Chapter 3 of *Tropics of Discourse*, "The Historical Text as Literary Artifact," argues that historical situations do not themselves have intrinsic meaning, but rather historians create a meaningful narrative possessing qualities of correspondence and coherence out of documents such as reports and testimonies that are always already encoded with meanings (83–85).

6. Linda Egan also discusses the topic of theatricality in Monsiváis's CND chronicle in the subsection "Hunting Democracy in the Jungle" of the first chapter of *Carlos Monsiváis: Culture and Chronicle and in Contemporary Mexico* (27–33).

7. English original from the screenplay of *Batman Returns.*

8. "Al salir de mi trabajo en el periódico *La Jornada* veo un puesto de souvenirs ideológicos, fotos del Che Guevara, Zapata y, sobre todo, el subcomandante Marcos" (279). [Upon leaving work at *La Jornada* I see a stand selling ideological souvenirs, photos of Che Guevara, Zapata and, above all, Subcomandante Marcos.]

9. Guillermoprieto's titles include: *Samba* (1990); *The Heart That Bleeds: Latin America Now* (1994), translated as *Al pie de un volcán te escribo* (1995); and *Los años en que no fuimos felices: Crónicas de la transición mexicana* (1999), a number of whose pieces also appear in *Looking for History:Dispatches from Latin America* (2001).

10. I will take textual quotations from the published English versions of these articles that appear in the book *Looking for History: Dispatches from Latin America.*

11. Recall the definition of evidence given in Chapter 1: "a set of facts deliberately assembled and placed into an interpretive context in the service of a claim."

12. Carlos Monsiváis and Marcos are the primary participants, with Hermann Bellinghausen playing a secondary role and asking many fewer questions.

13. In her articles on the EZLN and the region of Las Cañadas in Chiapas, Guillermoprieto frequently characterizes the area as a deforested wasteland, in contrast to most references to the Lacandón as a jungle.

Works Cited

Abreu Gómez, Ermilo. *Cuatro siglos de literatura mexicana*. Mexico City: Editorial Leyenda, 1946.

Alessio Robles, Miguel. *Historia política de la Revolución*. Mexico City: Ediciones Botas, 1938.

Alonso Cortés, Rodrigo. *Francisco Villa, el quinto jinete del apocalipsis*. Mexico City: Diana, 1972.

Anderson, Linda. *Autobiography*. London: Routledge, 2001.

Aristotle. *On Poetry and Style*. Trans. G. M. A. Grube. Indianapolis: The Bobbs-Merrill Co., 1968.

Azuela, Mariano. *Los de abajo*. Mexico City: Fondo de Cultura Económica, 1960.

Bakhtin, Mikhail. *The Dialogic Imagination: Four Essays*. Ed. Michael Holquist. Trans. Caryl Emerson and Michael Holquist. Austin: U of Texas P, 1981.

Barnet, Miguel. *Biografía de un cimarrón*. Havana: Instituto de Etnología y Folklore, 1966.

Barthes, Roland. *Camera Lucida: Reflections on Photography*. Trans. Richard Howard. New York: Hill and Wang, 1981.

———. *Image-Music-Text*. Trans. Stephen Heath. London: Fontana P, 1977.

———. *S/Z*. Trans. Richard Miller. New York: Hill and Wang, 1974.

Baynham, Mike. "Narratives in Space and Time: Beyond 'Backdrop' Accounts of Narrative Orientation." *Narrative Inquiry* 13.2 (2003): 347–66.

Bencomo, Anadeli. *Voces y voceros de la megalópolis: La crónica periodístico-literaria en México*. Madrid: Iberoamericana, 2002.

Bending, Lucy. "Approximation, Suggestion, and Analogy: Translating Pain into Language." *Yearbook of English Studies* 36.1 (2006): 131–37.

Beverley, John. "The Margin at the Center: On *Testimonio* (Testimonial Literature)." *Modern Fiction Studies* 35.1 (Spring 1989): 11–28.

Bhabha, Homi K. *The Location of Culture*. London: Routledge, 1994.

Bielsa, Esperança. *The Latin American Urban Chronicle: Between Literature and Mass Media*. Lanham, MD: Lexington Books, 2006.

Blanco, José Joaquín. *Función de medianoche.* Mexico City: Era, 1986.

———. *Los mexicanos se pintan solos: Crónicas, paisajes, personajes de la Ciudad de México.* Mexico City: Ciudad de México Librería y Editora, 1990.

Borges, Jorge Luis. "Funes el memorioso." In *Ficciones.* Buenos Aires: Emecé, 1956. 117–27.

Brenner, Anita. *The Wind That Swept Mexico.* Austin: U of Texas P, 1971.

Brushwood, John. *Mexico in Its Novel: A Nation's Search for Identity.* Austin: U of Texas P, 1966.

Bruce-Novoa, Juan. "Martín Luis Guzmán's Necessary Overtures." *Discurso Literario* 4.1 (Autumn 1986): 68–83.

Burgos, Elizabeth and Rigoberta Menchú. *Me llamo Rigoberta Menchú y así me nació la conciencia.* Mexico City: Siglo Veintiuno, 1985.

"Buscabiografias." <http://www.buscabiografias.com>.

Campobello, Nellie. *Apuntes sobre la vida militar de Francisco Villa.* Mexico City: EDIAPSA, 1940.

———. *Cartucho.* Mexico City: Factoría Ediciones, 1999.

———. *Las manos de mamá. Tres poemas. Mis libros.* Mexico City: Factoría Ediciones, 1999.

———. *Mis libros.* Mexico City: Compañía General de Ediciones, 1960.

Cancian, Ricardo Frank. "*Juan the Chamula: An Ethnological Re-creation of the Life of a Mexican Indian.*" *American Anthropologist.* New Series 65.6 (December 1963): 1371–72.

Carballo, Emmanuel. *Protagonistas de la literatura mexicana.* Mexico City: Ermitaño, 1986.

Castellanos, Rosario. "La novela mexicana contemporánea y su valor testimonial." *Hispania* 47.2 (May 1964): 223–30.

Castro, Carlo Antonio. "Ricardo Pozas y el universo tzotzil." *La Palabra y el Hombre* 3 (July–September 1994): 5–20.

Castro Leal, Antonio. *La novela de la Revolución Mexicana.* Mexico City: Aguilar, 1960.

Cohn, Dorrit. *The Distinction of Fiction.* Baltimore: The Johns Hopkins UP, 1999.

———. *Transparent Minds: Narrative Modes for Presenting Consciousness in Fiction.* Princeton: Princeton UP, 1983.

Cook, Scott. "Struggling to Understand Complexity." *Mexican Studies* 19.1 (Winter 2003): 203–41.

Cordry, Donald. *Mexican Masks.* Austin: U of Texas P, 1980.

Corona, Ignacio. "At the Intersection: Chronicle and Ethnography." In Corona and Jörgensen. 123–55.

——— and Beth E. Jörgensen, eds. *The Contemporary Mexican Chronicle: Theoretical Perspectives on the Liminal Genre.* Albany: State University of New York P, 2002.

Couser, G. Thomas. *Recovering Bodies: Illness, Disability and Life Writing.* Madison, WI: U of Wisconsin P, 1997.

Curiel, Fernando. "La querella de Martín Luis Guzmán." *The Americas Review: A Review of Hispanic Literature and Art of the USA* 17.3–4 (Fall–Winter 1989): 179–84.

de Beer, Gabriella. "Nellie Campobello's Vision of the Mexican Revolution." *The American Hispanist* 4.34–35 (1979): 14–16.

———. "María Luisa Puga." *Contemporary Mexican Women Writers: Five Voices.* Austin: U of Texas P, 1996. 11–57.

Derrida, Jacques. "The Parergon." Trans. Craig Owens. *October* 9 (1979): 3–40.

Dessau, Adalbert. *La novela de la Revolución Mexicana.* Trans. Juan José Utrilla. Mexico City: Fondo de Cultura Económica, 1972.

Díaz Arciniega, Víctor. "La voz: el eco. Vasconcelos: Lección de historia y vida." In Vasconcelos, *Ulises criollo.* 732–75.

Domínguez Michael, Christopher. "Martín Luis Guzmán: El teatro de la política." *Vuelta* 11.131 (Oct. 1987): 22–31.

Dubrow, Heather. "Introduction." Special Issue on "The Status of Evidence." *PMLA* 111.1 (January 1996): 7–20.

Duffey, J. Patrick. "Pancho Villa at the Movies." In *Latin American Literature and Mass Media.* Ed. Edmundo Paz-Soldán and Debra A. Castillo. New York: Garland, 2001. 41–56.

Egan, Linda. *Carlos Monsiváis: Culture and Chronicle in Contemporary Mexico.* Tuscon: U of Arizona P: 2001.

Eakin, Paul John. *How Our Lives Become Stories: Making Selves.* Ithaca, NY: Cornell UP, 1999.

———. "What Are We Reading When We Read Autobiography?" *Narrative* 12.2 (May 2004): 121–32.

Edwards, Robert. "Exile, Self, and Society." In *Exile in Literature.* Ed. María-Inés Lagos-Pope. Lewisburg, PA: Bucknell UP 1988. 15–31.

EZLN: Documentos y comunicados I. Prologue by Antonio García de León. Mexico City: Era, 1994.

Faverón Patriau, Gustavo. "La rebelión de la memoria: Testimonio y escritura de la realidad en *Cartucho* de Nellie Campobello." *Mester* 32 (2003): 53–71.

Foster, David W. "Escrutando el texto de la Revolución: *El águila y la serpiente* de Martín Luis Guzmán." *Revista de Crítica Literaria Latinoamericana* 15.30 (1989): 79–90.

———. ed. *Mexican Literature: A History.* Austin: U of Texas P, 1994.

Foucault, Michel. *Language, Counter-memory, Practice.* Ed. Donald F. Bouchard. Trans. Donald F. Bouchard and Sherry Simon. Ithaca, NY: Cornell UP, 1977. 113–38.

Frey, James. *A Million Little Pieces.* New York: Doubleday, 2003.

Galeana, Benita. *Benita.* Mexico City, Imprenta Mels, 1940.

———. *Benita.* Trans. Amy Diane Prince. Pittsburgh: Latin American Literary Review P, 1994.

Gallo, Rubén, ed. *The Mexico City Reader.* Trans. Lorna Scott Fox and Rubén Gallo. Madison. WI: U of Wisconsin P, 2004.

Garciadiego, Javier. "Tres asedios a Vasconcelos." In Vasconcelos, *Ulises criollo.* 613–27.

Glusker, Susannah Joel. *Anita Brenner: A Mind of Her Own.* Austin: U of Texas P, 1998.

González, Aníbal. *La crónica modernista hispanoamericana.* Madrid: Porrúa Turanzas, 1983.

González, Manuel Pedro. *Trayectoria de la novela en México.* Mexico City: Ediciones Botas, 1951.

González de Alba, Luis. "Para limpiar la memoria." *Nexos* 238 (October 1997): 45–49 or: <http://historico.nexos.com.mx/articuloEspecial.php?id = 5507> (June 17, 2010).

Grundberg, Andy. *Crisis of the Real: Writings on Photography, 1974–1989.* New York: Aperture Foundation, 1990.

Guillermoprieto, Alma. *Los años en que no fuimos felices: Crónicas de la transición mexicana.* Mexico City: Plaza & Janés, 1999.

———. "Historia de un rostro." *Letras Libres* 3.27 (March 2001): 40–48.

———. *Looking for History: Dispatches from Latin America.* New York: Vintage Books, 2001.

Gusdorf, Georges. "Conditions and Limits of Autobiography." In Olney. 28–48.

Guzmán, Martín Luis. *A orillas del Hudson.* In *Obras completas I.* 31–107.

———. *El águila y la serpiente.* Mexico City: Anáhuac, 1941.

———. "Un experto de la historia." In *Martin Luis Guzmán: Critica y autocritica.* Ed. Emmanuel Carballo. Mexico City: Universidad Nacional Autónoma de México, 1987. 17–32.

———. *Memorias de Pancho Villa.* Mexico City: Porrúa, 1991.

———. *Obras completas I.* Mexico City: Fondo de Cultura Económica, 1984.

———. *La querella de México.* In *Obras completas I.* 7–30.

Gyurko, Lanin. "Twentieth Century Fiction." In *Mexican Literature: A History.* Ed. David W. Foster. Austin: U of Texas P, 1994. 243–303.

Hellmann, John. *Fables of Fact: The New Journalism as New Fiction.* Urbana, IL: U of Illinois P, 1981.

Heyne, Eric. "Toward a Theory of Literary Nonfiction." *Modern Fiction Studies* 33.3 (1987): 479–90.

Hind, Emily. *Entrevistas con quince autoras mexicanas.* Madrid: Iberoamericana, 2003.

Hollowell, John. *Fact and Fiction: The New Journalism and the Nonfiction Novel.* Chapel Hill: U of North Carolina P, 1977.

Howells, William Dean. "Editor's Easy Chair." *Harper's Monthly* 119 (1909): 795–98.

Hutcheon, Linda. *A Poetics of Postmodernism: History, Theory, Fiction.* New York: Routledge, 1988.

Ilie, Paul. *Literature and Inner Exile: Authoritarian Spain, 1939–1975.* Baltimore: Johns Hopkins UP, 1980.

"Interview with James Frey." *CNN Larry King Live*, January 11, 2006. <http://transcripts.cnn.com/TRANSCRIPTS11/lkl.01.html>.

Izquierdo Albiñana, A. "Vasconcelos que no es Vasconcelos: Juicio femenino acerca de *Ulises criollo.*" In Vasconcelos, *Ulises criollo.* 840–42.

Jaramillo Hoyos, Alejandro. "Interview with Rossana Reguillo." *The Communication Initiative.* (July 2002). No pagination.< http://www.comminit.com/en149506>.

Jelinek, Estelle, ed. *Women's Autobiography: Essays in Criticism.* Bloomington: Indiana UP, 1980.

Jitrik, Noé. "Lectura de Vasconcelos." *Nuevo Texto Crítico* 1.2 (1988): 261–86.

Jörgensen, Beth E. "Benita Galeana; en la lucha." In *Las desobedientes: Mujeres de nuestra América.* Ed. María Mercedes Jaramillo. Bogotá: Panamericana, 1997. 272–87.

———. "Matters of Fact: The Contemporary Mexican Chronicle and/as Nonfiction Narrative." In Corona and Jörgensen. 71–94.

———. "Speaking from the Soapbox: Benita Galeana's *Benita.*" *Latin American Literary Review* 28.55 (2000): 46–66.

———. *The Writing of Elena Poniatowska: Engaging Dialogues.* Austin: U of Texas P, 1994.

Katz, Friedrich. *The Life and Times of Pancho Villa.* Stanford: Stanford UP, 1988.

Keller, Gary D. "El niño en la Revolución Mexicana: Nellie Campobello, Andrés Iduarte y César Garizurieta." *Cuadernos Americanos* 29.170 (May–June 1970):142–51.

Kerr, Lucille. "Gestures of Authorship: Lying to Tell the Truth in Elena Poniatowska's *Hasta no verte Jesús mío.*" *MLN* 106 (1991): 370–94.

Kozloff, Max. *The Privileged Eye: Essays on Photography.* Albuquerque: U of New Mexico P, 1987.

Kristeva, Julia. "A New Type of Intellectual: The Dissident." In *The Kristeva Reader.* Ed. Toril Moi. Trans. Sean Hand. New York: Columbia UP, 1986. 292–300.

Legrás, Horacio. "Martín Luis Guzmán: el viaje de la revolución." *MLN* 118 (2003): 427–54.

Lejeune, Philippe. *On Autobiography.* Ed. Paul John Eakin. Trans. Katherine Leary. Minneapolis: U of Minnesota P, 1989.

Leñero, Vicente. *Asesinato: El doble crimen de los Flores Muñoz.* Mexico City: Plaza & Janés, 1984.

———. *Los periodistas.* Mexico City: Joaquín Mortiz, 1980.

Lomnitz, Claudio. *Deep Mexico, Silent Mexico: An Anthropology of Nationalism.* Minneapolis: U of Minnesota P, 2001.

Long, Mary K. "Salvador Novo's *Continente vacío.*" *Latin American Literary Review* 24.47 (January–June1996): 91–114.

———. "Writing the City: The Chronicles of Salvador Novo." In Corona and Jörgensen. 181–200.

López, Irma M. "Autobiografía interminable: La novelística de María Luisa Puga." *Texto Crítico* 3.4–5 (January–December 1997): 73–82.

Lounsberry, Barbara. *The Art of Fact.* Westport, CT: Greenwood P, 1990.

Magaña Esquivel, Antonio. *La novela de la Revolución.* Mexico City: Porrúa, 1974.

Martínez, José Luis. *Literatura mexicana, siglo XX, 1910–1949.* Mexico City: Antigua Librería Robredo, 1949.

Matthews, Irene. *Nellie Campobello: La centaura del norte.* Mexico City: Cal y Arena, 1997.

Mazón Cervantes, Miguel. "El libro de un criollo." In Vasconcelos, *Ulises criollo.* 829–31.

McCord, Phyllis Frus. "The Ideology of Form: The Nonfiction Novel." *Genre* 19.1 (Spring 1986): 59–79.

Medina, Andrés. "Ricardo Pozas en la trama de la antropología mexicana." *La Palabra y el Hombre* 3 (July–September 1994): 21–68.

Medina, Dante. "Patience and Urgency." Trans. Beth E. Jörgensen. In Corona and Jörgensen. 47–50.

Meyer, Doris. "The Dialogics of Testimony: Autobiography as Shared Experience in Nellie Campobello's *Cartucho.*" In *Latin American Women's Writing: Feminist Readings in Theory and Crisis.* Ed. Anny Brooksbank Jones and Catherine Davies. New York: Oxford UP, 1996. 49–65.

Millay, Amy Nauss. *Voices from The Fuente Viva: The Effect of Orality in Twentieth-Century Spanish American Narrative.* Lewiston, PA: Bucknell UP, 2005.

Molloy, Sylvia. *At Face Value: Autobiographical Writing in Spanish America.* Cambridge, England: Cambridge UP, 1991.

Monsiváis, Carlos. "¿A quién le tienen que pedir perdón?" *Letras Libres* 1.1 (January 1999): 46–48.

———, ed. *A ustedes les consta: Antología de la crónica en México.* Mexico City: Era, 1980.

———. *Amor perdido.* Mexico City: Era, 1977.

———. "Crónica de una convención (que no lo fue tanto) y de un acontecimiento muy significativo." In *EZLN: Documentos y comunicados I.* 313–23.

———. "De la Santa Doctrina al Espíritu Público (Sobre las funciones de la crónica en México)." *Nueva Revista de Filología Hispánica* 35.2 (1987): 753–71.

———. *Entrada libre: Crónicas de la sociedad que se organiza.* Mexico City: Era, 1987.

———. *Escenas de pudor y liviandad.* Mexico City: Grijalbo, 1988.

———. *Los rituales del caos.* Mexico City: Era, 1995.

———. and Hermann Bellinghausen. "Marcos, 'gran interlocutor.' El diálogo persiste." *La Jornada* (January 8, 2001).

Montaño, Erika, Fabiola Palapa and Arturo Jiménez. "Murió María Luisa Puga a los 60 años; escribir, su máxima pasión." *La Jornada* (December 26, 2004): no pagination. <http://www.jornada.unam.mx1202an1cul.php>.

Mortenson, Greg, and David Oliver Relin. *Three Cups of Tea: One Man's Mission to Promote Peace . . . One School at a Time.* New York: Viking, 2006.

Morton, F. Rand. *Los novelistas de la Revolución Mexicana.* Mexico City: Editorial Cultura, 1949.

Napier, A. David. *Masks, Transformation, and Paradox.* Berkeley: U of California P, 1986.

Negrín, Edith. "Benita Galeana o la escritura como liberación." In *Mujer y literatura mexicana y chicana: Culturas en contacto.* Eds. Aralia López et al. Mexico City: Colegio de México, 1990. 31–35.

Nickel, Catherine. "Nellie Campobello." In *Spanish American Women Writers: A Bio-bibliographical Source Book.* Ed. Diane E. Marting. Westport, CT: Greenwood P, 1990. 117–27.

Oleas Franco, Rafael. "*Ulises criollo*: el imperio de los sentidos y los libros." In Vasconcelos, *Ulises criollo.* 776–803.

Olney, James. *Metaphors of Self: The Meaning of Autobiography.* Princeton: Princeton UP, 1972.

Pacheco, Cristina. *Cuarto de azotea.* Mexico City: Gernika, 1986.

———. *Sopita de fideo.* Mexico City: Océano, 1984.

Paúl Arranz, María del Mar. "La novela de la Revolución Mexicana y la revolución en la novela." *Revista Iberoamericana* 65.186 (January–March 1999): 49–57.

Paz, Octavio. *The Labyrinth of Solitude.* Trans. Lysander Kemp. New York: Grove P, 1961.

Pitt-Rivers, Julian. "*Juan the Chamula: An Ethnological Re-creation of the Life of a Mexican Indian.*" *Man* 64 (May–June 1964): 96–97.

Poniatowska, Elena. *Amanecer en el Zócalo: Los 50 días que confrontaron a México.* Mexico City: Planeta, 2007.

———. *¡Ay vida, no me mereces!* Mexico City: Joaquín Mortiz, 1985.

———. "La CND: de naves mayores a menores." In *EZLN: Documentos y comunicados I.* 324–28.

———. *Hasta no verte, Jesús mío.* Mexico City: Era, 1969.

———. *Nada, nadie: Voces del temblor.* Mexico City: Era, 1988.

———. *La noche de Tlatelolco.* Mexico City: Era, 1971.

Pozas, Ricardo. *Chamula: Un pueblo indio de los Altos de Chiapas.* Mexico City: Instituto Nacional Indigenista, 1959.

———. *Juan Pérez Jolote.* Mexico City: Fondo de Cultura Económica, 1998.

Puente, Ramón. "La autobiografía de José Vasconcelos." In Vasconcelos, *Ulises criollo.* 811–12.

Puga, María Luisa. *Antonia.* Mexico City: Grijalbo, 1989.

———. *Crónicas de una oriunda del kilómetro X en Michoacán.* Mexico City: Consejo Nacional para la Cultura y las Artes, 1995.

———. *De cuerpo entero: El espacio de la escritura.* Mexico City: Universidad Nacional Autónoma de México, 1990.

———. *Diario del dolor.* Mexico City: Alfaguara, 2004.

———. *Las posibilidades del odio.* Mexico City: Siglo Veintiuno, 1978

Ranke, Leopold von. *History of the Latin and Teutonic Nations from 1494–1514.* Trans. Philip A. Ashworth. London: G. Bell and Sons, 1887.

Reguillo, Rossana. "Border(line) Texts." Trans. Ignacio Corona and Beth E. Jörgensen. In Corona and Jörgensen. 51–59.

———. *Ciudadano N: Crónicas de la diversidad.* Guadalajara: ITESO, 1999.

———. "Ciudades y violencias: Un mapa contra los diagnósticos fatales." In *Ciudades translocales: Espacios, flujo, representatción—perspectivas de las Américas.* Eds. Rossana Reguillo and Marcial Godoy-Anativia. Guadalajara: ITESO, 2005. 393–413.

———. *La construcción simbólica de la ciudad: Sociedad, desastre y comunicación.* Guadalajara: ITESO, 2005.

———. *Emergencia de culturas juveniles: Estrategias del desencanto.* Barcelona: Grupo Editorial Norma, 2000.

———. "The Social Construction of Fear: Urban Narratives and Practices." In *Citizens of Fear: Urban Violence in Latin America.* Ed. Susana Rotker. New Brunswick, NJ: Rutgers UP, 2002. 187–206.

——— and Cristina Padilla, eds. *Quién nos hubiera dicho. Guadalajara, 22 de abril.* Guadalajara: ITESO, 1993.

Rich, Adrienne. *Of Woman Born: Motherhood as Experience and Institution.* New York: Norton, 1976.

Ricoeur, Paul. "Life: A Story in Search of a Narrator. In *A Ricoeur Reader: Reflection and Imagination.* Ed. Mario Valdés. Toronto: U of Toronto P, 1991. 425–37.

Robles, Martha. *La sombra fugitiva: Escritoras en la cultura nacional.* Mexico City: Universidad Nacional Autónoma de México, 1985.

Rutherford, John. "The Novel of the Mexican Revolution." In *Cambridge History of Latin American Literature II: The Twentieth Century.* Ed. Roberto González Echevarría and Enrique Pupo-Walker. Cambridge, England: Cambridge UP, 1996. 213–25.

Scarry, Elaine. *The Body in Pain: The Making and Unmaking of the World.* New York: Oxford UP, 1985.

Secanella, Petra María. *El periodismo político en México.* Barcelona: Editorial Mitre, 1983.

Shirk, Henrietta Nickels. "Cancer Diaries: Writing as Fighting for Wellness." *Conference of College Teachers of English Studies* 64 (September 1999): 30–39.

Silva Herzog, Jesús. *La Revolución Mexicana en crisis.* Mexico City: Ediciones Cuadernos Americanos, 1944.

Smith, Paul B. *Discerning the Subject.* Minneapolis: U of Minnesota P, 1988.

Smith, Sidonie. *A Poetics of Women's Autobiography: Marginality and the Fictions of Self-Representation.* Bloomington: Indiana UP, 1987.

———. *Subjectivity, Identity and the Body: Women's Autobiographical Practices in the Twentieth Century.* Bloomington: Indiana UP, 1993.

Sontag, Susan. *On Photography.* New York: Farrar, Straus and Giroux, 1977.

Spengemann, William C. *The Forms of Autobiography: Episodes in the History of the Literary Genre.* New Haven: Yale UP, 1980.

Stanley, Liz. *The Auto-biographical I: The Theory and Practice of Feminist Auto/biography.* Manchester: Manchester UP, 1992.

Stanton, Domna C. "Autogynography: Is the Subject Different?" *New York Literary Forum* 12–13 (1984): 5–22.

Steedman, Carolyn. "Stories." In *Women, Autobiography, Theory: A Reader.* Ed. Sidonie Smith and Julia Watson. Madison, WI: U of Wisconsin P, 1998. 243–54.

Stewart, Victoria. "Holocaust Diaries: Writing from the Abyss." *Forum for Modern Language Studies* 41.4 (October 2005): 418–26.

Stoll, David. *Rigoberta Menchú and the Story of All Poor Guatemalans.* Boulder: Westview P, 1999.

Szanto, George. "Civil Societies." *Brick* 54 (Spring 1996): 4–12.

Taylor, Diana. *Disappearing Acts: Spectacles of Gender and Nationalism in Argentina's "Dirty War."* Durham, NC: Duke UP, 1997.

Tittler, Jonathan. *Narrative Irony in the Contemporary Spanish-American Novel.* Ithaca: Cornell UP, 1984.

Torres, Teodoro. "*Ulises criollo.*" In Vasconcelos, *Ulises criollo.* 831–32.

Usigli, Rodolfo. *El gesticulador y otras obras de teatro.* Mexico City: Cultura SEP, 1983.

Valdés, Mario. "The Literary Social Symbol for an Interrelated Study of Mexico." *Journal of Ibero-American Studies* 7.3 (July 1965): 385–99.

Vasconcelos, José. *Memorias.* Mexico City: Fondo de Cultura Económica, 1982.

———. *A Mexican Ulysses, An Autobiography.* Trans. William Rex Crawford. Bloomington: Indiana UP, 1963.

———. *Ulises criollo.* Edición Crítica de Claude Fell. Mexico City: Fondo de Cultura Económica, 2000.

Viezzer, Moema and Domitila Barrios de Chungara. '*Si me permiten hablar . . .' Testimonio de Domitila, una mujer de las minas de Bolivia.* Mexico City: Siglo Veintiuno, 1971.

Villoro, Juan. *Los once de la tribu.* Mexico City: Aguilar, 1995.

Walsh, Rodolfo. *Operación masacre.* Buenos Aires: Ediciones de la Flor, 1985.

White, Hayden. *The Content of the Form: Narrative Discourse and Historical Representation.* Baltimore: Johns Hopkins UP, 1987.

———. *Figural Realism: Studies in the Mimesis Effect.* Baltimore: Johns Hopkins UP, 1999.

———. *Metahistory: The Historical Imagination in Nineteenth-Century Europe.* Baltimore: Johns Hopkins UP, 1973.

———. "The Real, the True and the Figurative in the Human Sciences." *Profession* 92 (1992): 15–17.

———. *The Tropics of Discourse: Essays in Cultural Criticism.* Baltimore: Johns Hopkins UP, 1978.

Wilkinson, James. "A Choice of Fictions: Historians, Memory and Evidence." *PMLA* 111.1 (January 1996): 80–92.

Woods, Richard Donovan. *Mexican Autobiography/La autobiografía mexicana.* Westport, CT: Greenwood P, 1988.

———. "Mexican Autobiography: An Essay and Annotated Bibliography." *Hispania* 77.4 (1994): 750–802.

Index

Abreu Gómez, Ermilo, 6
Alessio Robles, Miguel, 40
Alonso Cortés, Rodrigo, 41
Aristotle, *Poetics*, 2, 39
author, 17–18
autobiography, 17, 46, 50, 69–75, 110, 115
  in Mexico, 70–72
  memory in, 79–81
Azuela, Mariano, 27

Bakhtin, Mikhail, 127
Barnet, Miguel, 122
Barthes, Roland, 13, 17, 62
Baynham, Mike, 91
Bencomo, Anadeli, 139, 167
Bending, Lucy, 101, 205 n. 19
Bhabha, Homi K., 127
Bielsa, Esperança, 139
Blanco, José Joaquín, 142
Borges, Jorge Luis, 80
Bradu, Fabienne, 7
Brenner, Anita, 58
  The Wind That Swept Mexico, 8, 58–67
Bruce-Novoa, Juan, 29, 202 n. 3
Brushwood, John, 29

Calles, Plutarco Elías, 78
Campobello, Nellie, 49–50
  Apuntes sobre la vida militar de Francisco Villa, 8, 28, 54–57
  Cartucho, 8, 27, 28, 51–54
Cancian, Ricardo Frank, 123
Capote, Truman, 16
Carballo, Emmanuel, 31
Cárdenas, Lázaro, 78
Carranza, Venustiano 31, 33, 36, 40, 78
Castañón, Adolfo, 7
Castellanos, Rosario, 121
  "Los convidados de agosto," 174
Castro, Carlo Antonio, 120–21
chronicle, 9, 95, 138–142, 163–64, 208 n. 4
  hybrid nature of, 141
chulel, 126
Cohn, Dorrit, 11–12, 15, 203 n. 8
Cook, Scott, 119
Cordry, Donald, 165
Corona, Ignacio, 138–39, 149

Couser, G. Thomas, 100

Damasio, Antonio, 81–82
Derrida, Jacques, 19–20, 128
Dessau, Albert, 29
diary, as genre, 100

Díaz, Porfirio, 66
Díaz Arciniega, Víctor, 79
Doctorow, E.L., 4
document, 23
Domínguez Michael, Christopher, 7, 48–49
Dubrow, Heather, 22

Eakin, Paul John, 79–80, 81–82, 84
Ejército Zapatista de Liberación Nacional, 162–90
Egan, Linda, 139, 144, 147, 148, 167, 171
evidence, 21–23, 38
exile, literature of, 96–97
EZLN. *See* Ejército Zapatista de Liberación Nacional

fact, 21, 125
  factual status and factual adequacy, 16–17, 19, 25, 30, 33, 41, 49, 72, 100, 121–22, 123, 125, 126, 145, 193–94
Faverón Patriau, Gustavo, 52
Fell, Claude, 77, 79
fiction, 1, 2
  distinction from nonfiction 2–4, 11–12, 15–17
fiscal, 135
Foster, David William, 6, 29
Foucault, Michel, 13, 18
Frey, James, *A Million Little Pieces*, 4

Galeana, Benita, 108–10, 111, 206 n. 3
  Benita, 9, 108–18, 136, 206 n. 7
Gallo, Rubén, 139
Garciadiego, Javier, 79
Gill, Mario, 109–10
Glusker, Susannah Joel, 58
González, Aníbal, 139
González, Manuel Pedro, 29
González de Alba, Luis, 5
Grundberg, Andy, 63, 64–65
Guillermoprieto, Alma, 180–82
  "La desenmascarada," 180–85
  "Historia de un rostro," 188–89
Gutiérrez, Eulalio, 30, 33, 34, 37, 40, 42
Guzmán, Martín Luis, 31–32
  El águila y la serpiente, 8, 27, 28–39
  "Un experto de la historia," 30–31, 38; 31
  Memorias de Pancho Villa, 8, 28, 39–49
Gyurko, Lanin, 29

Heyne, Eric, 16
historiography, 23–24, 38
Huerta, Victoriano, 31, 44
Hutcheon, Linda, 20
hybridity, 126
  in Chamula culture, 126–35

Ilie, Paul, 96
ilol, 126
intertextuality, 75
  in *Ulises criollo*, 84–87

Jitrik, Noé, 78

Katz, Friedrich, 49
Kerr, Lucille, 47
komel, 126
Kozloff, Max, 65
Kristeva, Julia, 96–97

Legrás, Horacio, 34
Lejeune, Philippe, 17, 46–47, 69–70, 72
  autobiographical pact, 32, 46, 110, 202–03 n. 4
Leñero, Vicente, 11, 12

Limantour, José Ives, 67
López Obrador, Andrés Manuel, 171

Machete, El, 110, 114
Madero, Francisco I., 31, 79, 86
Martínez, José Luis, 6
masks, 164–65
Matthews, Irene, 50, 51
McCord, Phyllis Frus, 4, 11
Medina, Andrés, 120
Medina, Dante, 11
Melville, Herman, 175
memoir, 41–42, 46–49
memory, 79–81
  in *Ulises criollo*, 80–84
Menchú, Rigoberta, 5
Mexican Communist Party. *See* Partido Comunista de México
Mexican Revolution of 1910, 33, 132
  novel of the Mexican Revolution, 27–28
  portrayed in *El águila y la serpiente*, 33–39
  portrayed in *The Wind That Swept Mexico*, 59–67
Millay, Amy Nauss, 122
Molloy, Sylvia, 70–71, 78–79, 81, 85
Monsiváis, Carlos, 9, 29, 108, 138–40, 142, 145
  "Crónica de una convención (que no lo fue tanto) y de un acontecimiento muy significativo," 167–71
  Entrada libre, 143, 144, 162
  "Marcos, 'gran interlocutor,'" 186–88
  "A quién le tienen que ¿pedir perdón?," 186
  "San Juanico: Los hechos, las interpretaciones y las mitologías," 9, 144–48, 158–59
Mortenson, Greg, *Three Cups of Tea*, 4
Morton, F. Rand, 29

Napier, A. David, 164–65, 178–79
National Pro-Democracy Convention (CND), 166
Negrín, Edith, 109
North American New Journalism, 3, 5, 140
nonfiction, 2, 9–10, 12, 15, 19–25
  as classification in Mexico, 5–8

Obregón, Alvaro, 31, 36, 40

Partido Comunista de México), 108, 114, 115–17
Paúl Arranz, María del Mar, 28, 30
Paz, Octavio, 163, 177, 189–90
photography, theory of, 62–63, 65
  in *The Wind That Swept Mexico*, 63–67
Pitt-Rivers, Julian, 123
Poniatowska, Elena, 1, 141–42
  Amanecer en el Zócalo, 171
  "La CND: de naves mayores a menores," 171–73
  Fuerte es el silencio, 162
  Hasta no verte, Jesús mío, 1, 107–08
  Nada, nadie: Las voces del temblor 2, 9, 143, 162
  La noche de Tlatelolco 2, 9, 161–62
post-structuralism, 12, 13
Pozas Arciniega, Ricardo, 118–19, 120
  Juan Pérez Jolote: Biografía de un tzotzil, 9, 118–36, 207 n. 14
pukuje, 135
Puga, María Luisa, 88–90, 204 n. 10
  Crónicas de una oriunda del kilómetro X en Michoacán, 9, 95–99

Puga, María Luisa *(continued)*
Diario del dolor, 9, 99–105
El espacio de la escritura, 8, 90–95
Las posibilidades del odio, 88;

real, 12
traces of the, 20–21
reality, 1, 3, 9, 13–14
referentiality, 13, 20
Reguillo Cruz, Rossana, 121, 148–51
La construcción simbólica de la ciudad, 9, 151–59
Ciudadano N: Crónicas de la diversidad, 150–51
En la calle otra vez: Las bandas, 148–49
Rentería de Villa, Austroberta, 54
Rich, Adrienne, 117
Ricoeur, Paul, 13, 14, 50, 75, 153
Robles, Martha, 108–09
Rodríguez, Jesusa, 166
Rutherford, John, 28, 202 n. 2

Salinas, Carlos, 162
Secanella, Petra María, 207 n. 5
Silva Herzog, Jesús, 40
Smith, Paul B., 73–74
Smith, Sidonie, 74–75, 115, 204 n. 5
Sontag, Susan, 62, 65
St. Augustine, *Confessions*, 86–87
Stoll, David, 5
student movement of 1968, 161
Subcomandante Marcos, 9, 161, 163–90
subjectivity, 73–76
Szanto, George, 92

Taylor, Diana, 165
testimonial literature 1, 14, 15, 22, 48, 107, 110–11, 122–23
testimonio. See testimonial literature
Tittler, Jonathan, 99

Usigli, Rodolfo, 177

Valdés, Mario, 123
Vasconcelos, José, 76, 77, 79, 84–85, 87–88
Memorias, 76
Ulises criollo, 8, 71, 76–88
Villa, Francisco, 28–29, 33, 36–37, 39–57; 66, 67
Villoro, Juan, 173–74
"Los convidados de agosto," 174–78
"El guerrillero inexistente," 178–80

White, Hayden, 21, 24, 125, 164, 208 n. 5
Wilkinson, James, 22–23, 125
Winfrey, Oprah, 4
Woods, Richard Donovan, 71

Zapatistas. *See* Ejército Zapatista de Liberación Nacional
Zedillo, Ernesto, 178